MERCENARIES AND THEIR MASTERS

Warfare in Renaissance Italy

ITALY AT THE END OF THE FIFTEENTH CENTURY

See also detailed map of Northern Italy (p. 30) and Central Italy (p. 22)

MERCENARIES

AND THEIR MASTERS

Warfare in Renaissance Italy

————◦◦————

MICHAEL MALLETT

ROWMAN AND LITTLEFIELD
Totowa, New Jersey

BY THE SAME AUTHOR

The Borgias,
The Rise and Fall of a Renaissance Dynasty

First published in the United States 1974
by Rowman and Littlefield, Totowa, N.J.

© Michael Mallett 1974

ISBN 0-87471-447-8

Printed and bound in Great Britain

CONTENTS

ILLUSTRATIONS

MAPS

PREFACE

The debts which an historian incurs are always difficult to enumerate and can never be fully acknowledged. However I have to thank the British Academy and the University of Warwick for research grants which enabled me to carry out some of the travelling around Italian archives which this book has involved. My debt to John Hale is apparent at many points in this book; his insights and enthusiasm for the subject have inspired me for many years. In addition I owe much to countless colleagues and students who have patiently listened to and commented on my ideas, particularly at the annual Warwick University Venice Symposium. For editorial help I am grateful to John Huntington, while for both material help and moral support it is to my wife, Patricia, that I owe my greatest debt.

M.E.M.

INTRODUCTION

Warfare is an unpopular subject today for understandable reasons. The history of warfare is too often concerned with romantic glorification of individual military leaders and the *minutiae* of their martial exploits. This is particularly true of the history of Italian Renaissance warfare which has been dominated by the figures of the condottieri, those ambitious and self-seeking mercenary captains whose behaviour was deplored by contemporaries and whose military and historical significance has been generally derided by subsequent critics. Thus the subject is not only unpopular in a world tired of war, but also the historical method so often associated with it—biography—is currently unfashionable amongst historians.

However, this is not another book about the condottieri. That good biography is an essential part of historical writing is a belief that I hold, but do not propose to justify here, as it is not my intention to concentrate on the 'lives of the great captains'. Nor is it my intention to write military history in the accepted sense of that term. This is a study of institutions, attitudes, and ideas, as well as of men and of battles; it is about warfare as a part of total human history.

Warfare and military history cannot be isolated from the rest of history; nor is war just 'the continuation of state policy by other means' as Clausewitz once suggested. It is an essential part of the total relations between states, and of the total life of any historical community. Military history is not only about battles, or about armies. This was true long before the concept of total war was accepted. Medieval and Renaissance wars were wars of attrition in which battles were few and civilian involvement considerable. Wars had to be directed, organised and paid for; they also had to be suffered. Soldiers, even mercenary soldiers, are not a race apart; they act in accordance with the standards and dictates of the society of which they form a part. Machiavelli saw this as an ideal condition to be achieved only with a citizen army, but it applies to some extent to all armies. Recent research into the Hundred Years War in Britain and France has emphasised that 'war was the continuous exertion of military pressure, mainly on the civilian population', but this is not the end of the interrelationship between war and society. Armies were not just the scourge of civilians, they were also the employees of civilians. They had to be recruited, provisioned and paid; they had to be disciplined, controlled and eventually demobilised. The relationship with government and with the entire civilian population was continuous.

All this was particularly true of Italy where states of roughly similar economic potential jostled each other. Their concern was not to annihilate their rivals, but to achieve security and predominance within clearly defined spheres of influence. Their population resources were a good deal more limited than their wealth, and so their weapons were small professional mercenary armies, the activities of which were related to the needs and intentions of the states which employed them. The methods were devastation, the capture of small political and diplomatic counters, and the frustration of the enemy's attempts to do the same. Battles were calculated risks, fought to gain advantage not overwhelming victory; rarely decisive but far from bloodless.

The 'bloodless battle' is one of many preconceptions that have to be put aside to get at a true understanding of Italian warfare in the Renaissance. Another is the undue emphasis which has been placed on the condottieri, and particularly on a few outstanding figures whose ambitions and vices have been seen to sum up Italian warfare. The condottieri were deplored by many contemporary humanists for whom both classical tradition and current preoccupation with active civic participation ran counter to the practice of employing mercenaries. They were despised by Machiavelli and Guicciardini, because it seemed to them that the root of Italy's weakness in the face of the French invasion in 1494 and in the subsequent years lay in her military system. Later tradition has tended to echo the prejudices and strictures of contemporaries. The stateless, unprincipled mercenaries have always been the scapegoats for Italy's disunity, even if for some they have also been true Renaissance individuals. And it has largely been through biographies that we have been shown them and the system of which they were a part; biographies which have tended to conflate hasty judgments on individuals with sweeping assessments of institutions and society. But war does not just concern the men who wage it; even less is it only the concern of the men who lead it. Much work, even of a biographical nature, remains to be done on the lesser figures in the Renaissance military hierarchy, the 99 per cent of soldiers who did not aspire to become princes or control the destinies of states. But above all we need to look beyond individuals to the organisation and practice of war, and the role of war in Renaissance society.

Not only have Italian soldiers in this period been often misrepresented, but also Italian warfare has been seen as anachronistic and backward. Italy, protected for two centuries by the Alps and her maritime strength, had lost touch with military developments in the north and was still fighting in a medieval world of cavalry charges and pseudo-chivalric ideals. The exaggeration of these ideas can best be exposed by a comparative study of European warfare, which would be too much to attempt systematically in this book. But even a brief glance can show the similarities which existed on both sides of the Alps.

European warfare was passing through a transitional stage between the feudal host of the Middle Ages and the permanent professional armies of modern times. The main features of this transition were the replacement of cavalry by infantry as the predominant arm, the emergence of paid, professional standing armies, the change in strategy from one of attrition to one of a search for decisive blows, and finally a tactical switch from a reliance on brute force to the development of a 'science' of war. The transition was a slow one, despite the various 'military revolutions' which have been postulated by historians to emphasise moments in which the process was speeded up. The Hundred Years War, the Italian Wars, the age of Gustavus Adolphus and Cromwell, and the French Revolutionary wars, have all been picked out as moments of revolution in warfare, but the changes which are seen to have come about in these periods are basically the same. During this prolonged process it is rarely possible to argue that one country or one army was decisively different to or more advanced than another. This is particularly true in the late fourteenth and fifteenth centuries. All armies of the period were already contract armies; they were mercenary armies in the widest sense of the word and some of them included large numbers of foreign mercenaries. The contracts under which soldiers were employed were basically similar whether they were *condotte*, indentures or *lettres de retenue*. The methods they used varied less than we imagine. All armies were confronted with the problem of adjusting to the use of gunpowder; all were faced with the need for greater organisation and greater permanence. Standing armies were not invented in France any more than gunpowder was invented in Germany. Contracts, muster rolls, uniform pay scales, standardisation of the size of units, central control were features of the organisation of all European armies from the permanent forces of Charles V in France and Giangaleazzo Visconti in Milan in the later fourteenth century, through the English army in Normandy in the early fifteenth century, to the Spanish army of Ferdinand and Isabella. Italian troops fought in all the European wars, and foreign captains and armies fought, and were often defeated, in Italy in the fifteenth century.

The aim of this book, then, is to overthrow misconceptions and broaden understanding. It is not intended to be a very detailed study, and certainly not a definitive one. It opens up, I hope, new ways of looking at Italian warfare, new avenues of approach which will be explored by detailed research. Some will no doubt turn out to be dead ends; others will require whole books on their own; all will, however, be worthwhile if they help us to see past the dominant figures of the condottieri to the institutional framework in which they served and the society of which they formed a part.

CHAPTER ONE

THIRTEENTH-CENTURY WARFARE

By the end of the twelfth century Italy had reached a stage of political disintegration more complete than at any time since the collapse of the Roman Empire. Yet two events occurred in the last years of that century which gave hope, in one case only transitory hope, that a new unity was about to emerge. In 1176 Henry, the son of the German emperor Frederick Barbarossa, had been married to Constance, the heiress to the Norman kingdom of Sicily. Thus when thirteen years later both Frederick and Constance's father, William II, died, the young couple were the overlords of all Italy except for the states of the Church, and when Henry himself died in Messina in 1197 this joint title passed to his infant son Frederick, later to be Frederick II—'the wonder of the world'. In the following year Innocent III, the most powerful and politically conscious of all medieval popes, ascended the papal throne.

The second of these events, the beginning of the pontificate of Innocent III, can be assessed and its importance described more easily than the first. Innocent III was in a real sense the founder of the Papal State. He was able for the first time to impose a degree of political unity and control on that considerable area of central Italy which popes had claimed to rule for over 400 years. The Papal State embraced the most geographically and politically diverse parts of Italy; it included the flourishing cities of Umbria, Romagna and the

Marches, the rugged feudal areas of the Abruzzi and the western Apennines, and that contentious and self-assertive relic of ancient greatness which was medieval Rome. In terms of real political unity Innocent's achievement was far from complete, but the Papal State which he established was, in geographical terms at least, *the* Papal State until the nineteenth century.

The apparent unity created by Henry VI and Frederick II between the theoretical imperial overlordship in Lombardy and Tuscany and the advanced Norman monarchy of Naples and Sicily was to be far less durable. The emperors since Charlemagne had claimed sovereignty over northern Italy, but Frederick Barbarossa's attempts to give substance to that sovereignty had been frustrated by the growing strength and independence of the cities of the area. The victory of the Lombard League at Legnano in 1176 indicated the limits of imperial pretensions, and after the death of Frederick II in 1250 the German emperors largely gave up any further attempts to assert their claims. The southern part of the peninsula had few cities, and the energetic administration of the Normans, who had evicted both Byzantine and Saracen rulers in the eleventh and twelfth centuries, had created one of the strongest states of the High Middle Ages. The court of the Norman kings, and later Frederick II, at Palermo was the cultural showpiece of the age, combining as it did all that was most vibrant in the civilisations of Northern and Mediterranean Europe.

But the appearance of the Hohenstaufen emperors in southern Italy started a new phase in the prolonged confrontation between emperors and popes, and the latter saw themselves as geographically encircled. Innocent III and his successors tried all that they knew to prevent Frederick II's control of both ends of the peninsula becoming a reality. The popes had always taken a particular interest in the affairs of southern Italy and claimed the area as a fief of the Church. After the death of Frederick, while his sons, both legitimate and illegitimate, sought to hold together his vast empire, the popes, and particularly the French Urban IV, invited Charles of Anjou, brother of Louis IX of France, to evict the Germans and take over the rule of the southern kingdom. In 1266 Charles defeated and killed Frederick's illegitimate son Manfred at Benevento, and two years later he completed the task by shattering the last German army to appear in the south at Tagliacozzo. These two battles made the Angevin dynasty secure, but no sooner was it secure than new tensions split the southern kingdom. Charles alienated the Sicilians both by his brutality and by seeking to transfer the centre of his rule from Palermo to Naples. In 1282 the revolt known to history as the Sicilian Vespers resulted in Peter of Aragon, the husband of Manfred's daughter Constance, being invited to rule an independent Sicily. From this event stemmed a long conflict between Angevins and Aragonese for control of southern Italy, a conflict which was to last two centuries and served both to weaken the area economically and to remove it to some extent from the main stream of Italian development.

The fact that Frederick II failed to build on his fortunate inheritance and create a largely united Italy in the thirteenth century was due to the concerted efforts of his two greatest enemies, the popes and the Italian cities. A struggle which had been an almost personal one between popes and emperors for moral and spiritual authority in Europe had become a more specifically Italian one. It had become a struggle in which all Italy took sides as either Guelfs or Ghibellines. The popes to add strength to the Guelf cause had brought in the Angevins, and indeed soon found themselves so dependent on French support that, in the early fourteenth century, the papal court was moved to Avignon, and the Papal State lapsed into a period of confusion and anarchy.

Finally what of the last element in this political equation— the burgeoning cities particularly of north and central Italy? Italy had always been a land of cities. Both the inhospitable nature of much of the terrain, and the commercial activity generated at the centre of the Mediterranean had ensured this. Most of the famous Roman cities of Italy had survived the difficult conditions of the early Middle Ages, and in the eleventh and twelfth centuries began to grow again, as international trade and contact revived. The intensive urban renewal of this period not only laid the foundation for the new cultural orientations which culminated in the fifteenth century, but also created a mass of new political entities. The wealthy walled city was a barrier to all traditional lordships. The league of Lombard cities founded in the twelfth century successfully resisted imperial domination; the Guelf League of Tuscan cities gave invaluable support to popes and Angevins in the thirteenth century. But these leagues were little more than military defensive alliances; they were in no sense political federations. It was the mass of virtually independent city states which gave Italy its political complexity in the thirteenth century. Some like Venice and Genoa had an international standing because of their empires in the Eastern Mediterranean; others like Milan and Florence had it because of their industrial wealth. These were the largest cities in Europe; Milan at the meeting point of the Alpine routes was the leader of the Lombard League; Florence, whose bankers financed both the popes and the Angevins, dominated Tuscany by the end of the thirteenth century. It was within the walls of these cities that the immediate future of Italy lay.

The two most notable characteristics, then, of thirteenth-century Italy were the immense variety of political organisations and political traditions, and the precocious growth of urban life. Both these factors tended to undermine the strength of the feudal institutions which had been transplanted to Italy from northern Europe. In Lombardy and in the south there had been deliberate attempts to create a system of feudal tenure and feudal military obligations, by Charlemagne and his successors in the north and by the Normans in the south. At the same time in central Italy there had been some inevitable borrowings of feudal institutions. There were noble feudal vassals of the Emperor in Lombardy and Tuscany, and there were feudal vassals of the popes in the Papal States. But only in Naples and Sicily was feudal obligation a significant feature of the pattern of military service by the thirteenth century. In northern and central Italy the growth of the cities had led to a rapid curtailment of the power of many of the rural nobility. Some were now vassals of the cities and owed feudal military service to them, many more had actually been forced to live in the cities and integrate themselves into the urban upper classes.

Thus while it was already an anachronism to think of any European armies in the thirteenth century as strictly feudal armies, it was particularly the case in Italy that the main components of armies of the period were non-feudal. Mass levies and mercenary soldiers made up the bulk of Italian armies of the thirteenth century. The Lombards in the eighth century had relied on a universal obligation for military service to fill their armies, and this tradition had survived in northern and central Italy. With the growth of cities their defence had been entrusted to a mass levy of the citizens, and as the cities spread their control over the surrounding countryside, the urban militias were supported by similar levies from the rural areas. These militias of the Lombard and Tuscan towns were a major factor in the warfare of the thirteenth century.

While there was in theory an obligation on all men capable

of bearing arms in the Italian cities to undertake military service in times of need, the obligation was in practice only extended to what one might describe as the 'political' class, the citizens who played an active part in the running of the city. Regulations for citizenship in Italian cities varied greatly from city to city, but on the whole the term 'citizen' was only applied to those who had a permanent stake in the community. Long residence, ownership of property, and reasonable affluence entitled one not only to the privilege of some measure of participation in communal government, but also to the obligation to pay taxes and render military service. With the early growth of a money economy in Italy such military service was paid from at least the twelfth century. Nor, in normal times, was it an unduly onerous duty for citizens. The city militias were divided into companies from different quarters of the city, and it was rarely necessary to call out more than a part of the force at once. Each man was expected to keep his arms, and where applicable his horse, in readiness; but the service required of him was normally confined to defence of the walls of the city for the limited period during which a besieging army could be maintained in the field, and the occasional brief excursion against some recalcitrant noble in the rural hinterland. In the latter case the service involved would rarely be for more than a week, and when defence of the walls was required this could easily be organised on a rota basis so that each man could continue with his normal occupation at the same time. Thus the communal militia system was not necessarily economically disruptive, nor was it consequently the case that the citizens should seek as soon as possible to convert their obligation for personal service into a money payment. A patriotic pride in their native city was, and still is, a major characteristic of the Italian mentality, and this *campanilismo* ensured that the citizens of Italian cities were prepared to fight long after increased affluence and the availability of mercenaries made such personal involvement no longer necessary.

The communal militias were largely, but by no means exclusively, made up of infantry. Relatively few citizens could afford the upkeep of war horses, and the skills of the infantry soldier required less constant practice than those of the cavalryman. Nevertheless the wealthier citizens were expected to serve on horseback and as many of them came from rural and often noble families they were not unaccustomed to such skills. The famous victory of Legnano in 1176 won by the militia of the Lombard League against Frederick Barbarossa has often been seen as a triumph of infantry over cavalry, but the army of the League contained over 4,000 cavalry and without the support of these the Lombard infantry would probably not have been able to withstand the charge of the German heavy cavalry. The Florentine army which was defeated by the Sienese at Montaperti in 1260 contained about 1,400 communal cavalry and about 6,000 communal infantry supported by some 8,000 infantry levies from the rural areas of the Florentine state.

That the bulk of Lombard and Tuscan armies of the thirteenth century was made up of infantry was certainly a significant contrast to both the preceding and succeeding periods, but the role of such infantry was always primarily defensive. As communal levies they were not particularly well trained, and they owed their strength to numbers and determination rather than to skill or battle experience. Certainly the introduction of the crossbow in the twelfth century gave a certain offensive role to infantry, but their main function was to provide a defensive screen behind which cavalry could regroup. The heart of the defence of a communal army was the *carroccio*, a wooden cart in which the standards of the city were placed and which with its picked guard provided a rallying point for the citizen soldiers. The *carroccio* symbolised the city itself and provided that stimulus to valour and loyalty which in northern European armies was produced by the presence of the king on the battlefield.

Throughout the thirteenth century the militia armies of the Lombard and Tuscan Leagues were strengthened by the presence of a sprinkling of mercenaries. The idea that mercenaries only appeared in the next period of Italian warfare, the fourteenth century, as civic and republican spirit died and masterful 'tyrants' took over, has long since been exploded. Just as mercenaries are to be found in the feudal armies of northern Europe from an early date, so in Italy there is no lack of evidence of their presence alongside the communal militias. It is perhaps true that in northern and central Italy the large numbers of men available for the communal armies led to a slower development of the role and the numbers of mercenaries than in northern Europe; but in the south mercenaries formed a principal component of papal, imperial and Angevin armies throughout the thirteenth century.

In using the term mercenaries we mean primarily foreign mercenaries although of course to a Florentine, for example, foreigners were not only non-Italians, but also Genoese, Venetians or any other non-Florentine Italians. All soldiers were paid by this time, and although it is sometimes possible to distinguish between the man who fought purely for money and the one who fought in part out of some sense of obligation or patriotism, it is easier to draw a line between natives and foreigners. In Florentine armies of the thirteenth century there was a clear distinction between the communal troops and the mercenaries, and although there were occasionally Florentines to be found amongst the mercenaries, these men were normally expected to be foreigners.

These mercenaries of the thirteenth century were recruited and served as individuals; the days of the mercenary company only came late in the century. They were employed by

Fiesole against Florence in the twelfth century and began to appear in large numbers in the service of Genoa and Siena in the 1220's. It is perhaps significant that both these cities were more economically advanced than Florence at this time and this contributes to the explanation for their early use of mercenary troops. But by the middle of the century Florence was also employing them. At Montaperti there were 200 mercenary cavalry in the Florentine army. These men normally had contracts for three months' service and were largely recruited in Emilia and the Romagna. Although they were organised into companies of 50, they were not hired in companies. By this time also there were growing numbers of German and French mercenaries to be found in the pay of Italian cities, and in 1277 there were 100 English mercenaries in Florentine service.

With the formation of the league of Tuscan cities in the 1260's and the commitment of each city to furnish contingents to a joint army, it became even more common to maintain a small force of mercenaries to form this contingent. Inevitably as Florence and her sister cities took on a commitment to fight for the protection of other cities as well as their own, some of the motivation which had fired the communal levies was lost and it was a logical step to meet the obligations of the League with mercenary troops. Equally inevitably as these troops became semi-permanent features of the military organisation they tended to form themselves into organised companies under accepted leaders. By 1300, although it was still unusual to hire mercenaries in groups or constabularies of more than 25, the commander of the Florentine mercenaries was expected to have a larger following. Count Amauri of Narbonne who commanded the Florentine army in the victory of Campaldino over Arezzo in 1289 had a company of 100–200 Angevin cavalry during the two years in which he remained in Florentine service.

The presence of imperial armies in Italy throughout the century and the Angevin expeditions after 1265 clearly accounted for the appearance of many of these foreign mercenaries ready to serve in Italian armies. But equally clearly the practice of employing mercenaries was becoming sufficiently common to attract men of other nationalities like English and Catalans. However, in the communal armies of north and central Italy, the mercenaries were still in a minority by the end of the century. The militia tradition died hard as did the reliance on mass infantry levies, and the mercenary companies largely composed of cavalry were still only valuable adjuncts to the traditional communal army.

In the south the picture was very different. While both the emperors and the Angevin dukes could command the services of considerable feudal contingents, they also relied heavily on mercenaries to fill up their armies which were operating so far from home. At the battle of Benevento in 1266 nearly two-thirds of Manfred's cavalry were German and Italian mercenaries, while his infantry were almost entirely made up of the famous Saracen archers who had been settled in Lucera by the Normans and now served their Hohenstaufen successors. On the other side at this battle, while the bulk of Charles of Anjou's cavalry were undoubtedly French, many of them were mercenary adventurers rather than feudal vassals. Both sides also employed the specialist Genoese and Pisan crossbowmen who were beginning to make an impact on the battlefield.

Therefore Italian armies of the thirteenth century were made up of a mixture of feudal, militia and mercenary elements with a steady increase in the last and the gradual emergence of the organised mercenary company by the end of the century. Although a great deal has been written about a sudden transformation in the Italian military scene round about 1300 when professional mercenaries replaced largely native troops, either feudal or communal, as the main components of Italian armies, it is the change from employing mercenaries as individuals to employing them in companies which is perhaps more significant. Both changes were much more gradual than has been thought and the factors which caused them much more complex. Nevertheless a change did take place and its causes need to be analysed.

The first factor which has to be considered is perhaps inevitably the economic one. Italy lay at the heart of the commercial revolution of the thirteenth century and at the heart of the expanding money economy. It was natural that the growing wealth of cities like Florence, Genoa, Venice and Milan, and the widening business interests of their citizens, should lead them to seek a more efficient and less distracting military system, the additional costs of which they were increasingly able to pay. At the same time economic expansion contributed to the growing political aggressiveness of Italian cities. Expanding populations needed wider and more secure hinterlands to live off; widening mercantile and industrial commitments exacerbated economic rivalries and led to greater efforts to dominate markets and sources of raw materials.

This political aggressiveness was stimulated by the political conditions in Italy after 1250. From that moment the interest of the German emperors in Italian affairs steadily declined and the cities of northern and central Italy found themselves no longer subjected to the physical threats from large imperial and papal armies. First the Lombard League and then the Tuscan League gradually fell apart and the rivalries between the cities themselves came to the fore. The process by which literally hundreds of tiny principalities and independent communes were reduced to a small handful of states had begun, as they expanded against and absorbed each other. In this situation war became a continuous possibility;

it was not the brief passage of an imperial army which had to be feared, but the constant hostility of the neighbouring cities. War was no longer just a matter of the occasional defence of the walls of the city, but often of aggressive and prolonged campaigns against neighbours. The expansion of the authority of city states over the surrounding rural areas meant that it was frontiers rather than walls that had to be defended. In these political conditions the hastily summoned communal levy was no longer an effective military weapon. Permanent specialised infantry were needed for frontier garrison duty and for effective siege warfare. Above all, professional cavalry were needed for the aggressive summer campaigns and for the ravaging attacks which were so destructive to the rival city's economy.

Another result of the lessening of international tensions in Italy was that internal factionalism became more serious. The Italian cities were natural breeding grounds of faction, particularly as the authority vested in communal authorities expanded and the need for unity declined. Deep factional rifts within the political class of a city made it difficult to levy an effective communal militia, particularly when the aims of the war were no longer purely defensive. At the same time such rifts tended to lead to more power being conferred on the foreign officials to whom all Italian cities entrusted the administration of justice and the maintenance of internal security. In these conditions such officials, and in particular the Podestà, who was responsible for the maintenance of law and order, sometimes took over supreme authority and became the lord of the city. At the same time these officials sometimes increased the size of the company of mercenaries which they were expected to maintain as guards and police. Some of the earliest mercenary companies originated as the bodyguards of civic officials. Finally factionalism produced political exiles, men to whom war became a natural profession as they sought to regain their positions in their native cities. In some of the more faction-ridden Italian cities a substantial minority of the citizens would be in exile at any given moment. It was an obvious step for an exile to enrol as a mercenary with a city which was the rival of the one from which he had been evicted, and many of the early mercenaries were such men.

It has often been argued that it was the new rulers in fourteenth-century Italy, the so-called *signori* who rose to power in so many of the city states, who introduced mercenaries because they could not trust the citizens with arms. Similarly in the surviving republics like Florence, growing class conflict made it unwise for the patrician oligarchies to depend for their defence on a communal militia in which their own employees participated. But these arguments carry little weight particularly when set beside the economic and political factors already mentioned. The fact that mercenaries were appearing well before the fourteenth century to some extent weakens the case for the *signori* as the innovators, but more importantly a study of the rise of any of the Italian *signori* shows that the basis for their power was consent not force. Many of the *signori* were the leaders of factions, and it was the factionalism which had contributed to the decline of the communal militia not the change to one man rule. In Florence not only was class conflict far less significant than some historians have thought, but also the lower classes had not usually participated in the militia anyway.

The growth in the use of mercenaries therefore had little to do with new rulers feeling a distrust for their subjects. It was the result of a combination of new economic possibilities and new political necessities with current military opportunities and needs. In part it depended on mercenaries being available; the presence of large numbers of political exiles was one factor, the presence of large groups of under-

employed foreign troops was another. Crusading was declining by the end of the thirteenth century; the last crusader
foothold in the Holy Land was erased in 1291. Large imperial,
Angevin and Hungarian armies made spasmodic descents into
the peninsula and on each occasion many of the contingents
remained as mercenaries of the Italian states. All this happened long before the famous truces in the Hundred Years
War which released companies of French and English soldiers
for such service after 1360. By this time, in the middle of the
fourteenth century, Italy itself was suffering from severe
economic depression and rural under-employment which
again produced manpower for the mercenary companies.

Finally what of the purely military factors? Here it is
necessary to look briefly at the developments in the art of
war in the thirteenth century to see why mercenaries and
professional soldiers were becoming an integral part of all
European armies in this period. One of the most decisive
innovations was the introduction on a large scale of the crossbow, and in northern Europe the long bow. There was without doubt a continuous archery tradition in Europe, but the
great boost given to these weapons in the late twelfth and
early thirteenth centuries stemmed from the experiences of
the Crusades. The crusading armies quickly learned to respect and to imitate the prowess of the Saracen mounted
archers; the first crossbows were imported from the Eastern
Mediterranean, and the first specialist crossbowmen were
Genoese and Pisans, the inhabitants of the two Italian maritime states most involved in the transportation and the
provisioning of the crusading armies.

At first there was a papal ban on the use of crossbows in
warfare between Christian states, and there was little large
scale production of the new weapon in Europe until well
into the thirteenth century. However by the middle of the
century both the crossbow and the long bow were fully

established as infantry weapons and their use created new problems and new specialisations. Not only did both weapons require long practice to use efficiently and therefore encouraged specialisation and professionalism in that sense, but they also had a considerable impact on the military techniques of those who were on the receiving end. Traditionally infantry were equipped with a short lance, or a sword, and a shield, but the new missile firepower which was directed at them led in Italy to a division of infantry into lance or pike men and shield bearers. The sole purpose of the latter was to carry great long shields which rested on the ground and provided a protection for both the pikemen and the crossbowmen. At the same time the new threat from crossbow bolts led to the gradual replacement of leather and mail armour by plate armour for cavalry. It also provoked a concern for the protection of horses and the introduction of horse armour. Finally as a result of these same innovations the cavalryman found an increased need for spare horses ready at hand in battle to replace those killed, or exhausted by bearing the weight of the new armour, and for close support from a small entourage of pages and archers to lead the horses and provide covering fire. Out of these needs grew the cavalry 'lance', the small group of men attached to the armoured man-at-arms, which was to become the characteristic formation of late medieval cavalry.

All these developments made it increasingly necessary to think in terms of professional and specialist troops. Plate armour was both more costly, and more physically demanding to wear; it was the armour of the professional not of the feudal or 'city' knight. It was innovations like these which widened the gap between part-time and professional soldiers, and made it ever more necessary for employers to seek the latter if they could afford them. Although it is not true that the defeat of the Florentine communal militia by Sienese

mercenaries at Montaperti in 1260 'proved' to the Florentines that the days of the militia were numbered, it remains
a fact that there was a certain military inevitability about the
eventual change-over.

Once large numbers of mercenaries were an accepted part
of the Italian military system, their formation into organised
companies under recognised leaders was inevitable. It was
both easier for states to recruit whole companies, and their
military efficiency was likely to be improved by long experience of fighting together. Thirteenth century warfare and
its innovations demanded an increased sophistication of tactics and disciplined collaboration amongst troops, which an
experienced mercenary company at least offered the hope of
achieving even if the eventual result often fell short of that
hope.

This discussion of thirteenth-century warfare can be best
concluded by looking briefly at one battle of the latter part
of the century which illustrates much of what has been said, the
battle of Campaldino (1289). This battle, fought midway between Florence and Arezzo in the valley of the Arno, was
between the Tuscan Guelf league led by Florence and the
Ghibellines led by Arezzo. The Guelf army consisted of 1,600
cavalry and about 10,000 infantry; of the 1,000 cavalry which
Florence herself provided, nearly half were mercenaries led
by Amauri of Narbonne and his Angevin knights. The Ghibelline force was rather smaller—about 800 cavalry and 8,000
infantry. The Guelfs were drawn up in a battle order which
illustrates well the developments which had taken place in
thirteenth-century warfare. Behind an advanced screen of 150
cavalry came the main body of the cavalry with the bulk of
the infantry drawn up on both flanks in a slightly advanced
position creating a crescent formation. The infantry included
large numbers of crossbowmen protected by the shield-
bearers and pikemen. Behind this crescent were arranged a

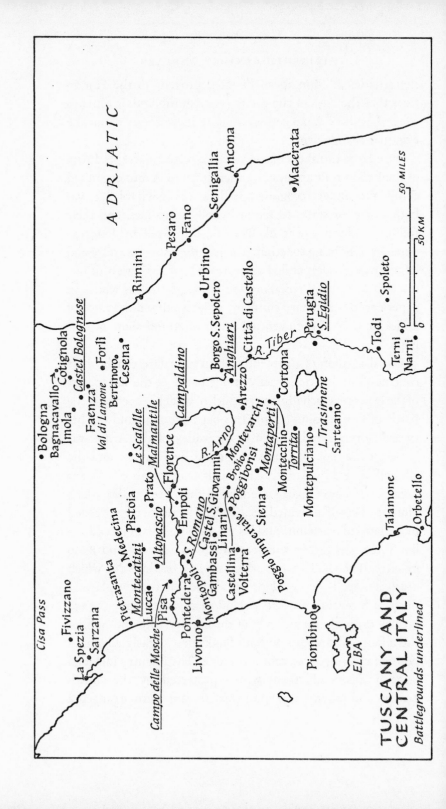

TUSCANY AND
CENTRAL ITALY

Battlegrounds underlined

row of carts in the lee of which the cavalry could regroup if broken, and behind that again a strong reserve of cavalry and pikemen. The Ghibelline army took up more traditional battle formations: a cavalry advance guard, a cavalry main body, a third line of infantry, and in the rear a cavalry reserve. The Ghibelline infantry was composed largely of pikemen with few crossbowmen.

The Ghibellines launched the first charge in which both the first two lines of cavalry and the infantry became involved. They swept aside the Guelf advance guard and pushed back the main cavalry force, and would perhaps have scattered it but for the line of carts and the pike reserve which provided a rallying point. However, at this stage the bulk of the Ghibelline army found itself caught in a crossfire from the two wings of crossbowmen. Confusion set in; the Ghibelline reserve panicked and fled, while the Guelf reserve swept round the flanks and came in on the rear of the trapped enemy. The result was a complete Guelf victory; over half of the enemy army were killed or captured.

The victory of Campaldino was a dramatic illustration of the new importance of missile weapons. It was the result of considerable tactical finesse achieved by an army in which communal militias still provided the bulk of the troops, but in which a strong stiffening of mercenaries played a substantial part. It was a battle which should serve as a warning to those who seek to draw too clear distinctions between medieval and renaissance warfare.

Like many of the problems connected with an interpretation of the Italian Renaissance, the military picture has been clouded by a too facile contrast between Italian Renaissance and northern European Middle Ages. It is the Italy of the thirteenth century from which the Italy of the Renaissance grew, and that Italy was not dominated visually by Gothic styles nor intellectually by scholastic thought. Therefore just as the contrast between Middle Ages and Renaissance in Italy is not one between Gothic and classical, or between scholasticism and humanism, neither is it a clear cut one between a feudal host and mercenary companies, between feudal barons and condottieri, or eventually between stereotyped cavalry tactics and the sophisticated cooperation between arms, including artillery, developed in the fifteenth century. At the same time, although there were peculiar features of Italian warfare in the fourteenth and fifteenth centuries, it was by no means totally distinct and isolated from developments north of the Alps, any more than Italian Renaissance styles were unaffected by the cultural world beyond that barrier. Many of the troops who fought in Italy in the thirteenth century, and a majority of those in the fourteenth century, were not Italians; the art of war in Renaissance Italy grew very much out of a fusion of local and ultra-montane traditions.

———◦◦———

CHAPTER TWO

THE AGE OF THE COMPANIES

The story of fourteenth-century warfare in Italy has traditionally been dominated by foreign mercenaries and adventurers,
and it is therefore not inappropriate to introduce it with two
little-known but significant figures from the early years.
William della Torre, a Catalan adventurer, first appeared in
Sienese service in 1277 as an undistinguished member of a
group of 19 mercenaries. By 1279 he was a constable, and in
1285 he appeared again on the Sienese pay-roll with 114
cavalry. After a period of service with Bologna he moved in
1290 to Florence and for two years his small company was to
be found garrisoning Tuscan castles. The size of William's
following fluctuated considerably but was never much more
than 100; the composition of the band also changed rapidly.
In 1292 William had about 100 men of whom the nationality
of 53 can be identified. Twenty-eight were Provençals and a
further eight came from northern France; there were two
Flemings, seven Italians, seven Spaniards and one Englishman.
This was not then a permanent company; the figure of
William himself was the one factor of continuity, and it was
presumably his reputation which won employment for this
little group of men who must have had some difficulty com-
municating with each other.

A few years later another Catalan catches the eye. In 1305
Diego de Rat was lent to Florence with a group of mercenaries by the Duke of Calabria. Diego was clearly a man of

some standing and experience, and he remained in Florence with his company for eight years. The company was a much more stable and larger group than that of William; Diego had 200–300 cavalry and as many as 500 infantry under his command and they formed a permanent nucleus both for the Florentine army and for that of the Tuscan League. Diego became a familiar figure in the streets of Florence and won immortality for himself by catching the attention of Boccaccio and receiving a mention in *The Decameron*. The story of how he won the favours of the Bishop of Florence's niece by paying her husband 500 forged florins represents, if nothing else, Boccaccio's opinion of mercenaries; but judging by later experiences if Diego de Rat had access to bad money he may well have received it in his pay from Florence.

Diego de Rat and his company are certainly an interesting and unexpected phenomenon; permanent mercenary forces even in relatively small numbers are not what we expect to find in the early fourteenth century. But the theme of this chapter is to be the variety of fourteenth-century warfare. If the great roving companies of foreign mercenaries inevitably caught the eyes and inspired the indignant pens of contemporary chroniclers, it remains true that most of the soldiers of the period did not belong to these companies. It was much smaller groups of mercenaries, already attached to favoured leaders and entirely reliant on contracts to the various Italian states, together with mass militia levies, that filled the ranks of Italian armies.

Nevertheless, it was the companies which were the exceptional and extraordinary feature of the period and it is with them that this enquiry must start. The striking features of the great companies were their size, their foreign quality and their democratic nature. That these features were less exceptional and notable than they seem will become apparent as the story unfolds, but a word needs to be said in general terms about the undoubted corporate quality of the early companies. The larger companies were amalgamations of many smaller companies and it is not surprising to find that they elected their leaders and took their decisions as a result of wide consultation within the company. Contracts with states were signed by large numbers of constables and councillors in addition to the elected leader. Booty was divided up within the company according to rank and service.

As in France during the Hundred Years War it was periods of truce and demobilisation which produced the 'free' companies. Mercenaries live on war; when peace is signed they have only three choices: to retire to some base and live off their inflated seasonal earnings, to seek another war, or to create for themselves artificial conditions of war by becoming outlaws. For the foreigners and exiles who formed a significant proportion of mercenaries in fourteenth-century Italy there was no safe base for the winters and the times of peace. Likely as it was that they could find another war somewhere in Italy in which they could join, the chances of this were reduced in winter and necessitated perhaps a long journey. Outlawry was more profitable if conducted in bands, and for foreigners in a strange land the larger the band the better. It was for this reason that the larger companies were those in which foreign mercenaries predominated, and Italy was certainly most attractive to foreign mercenaries in this period. The interests of German emperors, Hungarian kings, Angevin dukes and Avignonese popes, and the armies which they led or dispatched into Italy undoubtedly account for many of these. The wealth of Italy reflected both in good contracts and rich booty attracted others. But there was also the question of the lack of opportunities elsewhere in Europe; economic recession and unemployment in Germany made Italy peculiarly attractive to German soldiers and these were the predominant race amongst Italy's mercenaries.

One of the first of these free companies to emerge was called the Company of Siena and it was formed in 1322. There is some dispute amongst the chroniclers as to whether this company grew up round a nucleus of Sienese exiles of the Tolomeo family or round a group of German mercenaries sacked by Florence. Exiles and disbanded mercenaries were the two most likely starting points for any company and it was probably a combination of the two. The company was not large, about 500 cavalry and an indefinite number of infantry. It spent the winter of 1322–3 ravaging the Sienese and Umbrian countryside and then broke up in the spring as possibilities of piecemeal employment with neighbouring states reopened.

Of the origins of the so-called Company of the Cerruglio which appeared in 1329 there can be no doubt. Eight hundred German cavalry deserted the imperial army of Louis of Bavaria at Pisa and launched themselves in an unauthorised attack on the prosperous city of Lucca. They failed to take the city, and indeed it was true of all these fourteenth-century companies that they could rarely make much impression on a walled city as they lacked either siege equipment or the administrative resources to provision themselves for a long period in one place. However, the suburbs of Lucca offered rewarding loot and, having digested this, the company established itself for the winter in the neighbouring hills in a fortified base known as the Cerruglio. Here they elected as their leader the Italian, Marco Visconti, who had been sent to negotiate with them by the emperor, and in the following spring succeeded in taking Lucca by surprise. To the loot from the city they were able to add an additional gain by selling Lucca to the Genoese for 30,000 florins. This no doubt seemed the limit of the possible achievements of this small group and so they divided up their booty and dispersed.

It has been estimated that between 1320 and 1360 about

700 German cavalry leaders are known to have been active in Italy, with at least 10,000 men-at-arms. Another group of these Germans formed the nucleus of the company who called themselves the Cavalieri della Colomba after the abbey of the Colomba in which they established their base near Piacenza in 1334. Once again the original intention of the company was little more than a season of looting within a small area. But now the possibilities for the company expanded as Perugia, engaged in a local war with Arezzo, called for their services. The Knights responded, moved across Tuscany, drove off the Aretine army, and took the opportunity to sack two small towns in the area. These military achievements were sufficient to impress the Florentine recruiting officials who took 350 of the company into Florentine service, and this broke up the force.

The companies which have been described so far could scarcely qualify as significant military forces, but that which was formed in 1339 out of the demobilised veterans of the Della Scala war was a rather more imposing venture. This was the Company of St. George, the first to take that name during the century, and it was formed by another Visconti, Lodrisio, who had been exiled from Milan. Lodrisio collected 2,500 cavalry and 1,000 infantry, many of them Swiss, and led them across Lombardy to the gates of Milan. Associated with him in the leadership of this horde were two German nobles who were to be key figures in the history of the companies, Conrad of Landau and Werner of Urslingen. Lodrisio Visconti's aim was no less than to capture Milan from his cousins Azzo and Lucchino, and the appearance of his company certainly caused rather more than a tremor of anxiety. Lucchino hurriedly collected mercenaries and turned out the Milanese militia. The Company of St. George moved round to the north-west side of Milan and attacked the advance guard of the Milanese army at Parabiago. It was

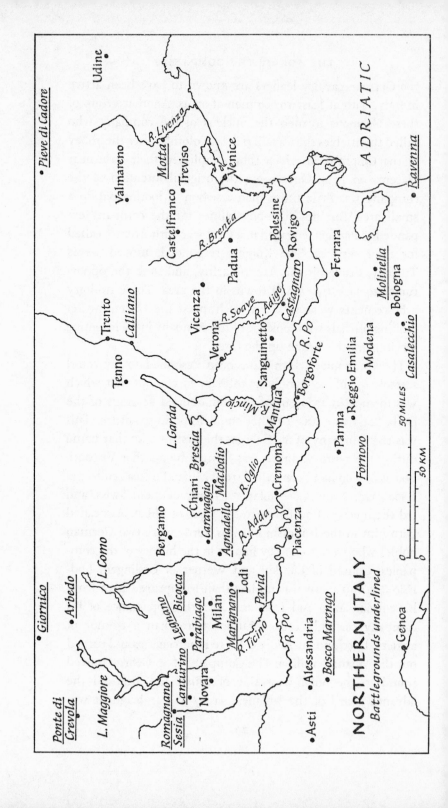

NORTHERN ITALY
Battlegrounds underlined

February and bitterly cold; thick snow lay on the ground and the Milanese troops were exhausted after their march from the city. The Company shattered the advance guard and drove them back towards the city; but Lucchino Visconti, coming up behind, rallied his troops and threw his whole army into the battle. The battle of Parabiago was one of the most bitter and bloody contests of the whole period. The Milanese army, considerably superior in numbers, was almost broken by the impetus of the Company's assault; Lucchino himself was un-horsed, captured, and tied to a tree. But at this moment Ettore da Panigo, a Bolognese exile, with 700 cavalry arrived on the scene late from Milan, and the presence of these re-inforcements tipped the scale. The Company of St. George was shattered, Lodrisio himself captured, and over 4,000 dead from the two sides were left on the field.

The size and the ambitions of the Company of St. George presaged the achievements of the Great Companies of the 1340's and 1350's. Although the Great Company which Werner of Urslingen formed out of the demobilised veterans of the Pisan–Florentine war of 1342 did not remain in being for more than a year, the next two decades were dominated by a series of Great Companies in which there was a certain continuity. Once again, although the bulk of Werner's follow-ers were probably Germans, there was a strong Italian ele-ment in his company led by the Bolognese Ettore da Panigo whose intervention at the battle of Parabiago had proved decisive. Another leader in the company was Francesco degli Ordelaffi, a representative of a relatively new breed of men —the soldier princes of the Romagna. He was the ruler of Forlì and seemed to occupy a rather ambivalent position as both member and employer of the Company. The Company in 1342 comprised 3,000 *barbute*: *barbuta* was the name given to the German cavalryman of the period, and others whose equipment was similar to that of the Germans, who tended to wear a composite armour including some plate, a *barbuta* or conical helmet with a simple nose piece, and who was accompanied by one retainer. Werner and his men moved all over central Italy in 1342 blackmailing cities, ravaging the countryside and fighting minor campaigns on behalf of anyone who would employ them. However, by the autumn, as they tried to move north through the Romagna, Bologna had organised a league against them. The Bolognese prepared a defensive position in the Val di Lamone with sharpened stakes driven into the ground at an angle with the points towards the advancing Company. This, backed by determined infantry, was enough of a barrier to hold up the cavalry of the Company for two months. Eventually a truce was agreed and the Company was allowed to pass through Bolognese territory as long as they did no damage and kept to an agreed route. However, once they were beyond Bolognese frontiers in Lombardy, they rampaged once more and were finally bought off by the Lombard cities. Werner returned to Germany with many of his followers and rich booty, while the Italian elements in the Company dispersed.

The success of Werner of Urslingen indicated what a large independent force of well armed troops could do in the politically fragmented area of central Italy where there was no single army large enough to resist it. The check it had suffered at the hands of the Bolognese and their allies had showed that a large company could be resisted by a confederation of states using mainly militia forces and prepared defences. The first lesson was to have more positive application than the second in the next thirty years, when rarely were the Italian states able either to combine effectively or resist the successors of the Great Company except behind their own walls.

Werner of Urslingen returned to Italy in 1347, this time in the pay of the new invaders of Italy, the Hungarians. The younger brother of King Lewis of Hungary had married the Angevin Queen of Naples, Joanna I. Joanna, whose dissolute nature was only equalled by her political ineptitude, allowed —or perhaps arranged—the murder of her Hungarian husband by Neapolitan rivals, and Lewis now marched to avenge his brother. The Hungarians brought added variety to the Italian military scene. They were essentially light horsemen equipped with bows and throwing lances and relying on speed of manoeuvre rather than heavy armour to protect themselves. Once again large numbers of them remained in Italy after the main Hungarian armies had departed, and they often formed important elements of subsequent companies.

The alliance between King Lewis and Werner of Urslingen was shortlived and the latter was soon on his own again operating with his Germans in central Italy. In 1349 he reunited with the remnants of the Hungarians and defeated the Neapolitans at Meleto near Naples. Amongst the Hungarian leaders were his old colleague Conrad of Landau and a new figure, Montreal d'Albarno, a Provençal knight who had for a time been a Hospitaller and whom the Italians called Fra Moriale. The union of these three created the largest company yet seen in Italy and its victory at Meleto over the Neapolitan feudal baronage was both significant and, for the Company, extremely lucrative. Over half a million florins' worth of booty and ransom money were divided up amongst the Company which then split briefly into two. Werner and Conrad went northwards to campaign in Werner's favourite area of central Italy; Fra Moriale remained in the south to draw profit from the confusion in Naples. In 1351 Werner of Urslingen returned once more to Germany, this time to a permanent retirement, and Conrad rejoined Fra Moriale who now took command of the Great Company.

The Great Company of Fra Moriale operating in central Italy in 1353 and 1354 was described by the Florentine chronicler Matteo Villani: 'Because of the enormous booty which the company was taking, many soldiers, having completed their terms of service, without wanting further pay, went off to join Fra Moriale; and sometimes they had themselves dismissed in order to join him. He enrolled them and in an ordered way gave each one a share of the booty; all the booty and loot which was saleable he sold, and he guaranteed safety to the purchasers and treated them correctly in order to facilitate his commercial dealings. He established a chamberlain who received and paid the money, and set up councillors and secretaries through whom he directed everything. He was obeyed as lord by all the knights and horsemen and he maintained justice amongst them which was summarily executed.' The Company numbered about 10,000 fighting men and 20,000 camp followers many of whom were women. The women washed the clothes, ground the corn and cooked for the Company. In fact the organisation and discipline of this huge army was impressive and irresistible. All the Tuscan and Umbrian cities had no alternative but to buy immunity from it. Florence paid protection money of 3,000 florins to the constables of the Company and 25,000 to Fra Moriale himself. By this time it is apparent that, although 234 leaders of the Company were mentioned in the agreement with Florence, and although division of booty was scrupulously organised, the role of the leader—of Fra Moriale himself— had become paramount. It was his personality and powers of organisation which held this private army together and he took a major share of the rewards. He had 60,000 florins invested with Venetian merchants in addition to the treasure chest of the Company and the large sums owing to him from the Papacy for military service. In 1354 he left the Company at Città di Castello under the command of Conrad of Landau while he rode to Rome with a small bodyguard to collect his earnings. But in Rome power had temporarily fallen into the hands of that strange republican demagogue, Cola di Rienzo, who seized the opportunity both to make himself popular and to straighten up his accounts by arresting and executing Moriale.

The death of Fra Moriale meant that leadership of the Company passed to Conrad of Landau and was to remain with him for nine years until his death in 1363. During this period the Great Company had a continuous existence and was to be associated at various times with the company which was formed by another German leader, Hannekin Bongarten. However the nature of the companies had changed; they were no longer purely temporary associations for exploiting the weakness of civilian populations, but permanent military formations which spent most of their time in the pay of one or other of the Italian states. They still derived considerable profit from periods of unlicensed ravaging and looting, and they were never loth to accept ransom money from a city rather than pay. But the professional military role of the companies became increasingly important.

However, despite its size and experience, the Great Company was by no means invincible. Twice during these years it was humiliated by the army of Florence. In July 1358 when the Company had been called southwards to help Siena against Perugia, Conrad of Landau negotiated with Florence a free passage for his troops through the valleys of the Apennines on the eastern frontiers of the Florentine state. But the mercenaries got out of hand and began to despoil the countryside, so the Florentines quickly took action against them. A mixed army of peasant levies, Florentine crossbowmen and mercenaries trapped the Company in a narrow valley at Le Scalelle and shattered it. The German and Hungarian cavalry were helpless against a hail of stones and crossbow bolts directed at them from the slopes above, and the majority were killed or captured. The Company, however, soon reformed in the Romagna and, joined by Bongarten, made an attempt the next year to revenge itself on Florence. This time however Conrad and Bongarten tried their luck on the western frontiers of Florence—in the Arno valley where flatter country gave them a better chance of deploying their cavalry strength. But the Florentine captain general, Pandolfo Malatesta, was waiting for them with a powerful mercenary army and put them to flight at Campo delle Mosche.

However, it was not an Italian army which was to bring about the eventual destruction of the Great Company. In 1361 a new force had appeared on the Italian scene and this was the famous White Company made up of veterans of the Hundred Years War. The members of the White Company and its later offshoots were always known in Italy as the *Inglesi* (English) because they were mostly men who had taken part in the 'English' wars in France; but they were by no means all Englishmen. The first commander of the Company was a German, Albert Sterz, and large numbers of his followers were French and Germans. However, the methods used by the Company, which gave it an immediate superiority in Italian warfare, were those perfected by the English at Crecy and Poitiers, and many of the leaders of the Company were Englishmen including Sir John Hawkwood and Andrew Belmont. Sterz was able to speak English which was an important factor in his leadership of the Company, but no doubt Latin was also a useful means of communication as it was on other occasions between Florentine officials and Hungarian captains. The White Company was an amalgam of a number of free companies which had been operating independently in southern France since the peace of Bretigny in 1360. In 1361 the Marquis of Montferrat, who had recently been deserted by Conrad of Landau and the Great Company, invited the White Company to come to Italy and join his service. Albert Sterz crossed the Alps with about 6,000 men and in 1363 he defeated the Great Company at the bridge of Canturino. Conrad of Landau, deserted at the height of the battle by his Hungarians, was mortally wounded, and only a shattered remnant of the once great company remained in Milanese service with Hannekin Bongarten. In the same year the White Company moved south into Tuscany and took service with Pisa against Florence.

The distinguishing characteristics of the 'English' mercenaries of the White Company were described at length by a number of contemporary chroniclers, but they can be summed up quite briefly. In the first place the Company derived its name from the highly polished armour worn by its men-at-arms. They wore more plate armour than was common in Italy and had sufficient pages to keep it brightly burnished. The three-man lance formation, which this company was reputed to have introduced into Italy, consisted of two men-at-arms and a page. In fact the 'lance' can be found somewhat earlier amongst mercenary cavalry in Italy, but it was developed by the White Company in the specific context of men-at-arms fighting on foot, which was one of the revolutionary features of English battle tactics of the period. The idea of dismounting men-at-arms was devised originally as a defensive ploy to enable them to stand their ground more firmly and to save their horses from being killed or wounded in battle. However, a body of dismounted men-at-arms advancing shoulder to shoulder with their lances also had considerable counter-offensive strength as the Italians quickly discovered. In order to accomplish this tactic each heavy cavalry lance was held by two men-at-arms who fought together, and when they came to grips with the enemy could also fight back to back to give each other support. Meanwhile the pages held the horses at the rear of the battlefield and came forward with them when they were needed either to pursue a beaten enemy or to withdraw quickly.

The other major novelty introduced into Italy by the White Company was the archer equipped with his long bow. The long bow had a greater effective range and a much quicker rate of fire than the crossbow, but its use demanded both good physique and long practice. For these reasons the method and the success of the English archers was not easily imitated in Italy, and gradually their numbers declined as further recruits from the north were not forthcoming, so that the impact of the long bow on Italian warfare was brief and temporary.

Together with these tactical innovations went considerable *ésprit de corps* and, above all, a greater discipline than was normal in the mercenary companies. This is not to say that discipline was perfect; the Pisans complained bitterly about the behaviour of the Company in Pisa and are even said to have engineered false alarms in order to get the English out of the city. However, Florentine experience later was on the whole good, and Florentine officials reported that the English troops were the best behaved that they had ever seen, always paying scrupulously for their provisions. Above all, however, it was their discipline in battle, and the stature and physique of many of the men, which impressed Italy. They were accustomed to riding at night and fighting deep into the winter, and, unlike most mercenary troops, they were equipped for siege warfare, carrying with them special collapsible scaling ladders and bombards.

This, then, was the company which brought a new dimension to Italian warfare in the 1360's. In 1364 the White Company, in Pisan pay, camped on the hills overlooking Florence and harassed and terrified the city. However, even as formidable a company as this had little chance of capturing a great city like Florence, and they contented themselves with looting the suburbs and collecting an enormous ransom. After this the White Company broke up; Sterz joined up with Hannekin

1 The *Victory of the Sienese at Sinalunga* (*1363*). This fresco by Lippo Vanni in the Palazzo Pubblico at Siena celebrates the defeat of the Compagnia del Capello led by Niccolò da Montefeltro.

IOANNES·ACVTVS·EQVES·BRITANNICVS·DVX·AETATIS·S
VAE·CAVTISSIMVS·ET·REI·MILITARIS·PERITISSIMVS·HABITVS·EST

2 *Sir John Hawkwood*. Paolo Uccello's massive equestrian memorial to Florence's only long-serving captain general was painted in 1436 to replace an earlier work by Agnolo Gaddi.

Bongarten to form the Company of the Star which they led southwards to harass Siena and the Papal States. The rest of the White Company remained for the time being in Pisan pay commanded by Sir John Hawkwood. Hawkwood was to be one of the leading figures in Italian warfare for the next thirty years. He was a tough, professional soldier who seemed to care less about money and more about military reputation than most of the other contemporary leaders. Much of his success can be attributed to the advantages that his troops enjoyed, but there can be no doubt that he established an unprecedented degree of unity and loyalty in his company. He also acquired a reputation for fidelity and honesty which was to some extent a reflection on the behaviour of his rivals because Hawkwood was no paragon of virtue. Although he clearly took a pride in his generalship and enjoyed war in a genuinely professional way, he was never averse to accepting money to desist from fighting and, in company with all contemporary leaders, he had scant respect for the lives and property of civilians. One thing that is very apparent in the emergence of Hawkwood is that the days of the free company were rapidly passing. Hawkwood was probably elected to command the White Company, and in 1375, when his company reached an agreement not to molest Florence, the contract was still signed by fifteen officers of the Company as well as Hawkwood himself. But increasingly Hawkwood's pre-eminent position was apparent; it was his generalship and personal qualities which won contracts rather than the size and prowess of his company. However, this is somewhat anticipating events and we must return to 1364 and the last period of intense company activity in Italy.

In the mid-1360's there were four large companies loose in Italy: those of Hawkwood, Sterz, Bongarten, and finally the Company of St. George of Ambrogio Visconti. Hawkwood in 1365 suffered one of his few defeats at the hands of the combination of Sterz and Bongarten, and thereafter joined forces with Ambrogio Visconti. In the next year Sterz, in the service of Perugia, was arrested and executed for supposed treachery. The Company of the Star broke up, and for some years the companies of Hawkwood and Ambrogio Visconti were the most powerful independent military forces in the peninsula. When united they were almost irresistible and Genoa, Siena and Perugia in turn were defeated by them. But once they split up, they became more vulnerable; Visconti was defeated by a combined papal–Neapolitan army and was finally killed in 1374 in a clash with peasants near Bergamo; Hawkwood chose a more secure if less profitable life by taking service first with Milan and then in 1375 with the papacy.

This was a moment when the Avignon popes were making great efforts to regain effective control of the Papal States after long years of anarchy. Immense sums of money were available from the papal treasury and the companies were admirable tools for this purpose. Hawkwood in 1375 found himself not only faced with the task of reducing the Romagna cities to their papal allegiance but also of conducting a war with Florence, which had taken fright at growing papal activity round her frontiers. Hawkwood allowed himself to be bought off by Florence but was rather more conscientious in obeying his ecclesiastical masters when it came to unleashing his troops on the populations of the Romagna towns. First at Faenza in 1376 and then at Cesena in 1377, the papal mercenaries carried out massacres of the civilian populations which were to be permanent stains on the records of Italian warfare. In both cases it was the papal officials who were as much to blame as the soldiers, and particularly the legate, Cardinal Robert of Geneva, who at Cesena demanded the blood of the entire population in revenge for the murder of some of his mercenaries. On this occasion Hawkwood's troops had been joined by a new company of Bretons who had been brought from France by the Avignon popes, and whose role in the massacre of Cesena seems to have been more positive than that of the English. Hawkwood is said to have obeyed Cardinal Robert's instructions with the greatest reluctance and to have succeeded in saving some of the women in Cesena. He had by this time already been in Italy for fifteen years and had developed a sympathy for the country and its inhabitants which the Breton mercenaries could scarcely be expected to share. However, in Cesena more than 5,000 of the population were slaughtered and the moats were filled with the bodies of those who tried to escape from the city.

Hawkwood, perhaps sickened by what he had had to do at Cesena, soon left papal service and most of the rest of his career was spent in the pay of Florence. However, while still serving the popes he had received the towns of Cotignola and Bagnacavallo as guarantees of his back pay and this was yet another indication of the growing role of the mercenary commander as opposed to the mercenary free company. Hawkwood's position as a papal feudatory, which is what in a sense he became with his possession of these two Romagna towns, was a new one for a foreign mercenary leader. Not only was the position of the mercenary captain, the condottiere, now recognised but the process of attaching him to the state had begun.

But the days of the companies were not quite done. The Bretons led by Bertrand de la Salle and Jean de Malestroit still served the popes, and after the Great Schism in 1378 when Cardinal Robert of Geneva was established as the rival Avignonese pope to the properly elected Urban VI, the Bretons served their old master, now Clement VII, the anti-Pope, in the war which ensued. Urban VI turned for support to a new company which had been formed by the Romagnol noble Alberigo da Barbiano, a company which once again took the title of the Company of St. George. Much has been written about Alberigo and his company who became almost folk heroes in the minds of Italians. To many, the Company represented a revival of Italian military prowess after over a century in which the battlefields of Italy had been dominated by foreigners. Alberigo da Barbiano is usually taken to be the first of the condottieri, while his company is seen as the last and infinitely the most worthy of the companies. After his victory over the Bretons at the battle of Marino in 1379, Alberigo was hailed by the pope as the liberator of Italy, and even the humanists, who generally deplored the whole mercenary profession, placed the achievements of Alberigo and his brave and unique band in a rather different category. But in fact there was nothing unique or revolutionary about Alberigo da Barbiano, nor was 1379 any great turning point in Italian military history. Alberigo was by no means the first leader of an Italian company; there had been two other companies of St. George led by Italians and largely composed of Italians. The fourteenth-century companies had always contained a proportion of Italian soldiers; throughout the century the Italian states had employed Italians as their captain generals. Alberigo da Barbiano formed a company which, like that of Hawkwood, was loyal to himself; its nucleus was men from his own estates in the Romagna. The trend towards this new conception of a company and its relationship with its leader had been discernible for some time. Alberigo had the good fortune and the skill to defeat the Bretons; this was by no means the first time that Italian troops had defeated a foreign company, but the Bretons did happen to be the last great foreign company. The numbers of foreign leaders and mercenaries in Italy gradually dwindled during the remaining years of the century, although Hawkwood remained dominating the scene, and the Florentine army was still led in 1402 by the Gascon Bernardon de Serres. Alberigo's company certainly did not behave any differently to previous companies; in 1380 they were fighting alongside German and Hungarian mercenaries against Florence, defended by Hawkwood and Lucius, the son of Conrad of Landau. Alberigo was defeated by Lucius at Malmantile only a year after his much acclaimed victory over the Bretons, and in 1381 he and his company sacked Arezzo in a style which varied little from that of the Bretons at Cesena.

Alberigo da Barbiano continued to be one of the leading captains in Italy until the end of the century, but by no means the outstanding one as we shall see in the next chapter. During that period there were still a few companies which fought under collective names and preserved traces of that corporate quality which had distinguished the great companies of the middle of the century. There was the second Company of the Star formed by Ettore Manfredi in 1379 and shattered by the Genoese when it tried to blackmail them twice in the same year. There was at the very end of the century the Company of the Rose which roamed Italy serving different masters until 1410 but was never a large or significant force. The days in which large companies of rootless foreign mercenaries ranged over Italy had passed. In Northern Europe the foundations of permanent armies had already been laid, and in Italy the increasingly powerful states were also seeking to establish permanent means of defence and permanent relationships with soldiers.

So the companies had come and gone, but as was suggested at the beginning of this chapter, they were by no means the only elements in Italian warfare in the fourteenth century. Mercenaries were employed by all the Italian cities either as individuals or in small detachments, and the hiring of a large company was only an exceptional expedient. Furthermore, the use of militia levies survived longer into the fourteenth century than has sometimes been thought. In Florence, although the employment of mercenaries was standard and highly organised practice by the 1320's, and both Pisa and Florence had issued complete and detailed regulations for the recruitment and control of mercenary troops by the middle of the century, the Florentine communal cavalry were still to be found in the armies of this period and militia obligations remained. In May 1302, when the Florentine army took the field to besiege Pistoia, it was made up of 1,000 cavalry and over 6,000 infantry. The paymaster's accounts, which have survived, show that about half the cavalry were Florentines, and of the infantry only 1,000 were foreign mercenaries while the rest were made up of cross-bowmen and shield-bearers from the city militia, and contingents of militia infantry and pioneers from the countryside. The army was commanded by the Podestà and accompanied by 113 stone-masons and carpenters, eight pay clerks, 42 porters, six provisioners, four tailors and four trumpeters. The Venetians in the War of Ferrara (1308–13) also relied largely on their own citizens, but this was partly because their enemy, the pope, had excommunicated them and this discouraged mercenaries from serving under their flag. Venetians joined the army at Ferrara for 15 days' service in rotation, and the captain general was a Venetian noble.

By 1359 when the Florentine captain general Pandolfo Malatesta took the field against the Great Company, the militia cavalry element had disappeared from the army and the 4,000 cavalry were entirely mercenaries. But the number was made up by many small contingents, some hired directly by Florence and others sent by her allies, and, although they included Germans and Hungarians, they also included many Italians. Malatesta himself was only one of several members of his family who served Florence as captain general during the century, and indeed the supreme military commanders of the period were usually Italians. Cardinal Albornoz, the most famous of the papal legates who sought to restore order in the Papal States during the absence of the popes in Avignon, employed mostly Italian captains for his army, although many of the troops were Hungarians. Among his leaders were members of the Malatesta family, Pietro Farnese, Andrea Salamoncelli da Lucca, Count Carlo da Dovadola, and Ugolino da Montemarte who was also a noted military architect and the designer of a number of Albornoz's castles including that at Ancona.

Thus the idea of Italian warfare in the fourteenth century being entirely dominated by foreign mercenaries and foreign captains is a very mistaken one. There were rarely more than two or three major companies operating at any one time, and few states could afford to hire one. There were certainly many small groups of foreign mercenaries available, and most armies would contain some, but, when one Italian city wished to attack another, it was still on its own militia that it relied in the first instance. A case in point was the war between Siena and Perugia in 1357–8. The trouble started over the little Tuscan hill town of Montepulciano which, although usually subject to Siena, in 1357 offered itself to Perugia. The Perugians accepted the offer and Siena prepared to fight to regain her lost possession and allied with neighbouring Cortona. The Perugian militia sallied out and laid siege to Cortona, and this started a steadily escalating war. The citizens of Cortona defended themselves gallantly, and Siena sent her standing mercenary cavalry force of 200 men under Mainetto da Jesi, a noted professional soldier from the Marches, to relieve her ally. Mainetto was unable to drive off the Perugians but did manage to raise the spirits of Cortona, which resisted a desultory siege all through the winter. With the spring of 1358, the Sienese made greater efforts and hired the services of Hannekin Bongarten and his famous company. Bongarten had about 1,200 men of his own and these, combined with the Sienese militia, succeeded in raising the siege of Cortona. This stirred the Perugians to greater action and their captain general, another prominent Marches noble, Smeduccio da Sanseverino, led out a large army of over 8,000 men of which a force of 400 Hungarians seem to have been the only foreign mercenaries. Smeduccio defeated and captured Bongarten at the battle of Torrita, and the Sienese sent out frantic appeals for further assistance. Florence now sent some troops, and Siena employed Giovanni da Vico, a Roman noble, as her new commander; she also sought to bring in Conrad of Landau and the Great Company, but Conrad, marching south, met disaster at Le Scalelle. However, despite these set-backs Siena's greater resources began to tell and she got the better of the enemy in the later stages of the war. Here then was a typical small Italian war of the fourteenth century; two cities fighting, at first largely with their own resources commanded by Italian captains; then as the war escalated more and more mercenaries, and even major companies, became involved, not always successfully; in the end the richer city gained the upper hand but rarely to the extent of being able to enter the rival's walls.

A final way of setting the foreign mercenaries in perspective is to consider some of the leading Italian soldiers of the period alongside the foreigners already mentioned. Werner of Urslingen, Conrad of Landau, Fra Moriale, and Hawkwood were formidable figures, but we must also remember Castruccio Castracane, Guidoriccio da Fogliano, Francesco Ordelaffi and Ambrogio Visconti, who were just a few of the Italian leaders in the fifty years before the appearance of Alberigo da Barbiano. Castruccio Castracane was the classic example of the exile turned soldier; born into the noble family of the Antelminelli of Lucca, he was forced to flee from Lucca at the age of 16 with his parents when the Guelphs took over the city. For 17 years he lived in exile, visiting England and the court of Edward I, fighting in France, and serving both the Della Scala in Verona and the Venetians as a mercenary. In 1314 he joined the army of Uguccione della Faggiuola, the Tuscan baron who had seized control in Pisa and was now setting his sights on Lucca. Uguccione was successful in this venture, took Lucca by surprise and installed himself as master of the city. In 1315 his army led by Castruccio defeated the Florentines, including Diego de Rat and his mercenaries, at Montecatini. In the following year Castruccio, with the support of the Lucchesi, deposed Uguccione and took over as ruler of the city, and for the next twelve years he was the leading Ghibelline in Tuscany. He crushed the Florentines again in 1325 at Altopascio, proving himself the military master of the Florentine Spanish general Raimondo da Cardona. Castruccio died in 1328, undefeated, and was later glorified by Machiavelli, who felt unable to find many examples of Italian prowess in the succeeding two centuries.

What Machiavelli did for the memory of Castruccio, the Sienese painter Simone Martini did for that of Guidoriccio da Fogliano. Both idealised their subjects; Machiavelli's Castruccio is the epitome of the classical military hero, Martini's Guidoriccio is proud master of all he surveys as he rides alone across the Tuscan landscape. But while Castruccio was the frustrated and ambitious exile eventually seizing the lordship of his native city, Guidoriccio was another type of soldier, the professional captain who led Siena's army for seven years between 1327 and 1334. Simone Martini's painting was commissioned by a proud city intent on emphasising its control over the surrounding countryside. The prominent position of Guidoriccio in the picture is something of an artistic accident; Siena certainly did not think of him as a triumphant war lord but as a useful and unusually faithful mercenary captain. Nor was his career a particularly notable one; Guidoriccio came from the noble Fogliani family of Reggio Emilia, a family which provided many military and civic officials to the cities of central Italy. After his period of service with Siena, he served the Della Scala in Verona and also for a time fought under Werner of Urslingen. He was a fore-runner of many of the fifteenth-century condottieri, a repre-sentative of the continuity of Italian military traditions.

Another characteristic type of Italian military leader was the soldier prince, the ruler by inheritance of a city who not only needed to defend himself and his state but also sold his military services as a mercenary to win wealth and experi-ence. The many soldiers of the Malatesta family are typical of this phenomenon, and another outstanding example was Francesco degli Ordelaffi, the lord of Forlì in the Romagna. Francesco was acclaimed lord of Forlì in 1331 on the death of his uncle but was briefly evicted by the papal legate. How-ever, he recovered the city two years later and added Cesena to his domain. For twenty years he fought, sometimes to expand his state, sometimes in the pay of others; he led a Visconti army against the Alidosi of Imola and a Pisan army against the Florentines; he employed the Great Company in one war and fought for the Hungarians in another. He had the reputation of being peculiarly brutal towards the clergy, but this was largely because the pope was his titular overlord and was constantly trying to evict him. In the end it was Cardinal Albornoz who, through years of persistent pressure, succeeded in dispossessing him. Francesco's wife Cia conducted a heroic but vain defence of Cesena, and his son Giovanni defied the papal forces in Bertinoro. But gradually Francesco and his family were squeezed out, and he ended his days in the less ambivalent position of mercenary captain to Venice, living in comparative penury but accorded a sumptuous funeral by the grateful republic.

Finally Ambrogio Visconti was typical of yet another type of Italian soldier; he was the illegitimate son of Bernabò Visconti, ruler of Milan. Born into an ambitious and well-placed family but barred from enjoying the ultimate consequences of that position, he turned to the career of arms. He formed the Company of St. George in 1365 and joined up with Hawkwood. His career was therefore that of leader of a great company; restless, landless, he had fluctuating fortunes and ended up the victim of peasant retaliation against his predatory troops.

Ambrogio Visconti was one of a very large family. His father Bernabò had fifteen legitimate children and at least five illegitimate daughters. His legitimate daughters were married to rulers all over Europe; three successive Dukes of Bavaria were his sons-in-law together with the Duke of Austria, the King of Cyprus, the lord of Mantua and the Duke of Kent. But five of his illegitimate daughters were married to soldiers in Italy; Donnina was married to Hawkwood, Elisabetta to Lucius of Landau, and Riccarda to Bertrand de la Salle. Here was an indication both of the rising personal prestige of the military leader, and also of the attempts to attach successful soldiers to the states and the ruling dynasties. In these circumstances the days of the great independent companies were clearly numbered. Furthermore, the threat of the companies had produced in the 1360's and 1370's a series of leagues specifically directed against them. The leagues stipulated the maintenance of permanent military forces by the member states and provided for common military action against the companies. Not that such action was often effective in itself; cooperation was difficult for Italian states, which were always such intense rivals. But the possibilities of permanent military employment, created by the leagues, already provided a solution to the problem. Here was an attractive alternative to all but the most ambitious soldier, and the companies began to break up as their leaders took service with the individual states in the new conditions of growing permanence of employment.

But this long process of growing reliance on mercenaries and the maintenance of standing forces of mercenaries had a natural corollary. The costs of warfare accelerated enormously, and the very presence of available mercenaries made war more common as states sought to utilise their expensive employees. The popes in the fourteenth century were sometimes spending as much as 60 per cent of their revenue on war, and this was a proportion which probably applied to most Italian states. This in turn meant an immense increase both in taxation and, perhaps even more significantly, in the administration both of finances and of war. It has been argued with great cogency that the principal driving force in the growth of organised bureaucracy, of fiscal and credit institutions, and ultimately of centralised political power, was the rising cost of warfare, and nowhere was this more clear than in Italy.

It was perhaps in this related area of war expenditure that fourteenth-century warfare showed the greatest developments. In the art of war the changes were not dramatic; the armoured strength of the cavalryman tended to increase as did the number of his followers; the English archers came and went, winning some battles but attracting few imitators; infantry tended to become more specialised and consequently relatively fewer in number; artillery made a very hesitant and relatively insignificant appearance. But to the states of Italy, war meant a very different thing in 1380 to what it had meant a century before.

CHAPTER THREE

SOLDIERS OF FORTUNE

The years around 1380 were decisive for the history of Italian warfare as they clearly saw the end of the great companies and the final emergence of the individual captain as the key to subsequent military developments. This was not because of Alberigo da Barbiano's victory at Marino nor because of any startling revival of Italian martial spirit. Alberigo was always a less renowned and significant figure than Hawkwood in the years after 1380, and his adversary at Marino, Bertrand de la Salle, also continued to play a role in Italian warfare with his Gascon and Breton followers until 1390. Indeed the next period which stretches from about 1380 until the defeat and death of Braccio da Montone at Aquila in 1424 is very much a period of transition in which the great condottieri, apparently liberated from the restrictions of corporate company organisation, began to struggle with the strengthening tentacles of state control.

The major factor in the decline of the influence of the companies was the growth of a more organised political structure in late fourteenth-century Italy. The tendency of the larger Italian states to expand and to develop a more coherent and centralised political organisation inevitably led to a greater emphasis on permanent defence. The companies could not survive against the growing military strength of the more powerful states or the leagues of the less powerful ones; nor did they have the will to survive as the attractions of contract service increased. The outstanding example of this new political phenomenon was the Milan of Giangaleazzo Visconti, united after Giangaleazzo's coup against his uncle Bernabò in 1385. Giangaleazzo, although by no means a martial figure himself, had a keen awareness of the need for an organised and powerful military force to carry out his ambitions to make Milan the predominant state in northern Italy. He had already, while the ruler of only the smaller half of the Milanese state, made Jacopo dal Verme his captain general in 1378, and Dal Verme was to serve him in this capacity for thirty years.

It is perhaps incongruous to start a chapter which will be in large part devoted to describing the independence and unreliability of a number of the key military figures around the end of the fourteenth century, with a discussion of the most outstanding example of the faithful condottiere in the period. But this perhaps helps to put the period into perspective and to bring out the crucial point that it was the political situation in various parts of Italy which dictated military conditions and organisation, and the political conditions varied from a highly advanced degree of political organisation to complete anarchy.

Jacopo dal Verme was a Veronese noble, born about 1350, the son of Lucchino dal Verme who had commanded the Venetian army which had suppressed the revolt in Crete in 1364. He fought his first campaigns in Piedmont but was already by 1370 usually in the service of the Visconti. Little is known about these early years, but his appointment as Giangaleazzo's captain general at the age of 28 was an indication of a growing military reputation. From then onwards he was part of the cultured Visconti court at Pavia and played a major role in the expansion of the Visconti state. He was clearly not a flamboyant figure and one's impression of his campaigns is that of a serious and rather cautious professional soldier. However, he won brilliant victories over the Duke of Armagnac and his French army at Alessandria in 1391, and over the German army of the Emperor at Brescia in 1401. He also proved himself on several occasions a worthy opponent of Hawkwood. As rewards for his services, he received numerous estates and castles from Giangaleazzo Visconti, and in 1388, on the occasion of his successful leadership of a combined Milanese–Venetian army against Padua, he was elected to the Venetian nobility and given a palace in Venice; he also received the citizenship of Milan in 1390.

It was Jacopo dal Verme who was one of the companions of the future Henry IV of England on a pilgrimage to the Holy Land in 1392. It was just at this moment, and perhaps even because of Jacopo's temporary absence, that Giangaleazzo brought off a considerable coup and added Alberigo da Barbiano to his cluster of long-serving condottieri. Alberigo had spent most of the 1380's fighting in Naples where he had been made Great Constable of the Kingdom and in 1390 Viceroy of Calabria. But in 1392 he was captured in local fighting in the Marches and a ransom of 30,000 florins was demanded for him. Giangaleazzo saw his opportunity and paid the ransom in return for an oath from Alberigo to serve him for ten years. So Alberigo da Barbiano came to Lombardy and took his place alongside Jacopo dal Verme as joint commander of the Milanese army. It was these two men together who carried out the last stage of Giangaleazzo's expansion policy, when they defeated the Florentines at Casalecchio in 1402 and occupied Bologna.

Giangaleazzo Visconti had been equally astute in gaining the services of another leading condottiere, Facino Cane. Cane came from a reasonably affluent Piedmontese family and saw his first fighting about 1380. He was a superlative horseman and specialised in leading lightning cavalry raids and devastation operations. He also had a reputation for brutality, but it was a sort of calculated brutality designed to create the maximum fear and therefore the minimum resistance to his activities. Cane was not the sort of man to fit well into the Milanese army and Giangaleazzo came to a special arrangement with him, lending him 4,000 florins in 1393 in return for a promise by the condottiere to come and serve when sent for. He spent most of his time fighting in local wars in Piedmont, but in 1397 the call from Milan came and for the next five years he was almost permanently with the Visconti army and led the advance guard with great bravery at Casalecchio.

Other condottieri who served Giangaleazzo Visconti in the 1390's were Ugolotto Biancardo, Pandolfo and Carlo Mala-testa, and Ottobuono Terzo. Some like Facino Cane came when required; others were Lombards who had been given estates and fiefs by Giangaleazzo and provided a permanent nucleus of captains. Giangaleazzo had thus been able to forge in a few years a remarkably effective military force which was the spearhead of Milanese expansion.

The only state which could seriously resist this Visconti drive was Florence, and the 1390's were taken up with a series of wars between the two states. As long as Hawkwood was alive and leading the Florentines, then the balance between the two states was fairly even. Hawkwood, although largely committed to Florence after 1380, did serve other masters and brought off his greatest coup in 1387 when he led the Paduans to victory over the Veronese at Castagnaro. This was a battle which illustrates better than any other both the tactical genius of Hawkwood and the advantages which his 'English' methods enjoyed in Italy. The stage was set by a feigned withdrawal by Hawkwood to draw the impetuous Veronese on to a battleground of his own choosing. This he found in marshy country to the south east of Verona, bisected by irrigation canals. Behind one of these canals and on

3 (a)   A fourteenth-century camp. Detail from Simone Martini's fresco *Guidoric-cio da' Fogliano* in the Palazzo Pubblico at Siena. At this time it was clearly usual for the bulk of the army to sleep in straw shelters rather than tents.

(b)   *The Finances of the Commune of Siena in peace and war.* This is one of the painted wooden covers on the Sienese public account books (*Libri della Biccherna e della Gabella*) and is attributed to Benvenuto di Giovanni (1468). The group on the right are the three men of a lance receiving their pay.

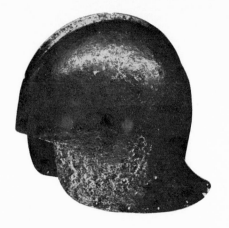

4 (a) A North Italian sallet of
second half of the fifteenth centu
This type of helmet was widely u
by infantry and lightly armed caval

(b) A North Italian *barbuta*, c. 14
70. The *barbuta* was originally int
duced from Germany in the fo
teenth century.

(c) A late fifteenth-century Italian arquebus. The arquebus began to replace the
hand-gun as the main hand firearm after about 1470.

somewhat firmer ground, he dismounted his cavalry and drew them up in close array. On each flank and pushed forward of the main position, he concealed crossbowmen, his 600 English archers, and a few cannon. The Veronese advanced confidently into this carefully prepared trap; they halted momentarily when confronted with the ditch, but quickly organised themselves to fill it with bundles of branches and began to storm across. At this moment Hawkwood's archers began to pour in their fire from the flanks while the men-at-arms firmly blocked the Veronese advance in the centre. As the hail of arrows began to take its toll and gaps began to appear in the demoralised Veronese ranks, Hawkwood gave the order to advance and his dismounted knights moved inexorably into the fray. The rout was complete; most of the Veronese army was either killed or captured; Hawkwood's reputation as the leading captain in Italy was confirmed.

Florence certainly recognised Hawkwood's pre-eminence by going to unheard of—and never to be repeated—lengths to retain his services. Immediately after his death Agnolo Gaddi and Giuliano d'Arrigo were commissioned to execute a memorial fresco of Hawkwood in the cathedral. This was replaced in 1436 by the great equestrian fresco by Paolo Uccello which can still be seen today. However this concern with Hawkwood's memorial 40 years after his death was not so much a desire to commemorate him more worthily as an interesting preoccupation with up to date artistic styles and a piece of Medici inspired propaganda to stimulate Florentine interest in military affairs. However in Hawkwood's lifetime, Florence poured rewards on him. During these last years of his life he received three castles: the towering fortress of Montecchio overlooking the Umbrian plain near Cortona, a castle near Poggibonsi guarding the road to Siena, and an estate with castle at S. Donato in Polverosa. He was given a house in Florence, a life pension of 2,000 florins, and dowries for his three daughters. His wife, Donnina Visconti, was also promised a pension in the event of his death.

Hawkwood perhaps needed little encouragement to settle down in Florentine service, but he certainly continued to soldier actively into the last years of his life. 1391 was a particularly busy summer for him, as he led the army of Florence and her allies into Lombardy to try conclusions with the Visconti. The plan for a joint assault on Milan by Hawkwood from the east and the Duke of Armagnac from the west broke down when Armagnac was defeated by Jacopo dal Verme at Alessandria. This left Hawkwood no alternative but to retreat before Dal Verme's greatly superior army, and the success with which he held his army together during the withdrawal, counter attacked at appropriate moments to hold the enemy back, and finally emerged from Lombardy with his army intact, was perhaps a better indication of his ability and the discipline which he exercised over his troops than any of his victories.

Hawkwood was preparing to leave Florence and retire to England when he died in 1394. He was given a state funeral, as the Florentines racked their brains to decide how to replace him. Giangaleazzo had created something of a monopoly on good Italian leaders, and after one or two unsuccessful experiments Florence offered the command to Bernardon de Serres. Bernardon was a Gascon who had come to Italy originally with the Breton Company in the 1370's and had fought at Marino. His career had not been particularly distinguished, but he did have a large company and he was a foreigner, which in Florentine eyes at this time was a recommendation. They needed a permanent successor to Hawkwood but were reluctant to commit themselves to an Italian who might be encouraged to try and take control of the city. Bernardone enjoyed limited success against Milan but was decisively defeated by Dal Verme and Alberigo da

Barbiano at Casalecchio in 1402, and soon after retired to France.

In Florence and Milan, and to a lesser extent in some of the smaller states of Lombardy like Padua and Verona, the realisation of the need for permanent forces and permanent commanders is clear in the last two decades of the fourteenth century. Venice at this stage still had little territorial interest in the Italian mainland and little need to maintain any considerable force of troops. In central and southern Italy the political situation was a good deal more confused, as both the Papal States and Naples were torn by almost constant civil war. In this situation the condottieri played a rather different role: they became in a certain sense the arbiters of the situation and their allegiances were much less clearly defined and more brief. It was in these political conditions that the powerful condottieri got a reputation for infidelity and ambition; the chances were there for them to grab cities and carve out states for themselves. The Papal States in particular were already a patchwork of semi-independent cities, many of them ruled by papal vicars whose allegiance to the pope was little more than a formality, and many of the condottieri sought to emulate such men.

In this area another group of condottieri were coming to the fore who, although they often became involved in the more rigid and disciplined political situation in the north, tended to drift southwards in search of greater personal opportunities. Alberigo da Barbiano had spent the 1380's in the south, and the Bretons and Gascons of Bertrand de la Salle and Bernardon de Serres still controlled the rough country north of Rome. One of the condottieri who made his name entirely in central Italy was Boldrino da Panicale, an Umbrian who never reached the top of his profession but whose errant, restless life was typical of some central Italian soldiers. His company was never more than 200 lances strong and oscillated between the service of Siena, Perugia, the popes, and various Romagna lords. He had a reputation for infidelity, but because he had a good company which was loyal to him he could always find an employer in that troubled region. Eventually the papal Marquis of the Marches, Andrea Tomacelli, who had used Boldrino to help him restore order in the Papal States, decided that he would anticipate Boldrino's next desertion and win popularity with the local inhabitants by having him murdered at a dinner party in Macerata. Boldrino's company is said to have carried the body of their murdered leader with them for two years as they sought to be revenged on Tomacelli.

But one of the best examples of these men was Biordo de' Michelotti, a Perugian noble who had been exiled during factional struggles in Perugia and whose main aim was to regain a position in his native city and indeed to take it over. He fought at Alessandria under Jacopo dal Verme and was also for a brief period Florentine captain general after the death of Hawkwood. But it was in Umbria that he really made his mark. He took over the company of Boldrino da Panicale, occupied Todi and Orvieto late in 1394 and was enfeuded with them by the pope. Then a revolt in Perugia enabled him to gain control there, and for the last years of his life he established himself as lord of Perugia. He did serve again briefly in the Milanese army in 1397, but it was in Perugia that he was murdered in 1398.

One could multiply indefinitely the examples of central Italian condottieri in this period, but the outstanding characteristics of these men are perhaps already apparent. A figure who is more difficult to ascribe to any particular type, but who seems to have exercised a considerable influence, was Cecchino Broglia da Chieri. Broglia was Piedmontese and first served under Alberigo da Barbiano and was present at Marino. He was also in the Paduan army at Castagnaro under

Hawkwood, and at Alessandria under Jacopo dal Verme. He can probably be described as one of those condottieri who appeared spasmodically in the Visconti army when needed, but he had very much a career of his own and this tended to be in central Italy. He spent a number of years in the 1390's with his company in the Romagna and Umbria, but not being a native of any of the local cities he does not seem to have been inspired by a desire to become lord of any of them. What was significant about him was his reputation as an instructor in the art of war; many of the leading condottieri of the next two generations served at one time or another in his company, and he was always regarded with considerable respect for this reason. Facino Cane, Ottobuono Terzo, Carmagnola, Gattamelata and Tartaglia were all 'pupils' of Broglia. Florence made a number of attempts to win his services including offering a life pension in 1396, but he was too restless a figure to accept a permanent position until the last years of his life. It was only finally in 1398 that he agreed to become one of Florence's permanent condottieri and was given a house in the city as well as a pension. He died of plague in Empoli in 1400, and the Republic buried him with full military honours in the cathedral in Florence.

It was around the turn of the century that the political situation in Italy changed completely, and a new generation of condottieri led by the predominant figures of Braccio da Montone and Musio Attendolo Sforza came to the fore. The death of Giangaleazzo Visconti, shortly after the great victory won by his army over the Florentines at Casalecchio in 1402, meant a temporary break in that move towards political organisation and centralisation in the north, and a predominance in the next twenty years of the divisive and anarchic factors in Italian politics of which the condottieri took full advantage.

Giangaleazzo's death was unexpected and threw the

Milanese state into confusion. His legitimate sons were both still children and neither showed any sign of being able effectively to succeed their father. In fact, in his will he went a long way towards dividing his state between them and his illegitimate son, Gabrielle Maria, although leaving the title of duke and a certain pre-eminence to the elder and less balanced of the two, Giovanni Maria. At the side of the new duke was his mother, Caterina Visconti, a woman with little political experience but a good deal of personality. Against this new and uncertain regime, revolts broke out in both Milan itself and a number of the subject cities. In this difficult situation the arbiters of events were the condottieri, who divided between those who remained basically faithful to the Visconti, and those who gradually turned to draw personal advantage from the confused situation. The first to break away was Alberigo da Barbiano, but he, now in his declining years, was a spent force and passed the last years of his life intriguing with no very definite aim rather than campaigning. More clear cut were the defections of Pandolfo Malatesta, Ottobuono Terzo and Gabrino Fondulo who took advantage of the revolts in Brescia, Parma and Cremona respectively to take control of those cities and set up their own rule. Terzo and Fondulo were men of limited significance whose brief lordships of their cities came to violent ends, but Pandolfo Malatesta was a rather different and more interesting figure of whom more will be said later.

Faithful to the Visconti in their own different ways and for different reasons were Jacopo dal Verme, Carlo Malatesta and Facino Cane. Dal Verme continued to lead the Milanese army in its attempts to protect the frontiers from the insistent pressure of Florence and her allies, and in dealing with internal revolts. But he soon became disillusioned with the atmosphere of suspicion and self interest which prevailed in Milan in the years after Giangaleazzo's death, and retired from the scene temporarily to serve the Venetians. Carlo Malatesta, the lord of Rimini, was always only partly committed to the Visconti and intervened only spasmodically to attempt to restore some sort of order and civility to Milanese affairs. The real controller of the situation in the first years after 1402 was Facino Cane, who played his part in the initial defence of the regime but soon began to move towards the ultimate goal of the lordship of Milan itself. With the help of the younger of the Visconti brothers, Filippo Maria, who had established himself in Pavia, Cane created a base for himself in Alessandria. Then, after the death of the Duchess Caterina, he began to exert a predominant influence over the Duke himself. Jacopo dal Verme and Carlo Malatesta returned briefly in 1407 to attempt to destroy Cane's influence and re-establish true Visconti control, but the perverse and perverted character of Duke Giovanni Maria made him a difficult man to like or support. So the two older condottieri abandoned the task; Dal Verme returned once again to Venetian service and died fighting the Turks; Malatesta returned to his other preoccupations in central Italy. Cane was left to exercise complete control in Milan until his sudden death from gout in 1411.

No sooner was his 'protector' gone, than Giovanni Maria was himself murdered and his younger brother was able to succeed to an undivided but mutilated inheritance. Filippo Maria Visconti emerged as a man cast in somewhat the same mould as his father; ambitious and enormously concerned to strengthen the Visconti state, but basically not a martial figure and therefore dependent on the creation of a faithful and reasonably permanent army. Now deprived of the help of any of his father's condottieri, he relied at first on one of Facino Cane's captains, Francesco Bussone, Count of Carmagnola. For ten years Carmagnola and the Duke worked to restore the Visconti state to its original territorial limits. The culmination of this work was the expulsion of Pandolfo Malatesta from Brescia in 1421. But, until then, Milan had ceased to be the aggressive force which it had been under Giangaleazzo, even though it gradually recovered from the disastrous political confusion of the first decade of the century.

Florence, freed from the incubus of Milanese aggression, was able to relax to some extent its defensive guard and its military commitments. The rising tide of civic humanist ideology with its emphasis on citizens playing an active role in both the government and the defence of the city contributed to heightening Florence's traditional fear of mercenaries and reluctance to spend money on them. So, despite the military demands of the attack on Pisa in 1405-6, and the prolonged defence of the state against King Ladislas of Naples between 1409 and 1414, Florence's progress towards the creation of a standing army and permanent relationships with condottieri became remarkably retarded. Great captains passed briefly through the pages of the accounts of Florentine military expenditure in this period, but none stayed to emulate the position of Hawkwood.

With Venice, however, the story was very different. In 1404-5 she had taken the first serious step towards the conquest of a territorial state on the Italian mainland with the capture of Vicenza, Verona and Padua from the Carrara family. A considerable army was assembled for this war, and amongst the commanders employed were Malatesta Malatesta, Paolo Savelli and Jacopo dal Verme. After the war, which resulted in the acquisition of a considerable block of territory and a land frontier with Milan, Venice was aware of the need for permanent defence on land. Fifteen hundred cavalry was at first the nucleus of the army, but two subsequent wars against the Hungarians in 1411-12 and 1418-20 both increased the size of the Venetian state, as Friuli and Istria were added, and emphasised the need for the defence of the long Alpine frontiers to the north and east. Carlo Malatesta and Pandolfo Malatesta commanded the Venetian army in the first of these wars, and Pandolfo remained as Venetian captain general on a part-time basis until about 1417.

The two Malatesta brothers were interesting figures who played a considerable part in the wars of this period. Carlo Malatesta was the ruler of the main Malatesta city, Rimini. He, even more than his brother, was rather different to most of the condottieri of the day in that he had a secure and long established base and had been brought up as a prince and a ruler as well as a soldier. He had spent some of his youth in Florence and was a pupil of the Florentine humanist, Malpighini, as well as being a friend of the Florentine Chancellor, Coluccio Salutati. He was a noted patron of the arts and had given Ghiberti some of his first work in the Malatesta palace at Rimini. Above all, perhaps, he was a profoundly religious man who represented the Roman pope, Gregory XII, at the Council of Constance. There is a story that when in Mantua in 1397 he ordered the statue of Virgil in the city to be destroyed, because it had become an object of worship; the implication being that he was a Christian first and a classical humanist afterwards. As a soldier Carlo Malatesta had great prestige, but it was a prestige that came more from his background and the fact that, as lord of Rimini, he could recruit and maintain a sizeable company of good troops, than from any spectacular degree of military success. He was a cautious general, who at various stages in his career commanded Visconti, Venetian, Florentine and papal armies. His attempt to intervene in Milanese politics in 1407-8 and avert the supremacy of Facino Cane was unsuccessful; he was severely wounded in Venetian service when his army was surprised by the Hungarians at Motta; then came a sound defeat at the hands of Braccio da Montone at S. Egidio in 1416. The Florentines once referred to him as a man who was 'very accustomed to losing' and employed his brother, Pandolfo, as well, as a sort of insurance policy. But the ransom of 100,000 florins which Braccio demanded for him, when he took him prisoner at S. Egidio, is some indication both of Carlo's potential wealth and his reputation.

Pandolfo Malatesta, the younger brother, was a man of the same stamp, although rather more ambitious and unpredictable. He was the Lord of Fano in the Marches, and then after the death of Giangaleazzo Visconti he established himself as the Lord of Brescia. Like his brother he had received a humanist education, was a fluent Latinist and also understood French and Provençal. At Brescia he created a court of some importance in early fifteenth-century culture, and he also maintained his company at a level of size and permanence which would almost justify the title of a standing army. Niccolò da Tolentino, Angelo della Pergola and Martino da Faenza all spent many years in the service of Pandolfo and were key figures at his court. After he was driven out of Brescia, Pandolfo returned to Fano and re-established himself there. For a number of years he was commander of the Venetian army and had a palace in Venice; in the early 1420's he commanded the Florentine army in the Romagna and was well thought of as a tactful and successful leader of men.

The opponent of the Malatesta brothers in 1411-12 and the commander of the Hungarian army was the Florentine, Filippo Scolari, better known as Pippo Spano. Pippo spent his life in Hungarian service and therefore does not really figure in a history of Italian warfare, but his part in that campaign against the Venetians and the singular interest of his career justify a brief glance at him. The Scolari were an old Florentine noble family, who, when not actually in exile from

Florence, were generally distrusted in the city and excluded from any role in politics. Filippo went to Hungary at the age of thirteen as apprentice and book-keeper for a Florentine merchant and soon attracted attention as a brilliant young man and a capable administrator. He entered the service of King Sigismund and rapidly began to gain military experience in the wars against the Turks. He was present in the crusading army at Nicopolis in 1396 and by 1408 had received the title of Ispan (count) and was Governor of Bosnia. Because of his long experience of fighting the Turks, Pippo Spano developed very different military skills to most of the Italian condottieri. He was a dashing cavalry leader, who was accustomed to fighting war to the death. His cruelty towards his prisoners and the speed and ruthlessness of his tactics completely nonplussed the Venetians and Carlo Malatesta in the early stages of the Hungarian war. But gradually the more methodical and cautious approach of the Italian condottieri gained the upper hand, and Pippo was defeated.

In Florence, which he visited in 1410 as representative of the Emperor, Pippo was regarded with suspicion and some fear. Both his family background and the ostentatious display of wealth and authority which he affected thoroughly frightened his countrymen. But, although unlike most exiles he seemed to have no desire to recover a position in his native city, he always retained an affection for Florence. Florentines were always welcome at his court in Hungary, and it was he who brought Masolino to Hungary to work on his chapel at Albercele. He also endowed the building of a chapel in Florence, the Rotonda di Sta. Maria degli Angeli, which was designed by Brunelleschi. In addition he was a passionate collector of manuscripts and a considerable architectural patron in Hungary.

But Pippo Spano, despite his Florentine background and upbringing, lived in a different world and fought a different type of warfare to that of the Italians, and we must now return to the Italian scene in the first two decades of the fifteenth century. If the political framework in northern Italy had changed dramatically in these years, with the temporary eclipse of Visconti power and the growth of the Venetian commitment to mainland politics, the situation in central and southern Italy remained on the whole much as it had been in the previous period. There was, however, an exceptional side to this picture: the brief emergence of Naples as an aggressive and organised power under King Ladislas between 1408 and 1414. Ladislas in his attempts to make himself master of central Italy by occupying Rome and large parts of the Papal States, and by threatening Florence, built up a large army which at the time of his death in 1414 was said to number 16,000 cavalry. In fact, there is not very much evidence of continuity of leadership or permanence in this army or in that of the papal–Angevin alliance which opposed it. But the sustained aggression of Ladislas did make some difference to the military pattern in this part of Italy: both armies and the individual companies of condottieri in these armies tended to increase in size, and the command of such armies conferred added prestige on the captains.

But on the whole the political pattern in central and southern Italy remained a confused one. The Papal States, until well after the arrival of Martin V in Rome in 1420, remained the area in which the independence and ambitions of condottieri could be most easily asserted. Naples, after the death of Ladislas, became once more the scene of continuous civil war until the final victory of Alfonso V and the Aragonese in 1442. These were the conditions which encouraged the emergence of the two greatest condottieri figures of this period, Braccio da Montone and Musio Attendolo Sforza, whose distinctive styles of warfare were to be handed on to their successors and pupils and were to some extent to dominate Italian military history for the rest of the century.

Musio Attendolo, better known as Sforza, was born into the influential and warlike Romagnol family of the Attendoli in 1369. Although they were not noble, but in fact affluent rural middle class, the Attendoli were already competing with the noble Pasolini family for the domination of Cotignola, the town which was shortly to be given to Hawkwood by the pope. Musio, like many of his family, was destined to be a soldier, and at the age of thirteen he became a page to one of the men-at-arms of Boldrino da Panicale. In the early 1390's he was with Alberigo da Barbiano, first as a squadron commander and then with his own *condotta* (contract) for 75 cavalry. By 1398 he was an independent condottiere employed in the defence of Perugia against the Visconti, and then in 1402 employed by Florence. He was in the Florentine army at Casalecchio where he was captured, and he remained with the Florentines as one of their leading commanders for the campaign against Pisa. By this time he had 180 lances and was well on his way to becoming one of Italy's leading captains. After the fall of Pisa in 1406, he took service with Niccolò d'Este, the Lord of Ferrara, and became captain general of the Ferrarese army against Ottobuono Terzo, the Visconti captain who had seized Parma. By 1409 Ottobuono had been defeated and killed by Sforza, who received the castle of Montecchio in Emilia as a reward from Niccolò d'Este. Sforza then moved southwards and joined the army of the papal–Angevin–Florentine alliance against Ladislas of Naples and was the principal architect of the great victory of Roccasecca over the Neapolitans in 1411. As a reward for this success, Sforza was made Count of Cotignola by Pope John XXIII, thus recognising the predominance in that town which the Attendoli had by now established. However, he deserted the papal cause in the next year and joined Ladislas, receiving a *condotta* for 830 lances.

So by 1412, Musio Sforza had reached the top of his profession. He had not in fact risen from nothing as his eulogists claimed, since he had always had the advantage of a large and warlike family, many of whom served in his company, and a solid base in Cotignola from which to recruit. Nevertheless, his success had been spectacular and had depended to a considerable extent on his own military prowess. It also depended on some well-timed changes of side and on three marriages, each of which had brought him estates and added prestige. Sforza was described by one of the chroniclers as: 'More than usually handsome with fierce features and an extremely powerful physique. He was intelligent and crafty, and a considerable orator who could inspire his troops with splendid speeches.' He certainly seemed to be able to inspire his troops with an unusual degree of loyalty and discipline, and it was from this discipline that his reputation as a military innovator sprang. Because of this discipline and the amount of careful planning he put into each action, he was able to control his troops on the battlefield to an unusual degree. He was a believer in cautious tactics executed by large masses of well-disciplined troops, and this meant not only cavalry but also infantry on which he placed particular, and for his day unusual, emphasis.

Sforza was far less successful as a politician, and in Naples after the death of Ladislas he inevitably became involved in politics. During these years he was twice imprisoned and was only saved by the steadfastness of his family and his troops, who were able to exert military pressure to gain his release. On the field of battle he usually found himself opposed by Braccio da Montone against whose fire and brilliance he tended to be at a slight disadvantage. His role in these events was always that of commander of the troops of one or other political faction in Naples, and he never seemed to be interested in winning an independent state for himself. It was as Great Constable of Joanna II, the successor to Ladislas, that he marched northwards early in 1424, hoping to settle scores with Braccio who was besieging Aquila. It was mid-winter, and Sforza was forced to use the coast road up the east coast rather than striking directly across the mountains. At Pescara he was confronted by the river Pescara in spate and the Bracceschi holding the city. So he elected to ford the river at its mouth in an attempt to bypass the city. There was a gale blowing in from the Adriatic and this made the crossing extremely hazardous, but Sforza successfully led his advance guard across only to find that the main army had halted, deterred by the prospect of crossing behind him. There was no alternative for Sforza but to return and lead the rest of his troops across himself. This he proceeded to do; he re-crossed successfully, got his army moving again and set out to ford the swollen river for the third time. However, one of his pages got into difficulties and as Sforza turned to help him his horse lost its footing and Sforza was thrown in full armour into the river and drowned. His son, Francesco, held the Sforza companies together for the decisive campaign that was still to come, but briefly it was the figure of Braccio da Montone which predominated in Italy.

The Fortebraccio family of Perugia were nobles and amongst the most powerful families in the city. Their original rural base was the town of Montone, but they had lived in Perugia for at least two centuries. Andrea d'Oddo Forte-braccio was born in 1368, just a year before Sforza, and at some early stage began to call himself Braccio. From his first military engagement, at which he was captured because of his impetuosity, Braccio had a reputation for courage and audacity. But it was a surprisingly long time before he established himself as a commander of troops. Perhaps this was partly because his fiery methods were distrusted by the senior condottieri under whom he served. But the more likely cause was that from the early 1390's the Fortebracci fell foul of the Michelotti family, who had gained control in Perugia, and had gone into exile, also losing their estates at Montone. So Braccio was unable to rely on his own recruiting ground and spent much of his life as an exile and a leader of exiles.

Braccio was severely wounded in the head in his second military encounter and was for a time half paralysed, and always walked with a limp. But he was a commanding figure, above average height and described by his contemporaries as a man who always stood out in a group. He served with a small following under Alberigo da Barbiano and with Florence in the 1390's, and was back with Alberigo in 1405 but still with only 12 lances. Whenever the opportunity presented itself, he rallied the Perugian exiles and tried to recover his position at Perugia, and the inconsistency towards his employers necessitated by this preoccupation with Perugia also contributed to the slow growth of his military reputation. So at the age of 37, when Sforza was already joint commander of the Florentine army, Braccio was still only a minor squadron commander.

However in 1406 the turning point in his career came. After some successful operations with Alberigo, which won him both the respect and the jealousy of his colleagues, he set out on his own, determined to make his own way. A series of blackmailing operations against small towns brought in cash, and he began to build up his own company always relying for the core of it on his fellow exiles from Perugia. In 1407 Roccacontrada in the Marches offered him the lordship of the town in exchange for protection against Ludovico Migliorati, and this at last gave Braccio a secure base. In the next years he steadily built up his strength as he moved from one side to the other in the balance between Ladislas and the papal–Angevin alliance. But it was always Perugia which was in the forefront of his mind, and he continued to lose opportunities for advancement as he concentrated on that. Braccio, unlike Sforza, was always the independent condottiere, but his restlessness was not just the search for a state for himself but the quest for a particular state, his native city, to which he felt he could only return as lord.

In 1414 Pope John XXIII made Braccio captain general of the Church and Count of Montone, and he had thus reached a position where rivalry with Sforza, now commander of the Neapolitan army, was inevitable. But it was two years later, in 1416, that the decisive moment for Braccio came. With his new strength and authority, and taking advantage of the lack of papal control during the Council of Constance, he launched his final assault on Perugia. The Perugians appealed to Carlo Malatesta to help them, and he marched to their relief with an army of some 5,000 men. The battle of S. Egidio which ensued was not a great battle in terms of numbers, but it was decisive for Perugia and was an interesting display of Braccio's techniques.

The strength of Braccio's methods lay, as did that of Sforza, in being able to control troops on the battlefield. However, there the similarity ends; Braccio believed in dividing his army into a number of small squadrons and committing them to battle piecemeal. In this way he found it not only easier to maintain personal control over the battle but was able to use his squadrons in rotation and thus rest them during the battle. The effect of this was that they fought fiercely for short spells and then fell back to be replaced by a refreshed squadron. It was this, together with the natural daring of Braccio himself, that produced the speed of manoeuvre and the bravura of Braccesco tactics. At the battle of S. Egidio, which was fought on a hot day in the height of summer,

Braccio had had the foresight to provide large quantities of water in barrels immediately behind his lines. Thus, as the long day's fighting wore on, Braccio's troops remained fresher and more vigorous than the Malatesta forces drawn up in traditional mass divisions according to a prearranged plan. It was significant that Carlo Malatesta, having drawn up his army in a great half circle into which he hoped to draw the impetuous Bracceschi and then surround them, had retired behind the battle line to his tent believing that once the battle had started there was little more that he could do. Braccio avoided the obvious trap, kept up a constant pressure all along the line and finally, as the Malatesta troops tired and began to lose their cohesion, he threw in his reserves to break through. Carlo Malatesta was caught up in the flight of his army and captured; 300 dead were left on the field.

The Battle of S. Egidio made Braccio the master of Perugia and many of the surrounding towns. He had created a state for himself, and he devoted a part of each of his remaining years to governing it. He built extensively in Perugia and employed his army to dig a canal which drained part of the Umbrian plain into Lake Trasimene. But one of his main interests was inevitably defence; he reorganised the Perugian militia and held jousts and the traditional Perugian 'battles of stones' in the streets to arouse the military spirit of his new subjects. His company was increasingly made up of Umbrians and began to look almost like a national army. It certainly saw constant action, as Braccio continued to campaign each year either in self defence against growing pressure from Martin V, or in the Neapolitan wars against Sforza. He maintained his state intact, despite the activities of the pope, but in the end it was a combination of papal and Neapolitan forces which caught him outside Aquila in June 1424.

Braccio's determined independence and self confidence was

ultimately the cause of his downfall. Isolated in his attempts to gain control of the Arbuzzi and add it to his Umbrian state, he rejected opportunities to defeat the allied army piecemeal, as it assembled, in the belief that he could inflict a defeat on it which would settle the power balance in central Italy permanently. It was again a hot summer's day when Braccio's army faced a much larger combined army on the plain of Aquila. His opponents that day were not only the Sforza squadrons led by Francesco and his cousin Micheletto Attendolo, but also the new Neapolitan captain general, Jacopo Caldora. Caldora had served with Braccio in the past and learnt a lot from him, and he also had a company made up largely of troops from the Abruzzi who were personally loyal to him. The tactics of Caldora and Francesco Sforza were inevitably a combination of the two schools of warfare. The army was divided into large squadrons and Caldora employed the Braccesco method of constantly rotating the squadrons, so that he always had fresh troops in reserve. Braccio, with a much smaller army, planned to hold the disciplined impetus of the Sforzeschi in check on his right while he broke Caldora in the centre and on the left. But he had underestimated Caldora's mastery of his own tactics and found that, although he gained an initial advantage against him, in the end it was Caldora who had the greater reserve strength and was able to counter attack with devastating effect. Meanwhile Braccio's right was also unable to hold the Sforzeschi who began to break through. As a last resort Braccio's chief lieutenant, Niccolò Piccinino, who had been detailed to guard the rear against an outbreak from the be-sieged city of Aquila, left his post in an attempt to restore the balance in the main battle. However, he not only failed to do this, but also left the rear exposed to a determined rush from the Aquilani, who began to sack the Braccesco camp. The day was totally lost for Braccio; his army was scattered and he himself wounded and taken prisoner. The chronicles record that when he was being treated for his head wounds by Caldora's doctor, an unknown hand jogged the doctor's arm and drove the scalpel into Braccio's brain. From this wound and also from sheer despair he could not recover. Three days later Braccio died, having refused to eat or exchange a word with his captors.

The list of the commanders in the two armies at Aquila could almost be used as a roll call of the leading soldiers of the next generation. Among the Bracceschi were Niccolò Piccinino, another Perugian who was to lead the Milanese army for 20 years, Gattamelata, commander of the Venetian army from 1434 to 1441, and Niccolò Fortebraccio della Stella, commander of the Florentine army in the early 1430's. In the allied army, in addition to Caldora and Francesco Sforza, were Micheletto Attendolo whose career will take up some of the following pages, Bartolomeo Colleoni, Venetian commander from 1455 to 1475, Niccolò Mauruzzi da Tolentino, leader of one of the most famous dynasties of condottieri in the fifteenth century, and Luigi da Sanseverino, whose family was also to become increasingly famous in Italian armies. The names of Sforza and Braccio were battle cries for almost the whole century, and even as late as the Pazzi War in 1478–9, many of the Florentine and Venetian troops still marched under the banner of the black ram (*montone*) on a yellow ground. At this time Braccio's grandson, Bernardino, was a leading Venetian commander, and the Milanese army contained several members of the Sforza family; but the old rallying cries and the old traditions of the Bracceschi and Sforzeschi embraced a wider group of late fifteenth-century commanders than just the survivors of the two families.

But while these traditions lived on, the political conditions in Italy, which so vitally affected the type of warfare and the military institutions, were entering a new phase in 1424. Milan, Florence and Venice were about to embark on thirty years of prolonged warfare from which permanent military institutions finally emerged. Martin V had clearly started the process of restoring order in the Papal States and building up a papal army. Alfonso of Aragon was already committed to his long campaign to capture the throne of Naples, a campaign which ended in success and a new and more powerful Neapolitan dynasty in 1442. From this moment onwards it is necessary to think more of armies, military institutions, and military administration rather than individual captains for whom the opportunities for independent action were rapidly declining. This is not to say that the leaders did not remain condottieri; but they were condottieri of the type of Jacopo dal Verme rather than that of Braccio da Montone.

CHAPTER FOUR

CONDOTTIERI AND THEIR EMPLOYERS

After the battle of Aquila and the almost simultaneous deaths of the two great leaders Sforza and Braccio, the large armies which they had built up fell apart. Braccio's eldest son, Oddo, was young and relatively inexperienced and, although his favourite lieutenant, Niccolò Piccinino, tried for a time to hold the Bracceschi together under the nominal command of Oddo, it was soon apparent that the real heir in terms of military prowess was Piccinino himself. This made many of his fellow Bracceschi leaders so jealous that they broke away to seek employment of their own. In the Sforzesco camp there was a worthy successor to Musio in his son Francesco, a man who had already to some extent shared command with his father and who was now able to hold together a large part of the company. But in this case there were cousins of almost equal standing who chose to seek their fortunes on their own. The most famous of these was Michele Attendolo, a man more often known as Micheletto because of his small stature, who was a good deal older than Francesco and who had spent some time in the service of Braccio before joining the rest of his family. Micheletto Attendolo spent the years following Aquila in the service of the pope. By 1430 he had 200 lances and 50 infantry in his company, but after five years in papal service he realised that if he was to increase his company and hence his own prestige he had to join a bigger army and seek more action. He sent his chancellor to negotiate with Venice, but the Venetians, although involved in a long drawn-out war with Milan, already had a well-established captain general in the person of Carmagnola, and also a second in command, Gianfrancesco Gonzaga, who had held the position for four years. So there was little chance for Micheletto to create for himself the sort of position to which he now felt he was entitled. Nor was Milan likely to prove any better, as the Duke had both Niccolò Piccinino and Francesco Sforza in his pay. So Micheletto turned to Florence. Florence was also engaged in war with Milan and at the same time was trying to capture Lucca, a venture which was going disastrously badly. So in April 1431 Florence was more than willing to negotiate with Micheletto and to win to her service a man with a solid reputation and apparently not outstanding ambitions.

The negotiations took place at the little village of Medecina between the Florentine representative, Averardo de' Medici, and Micheletto's staff. It was clear from the start that Florence had underestimated the soldier; as he at present led a company of 200 lances, the Florentines had assumed that if they offered a *condotta* for 300 Micheletto would be flattered and pleased. However Averardo quickly reported that Micheletto Attendolo had very different ideas; this was for him the turning point in his career, he was determined to seize the opportunity to make himself a great captain. Micheletto asked for a *condotta* for 600 lances and 400 infantry, an advance of 65 florins per lance (which represented about five months' pay) and an immediate bonus of 6,000 florins to cover his initial expenses, an additional florin a lance per month over normal pay rates, and finally and most significantly a guarantee of employment in peacetime. 'We know very well how you behave when you no longer have need of us,' he is reported to have said, 'and how you treated Niccolò da Tolentino and the others.' This last reference to the normal Florentine practice of dismissing her condottieri as soon as a truce was signed is a clear indication of the way attitudes were changing by the 1430's.

On receipt of this report the Florentine war council was in a dilemma. Niccolò Fortebraccio, who had led the army against Lucca in the previous year, had never made demands like these, but neither had he achieved the successes which the tottering Albizzi regime badly needed. Furthermore Niccolò was now threatening to resign his position as captain general unless he received enormous compensation for his losses in the recent campaign. So with the campaigning season about to start and a victory desperately needed, Florence was in danger of having no general. Averardo de' Medici was instructed to make three possible offers to Micheletto Attendolo. He could have 600 lances and 300 infantry with the same pay as the captain general, Fortebraccio; failing that he could have 660 lances and 300 infantry; or finally if he remained obdurate Averardo was to offer 600 lances, 300 infantry and the post of captain general. In any case he was promised a personal pension of 10,000 florins a year for five years after he left Florentine service, which was rather different to a peacetime contract which Florence was clearly not prepared to give.

The attempt to employ a captain with so enormous a following alongside the captain general who had considerably fewer lances, was clearly unrealistic and failed. Fortebraccio left, and Florence was forced to give way to most of Micheletto Attendolo's demands. The contract was signed in May for 630 lances and 400 infantry and Micheletto was made captain general. His extra florin a lance was agreed, but the clause was kept secret to avoid giving ideas to the rest of the Florentine condottieri. Rinaldo degli Albizzi, Florence's leading politician, was himself sent to Arezzo to give the baton of command to Micheletto. But Micheletto, anxious to savour his 'promotion', insisted on a proper ceremony in Florence at a time declared propitious by the astrologers. On 13 June, 1431, he rode into Florence at the head of his men-at-arms to accept command of the Florentine army and take the customary oath to his employers.

This is an instructive story which tells us much about the relations between soldiers and their employers in Renaissance Italy. The haggling that went on over the terms of the contract was partly about money, but it was also about the prestige and standing of the condottiere. Numbers, rates of pay, advances, bonuses, the degree of authority, and future standing, all came into the bargaining. Chroniclers reported that Micheletto had also asked for the lordship of Lucca if it should be captured, and this may well be true, but it was not a question which figured largely in the negotiations. Micheletto seemed to be primarily interested in his standing as a soldier and, although he had the Florentines 'over the barrel', his ultimate dependence on the good will of his civilian employers was clear.

All this brings us to the contracts under which Renaissance mercenaries served—the *condotte* of which thousands of examples survive and which must form one of the starting points for a study of Italian mercenaries. The *condotta* was the contract signed between the condottiere and his employer which arranged for the provision of a certain number of troops for a set period in return for payment, primarily in cash. The term was not a specifically military one; it was used for the contracts involved in the provision of many public services such as mining concessions, grants of tax collecting privileges and provisioning contracts. The contractors who hired merchant galleys from the Florentine state and operated them in the interests of the state were known as *conductores*, and in the naval sphere the hiring of sea captains and warships by the Italian states was an exact parallel to the military system of issuing *condotte.*

The military *condotta* was in many respects very similar to the English indenture or the French *lettre de retenue*, the main differences being that while in England and France contracts were usually issued to subjects of the crown for paid service to their king, in Italy, because the states were much smaller and economic and social conditions so different, they were normally issued to 'foreign' professionals. That this distinction necessarily implied shorter terms of service, less continuity, or less commitment, is a fallacy which it is one of the objects of this study to correct. Furthermore, while the main intention of the *condotta* was the provision of troops—and this placed the condottiere in the position of an entrepreneur in a certain sense—it was normally expected in Italy that the condottiere would lead his troops. The condottieri of Renaissance Italy were almost invariably soldiers, not, as was beginning to happen in Germany, capitalist recruiting contractors. The special, separate contract that authorised a captain to recruit, which had appeared in Germany by 1500, was not to be found in Italy in the fifteenth century. There were some *condotte* of the second half of the fifteenth century in which the condottiere was authorised to delegate leadership of the company, but these were exceptional. Finally the *condotta* was not only the contract signed between a soldier and an employing state. The companies of the condottieri were constructed on the same contractual basis, as squadron commanders or lesser soldiers received *condotte* from the condottiere himself. However, it was not usually the case that a condottiere received a contract and then subcontracted to form a company. The large companies were permanent entities with internal contractual arrangements quite separate from the state contracts of their leaders. Micheletto Attendolo's company had a continuous existence from at least 1425 to 1448 during which time 512 condottieri signed contracts with Micheletto. When he entered Venetian service in 1441, he had a company of 561 lances which included 167 condottieri. Some of these men had as many as 50 men at arms attached to them, others had only one.

The first substantial clause of any *condotta* set out the number of troops to be provided. This would be expressed either in terms of individual cavalry and infantrymen, or by using the composite terms common in various periods—*barbuta*, lance, *corazza*, man-at-arms, etc., all of which implied a unit led by an armoured knight but of size varying between two and six men. During the fourteenth and early fifteenth centuries it was comparatively rare for a mixed *condotta* calling for both cavalry and infantry to be issued. But in the later part of the fifteenth century more and more mixed companies were formed, and it became increasingly rare for a force of heavy cavalry not to be accompanied both by infantry and by mounted crossbowmen. While early *condotte* were often quite specific about the way in which the troops should be armed, detailed clauses of this type became rare in fifteenth-century contracts. This was part of a general tendency for *condotte* to become more abbreviated and formalised as time passed.

There were two exceptional types of contract in which the precise number of troops required was not stated, and these both appeared in the second half of the fifteenth century. They were both referred to as the *conducta ad provisionem* and the difference lay in the standing of the soldier to whom they were issued. The contract was used for some very senior captains, to whose discretion the exact size of the company was left, and at the other end of the scale it was used for experienced but low-ranking soldiers to secure their personal services. In the latter case it was always expected that the condottiere would have a few followers but their number was immaterial.

The next important feature of the *condotta* was the duration of the contract. Here there was an important distinction from the English indenture which applied to most *condotte* after the middle of the fourteenth century. The contract period was almost invariably divided into two; the first part, known as the *ferma*, was the set contracted period of service; the second part was a further period for which the employer could retain the services of the condottiere if he wished and if he gave proper notice. This second part of the contract period was known as the *ad beneplacitum*, or in Italian contracts—*di rispetto*. The employer was bound to notify the condottiere some weeks ahead of the end of the *ferma* if further service would be required. The introduction of this option period in the second half of the fourteenth century was clearly a step towards reducing the lack of continuity in the system and extending contracts. At the same time the duration of the contracts began to increase. In the fourteenth century it was customary for contracts to be signed for two or three months' service only; the implication being that all contracts ended in the autumn when the campaigning season was over. By the early years of the fifteenth century *condotte* were rarely issued for less than six months. The Florentines, who were the slowest to introduce both the option period and the longer contract, tended to use simple six month *condotte* up to the 1440's, but the other major states had largely gone over to contracts of six months *ferma* plus six months *ad beneplacitum*, and even one year plus one year, during the early decades of the century. Once contracts of six months plus six months, or longer, were standard, it was clear that the possibility of continuous service was envisaged. By the 1440's many Venetian contracts were for two years plus one year, and there were a few exceptional contracts given for even longer periods. By this time the process by which contracts were confirmed for the option period and renewed after that had become completely formalised in the Venetian system. It was accepted that condottieri were in permanent service, unless they seriously offended in some way or unless they made a positive request to leave.

The obvious corollary to these developments was *condotte* given for unlimited periods, but these in fact were comparatively rare. Soldiers presumably felt more secure with contracts for set periods which they knew were renewable when they were dealing with governments, and popes, which could change very rapidly. However, here in the contracts themselves lies some of the evidence for the growing permanence of the mercenary system in Italy. During the fifteenth century soldiers were becoming identified with states by continuity of service. This was particularly apparent with Venice in the first half of the century, but it applied to other armies to a lesser degree. Most backward in this development were the Florentines; Micheletto Attendolo was already bitter about it in the early 1430's, and even as late as the 1470's Florence had few permanent condottieri on whom she could rely.

The third important element in the *condotta* was the pay clauses. These were by no means always specific and often it was assumed, and sometimes stated, that troops would be paid the standard rates. Rates and methods of pay will be discussed elsewhere, as will be the devices by which the condottieri and their officers were rewarded over and above the normal pay of the soldiers. But in addition to the contractual agreement about pay, there was a financial consideration of even greater immediate importance to be decided—the advance or *prestanza*. All *condotte* provided for an advance of pay to be handed over immediately to enable the condottiere to re-equip his company and move it to take up new service. It was also a guarantee of good faith on the part of the employer and, although the *prestanza* became something of an anachronism in the conditions of permanent service of the later fifteenth century, condottieri still insisted on it. It was argued with some justice that the spring was an expensive time for the condottieri as they brought their companies out of winter quarters, and it became common for states to pay advances in the spring, even if the contracts were not actually being renewed then. The advance normally represented a quarter or a third of the total pay due to the company for the initial contract period. If the contract was for more than a year, then half the first year's pay was a fairly standard advance. This would be paid off by the condottiere receiving reduced monthly pay until the advance had been covered.

So far, this discussion of contracts has, by implication, concerned itself only with contracts for full-time service on full pay. These were the commonest type of *condotta*, but there were also contracts which laid down more limited obligations and service. The most important of these was the so-called *condotta in aspetto*, which provided for a condottiere and his company to be on call to come into service when needed. This was a device particularly favoured in the fourteenth century when few states maintained significant numbers of permanent mercenary troops. The condottiere with a *condotta in aspetto* would be free to base himself and fight where he wished as long as he was ready to come when called upon to serve his employer with the stipulated company. For this obligation he would receive reduced pay of perhaps one third or one half of normal rates, rising to full pay if and when his services were required. The *condotta in aspetto* was particularly appropriate for the condottiere prince, who had an independent base and his own state with which to occupy himself. Less formal types of part-time *condotte* were quite common in the fifteenth century and come under the general category of *condotte* on half pay; these included the traditional *condotta in aspetto*, *condotte* for service out of the campaigning season, and occasionally *condotte* for service on particular campaigns which in part served the individual interests of the condottiere or in which the booty was likely to be unusually lucrative.

But perhaps the most significant development in the fifteenth century, in terms of contractual clauses about pay and size of companies, was the appearance of the *condotta* which stipulated different company strengths and remuneration for wartime and peacetime service. Such contracts became common in the Venetian army in the early 1440's and were clearly a formalisation of a system of informal reduction and augmentation of the companies which was already operating. In the second half of the century such contracts spread to most Italian armies. In the Milanese and Venetian armies they reflected the situation in which many of the condottieri had become feudatories and maintained reduced forces in peacetime. For the condottiere prince they took the place of the *condotta in aspetto*, in that in peacetime it was accepted that he would return to his principality and maintain a reduced company.

Arrangements for the division of booty and prisoners between condottiere and employer normally filled one of the later clauses of the *condotta*. As a general rule the condottiere and his troops were entitled to the moveable goods which they captured, while the employing state claimed buildings, walls, fortifications, etc. Senior condottieri, rival princes and their families, and rebels of the employing state who were taken prisoner had to be handed over to the state, usually in return for a ransom; other prisoners were the property of the condottiere and his men. However, there was very rarely any suggestion that mercenary troops made their living out of booty and ransoms; these were the profits of war over and above the carefully regulated rates of pay which were fundamental to all military contracts.

The rest of these contracts were taken up with a variety of clauses about the authority of the condottiere over his men (usually complete except for crimes of violence committed against friendly civilians), the exemption of the company from taxes and tolls, the immunity of members of the company from pursuit for debts contracted before the beginning of the contract, the provision of free billets, firewood and straw for the company, and the provision of food at fair prices. The contract would also contain an oath of loyalty to the employer, and would frequently set out the arrangements for inspections of the condottiere and his troops. The extent to which current practice about inspections, the frequency of them, penalties for deficiencies, the listing of men and horses, etc., was set out in the *condotte* varied. Certainly by the fifteenth century it was rare for much of this administrative detail to appear, but this was no indication that the formalities were no longer observed. All states had their regulations for the employment and control of mercenaries, and an oath to observe these was often all that the individual contracts would contain.

A final section of the *condotta* was usually devoted to outlining arrangements for the conclusion of the contract. An employer had to give notice of his intention to take up the option on the second half of the contract period, and a few weeks before the final termination of the contract the condottiere was entitled to send his chancellor with a detachment of his men away to seek a new employer. Furthermore, for a period after the end of the contract, he was guaranteed a safe-conduct beyond the frontiers of his past employer. On the other hand the condottiere and his men swore not to fight against the former employer for six months after the

5 *Jacopo Cavalli.* Cavalli was a Veronese noble who distinguished himself fighting for Venice, particularly in the War of Chioggia. He died in 1384 and was given a state funeral. This funerary monument in SS. Giovanni e Paolo, Venice, was executed by Paolo di Jacobello delle Masegne.

6 *Paolo Savelli*. Equestrian statue in wood attributed to Jacopo della Quercia and erected in Sta. Maria de' Frari, Venice, in honour of the Roman condottiere who was Venetian captain-general during the siege of Padua in 1405.

contract terminated. This obligation was frequently recognised in the condottiere's next contract which absolved him from fighting against his former employer unless he wished to.

There are, of course, great dangers to attaching too much importance to contractual evidence. The *condotta* system had emerged at a time when the condottiere was employed for a short period and rarely served the same masters for two contracts in succession. The transition to a situation in the second half of the fifteenth century, in which condottieri were normally in the permanent service of a state, was reflected to some extent in a formalisation of the system and an abbreviation of the contracts, but inevitably some anachronisms remained and one cannot expect the later contracts to represent actual practice in all details. Furthermore, the official *condotte* were often modified by private and secret agreements of which we rarely have knowledge. Micheletto Attendolo's extra florin a month under the counter was an example of such an arrangement. Sometimes a condottiere would be privately authorised to maintain more or fewer troops than were agreed in the *condotta*. The usual motive for such deceptions was to avoid provoking the jealousy and discontent of other condottieri, but they were also done to mislead enemy spies and informants who could have easy access to the public *condotte*. However, after all this has been recognised, there remains sufficient evidence from the mass of other administrative and private material to show that the contracts are a guide to the strength, movements, and real obligations of the condottieri and their companies.

But the contracts are only the starting point for a study of the relations between mercenaries and their masters. For the duration of the contract, or series of contracts, the condottiere was constantly under the watchful eye of the government;

he was in the employ of states whose main preoccupation in the fifteenth century was war. Obviously the mechanics of military administration varied from state to state in Italy. In Naples and Milan, and even in the papacy, war was the direct concern of the prince or pope and his inner council. In Florence and Venice, standing committees were responsible for the military organisation in peacetime; these were respectively the *ufficiali della condotta* and the *savi della Terraferma*. When war broke out, these were supplemented by special emergency committees of senior citizens who took over the wider control of military affairs. In Florence the *Dieci della Guerra* would be appointed, and in Venice a war council was sometimes inserted in the government hierarchy between the Senate and the College. But given the nature of the Venetian constitution, it was more common for the Senate to retain control of most aspects of war policy, with the growing intrusion by the end of the fifteenth century of the permanent Council of Ten.

However, the direct supervisors of the army on the spot and the main links between governments and their soldiers were the civilian commissaries or *provveditori* appointed to accompany the army in the field. These men were either direct representatives and councillors of the prince, or in Florence and Venice temporarily nominated citizens from the upper echelons of the ruling class. They were attached to the armies to pass on instructions from the government, to send back reports both on the progress of the war and the behaviour of the soldiers, to give on the spot advice to the commanders, and to some extent to coordinate the administrative and supply services of the army. They had long been a feature of the Italian military scene and their necessary presence is referred to in some of the early contracts. Ricotti, the leading nineteenth-century military historian, refers to them as 'inconvenient, and often dangerous, in any active campaign, and

more fitted to spying and punishing failures, than to facili-
tating victories', and undoubtedly the condottieri themselves
often regarded them in this light. There is plenty of evidence
of clashes between condottieri and the commissaries; Giorgio
Corner, the Venetian *provveditore* with Carmagnola's army
in 1432, was thought to be largely responsible for the disgrace and subsequent execution of Carmagnola, and no doubt
there was an adverse commissary's report behind most of
the dramatic destructions of condottieri by their own employers. But in fact these were comparatively rare episodes
and one should not exaggerate the negative aspect of the
relations between soldiers and civilian officials. If we take
another celebrated case, the bitter feud between Sigismondo
Malatesta and Andrea Dandolo, when the latter was *provveditore* attached to Sigismondo's Venetian army in the Morea in
1464, we find an example of purely personal antagonism.
Ten years earlier Sigismondo had been the lover of Aritrea
Malatesta, who subsequently married Dandolo, and Sigismondo had been responsible for the payment, or rather non-
payment, of her dowry.

Here was a case when previous personal relationships between a condottiere and a civilian commissary marred a
working relationship, but more often, in a situation of emerging permanent armies, it was the other way round. The
commissaries, particularly in the princedoms and to a large
extent also in Venice, were a small group of men who, although civilians, developed a close contact with the soldiers
and a considerable experience of war. They often commanded
troops during the temporary absence of the condottiere commander, and to some extent participated in the brotherhood
of arms. The personal links between some of the Venetian
nobles who acted as *provveditori* and some of the leading
condottieri were close, sometimes too close for the peace of
mind of the Venetian government. The reports of these

civilians led more often to rewards for soldiers than to admonitions and executions.

Rewards at various levels and of various types were an essential feature of the Italian military system. This could be described as a necessary counter measure to prevent the enemy bribing soldiers away from the service of a state. But the reward systems which emerged in the fifteenth century had a much more positive element than that and played a major part in the creation of permanent armies. To some extent the rewards were built into the contractual system. An increase in the size of his *condotta* was the quickest way to please a condottiere, as this meant both more money in his pocket and added prestige. In a permanent army it was the standard means of promotion as well as a method of raising extra troops without having to employ new condottieri. A similar device was to give *condotte* to the relatives of condottieri; this not only pleased him but increased his family's commitment to the state and made it more difficult for any of them to desert. Somewhat more altruistic were the efforts made by states to gain privileges, concessions, etc., for its condottieri outside the state. Ambassadors of the employing state would seek benefices and papal bureaucratic posts for relatives of its condottieri in Rome; they would exert pressure on other governments to give arrears of pay due to recently employed condottieri.

The simplest and most obvious forms of reward were cash bonuses and gifts. These ranged from prizes of 25 florins to the first man to scale the walls of a besieged city to gifts of valuable silver helmets to captain generals when they received the baton of command. The gifts often took the form of pensions for life given not only on retirement but often during active military service. The pension given as a specific reward again had the effect of physically tying the soldier to the state as he would have little hope of continuing to receive the pension if he deserted. But pensions given on retirement, such as the 1,000 ducats a year given by Venice to Gattamelata when ill health forced him to retire, were again an indication of a more long term view of military service. Furthermore it was not only the soldiers themselves who received pensions; families and heirs were also brought into the system. Venice by the 1440's was encouraging the families of her condottieri to come and live within the Venetian frontiers by offering accommodation and family allowances to wives and children. The families of condottieri who died in Venetian service were given fairly lavish maintenance grants and the daughters were provided with dowries. Sometimes the company of a condottiere who died prematurely was kept in being until his sons reached maturity and could take over command of it.

For the upper echelons of the military hierarchy, the granting of estates and fiefs was a common form of reward. Small estates were often given to provide a pension or in lieu of a cash bonus, but the granting of a fief with wide varieties of feudal jurisdiction was a more significant trend. In areas which were already strongly feudal, like the Kingdom of Naples and the Duchy of Milan, there was an element here of inserting into a feudal class a new group of men who could be reckoned to be more dependent on the ruler than the established baronage. This was clearly one of the factors behind the enfeuding by Francesco Sforza of many of his captains when he became Duke of Milan in 1450. At the same time for all the states there were other, more specifically military, considerations. Key fortresses could be made secure by enfeuding them to a condottiere of proved prowess. Venice with her long Alpine frontiers was particularly aware of this possibility and hence the granting of Valmareno to Brandolino Brandolini and Castelfranco to Micheletto Attendolo. Other key points on the Venetian frontiers were Chiari guarding the approaches to Brescia which was given to Carmagnola, and Sanguinetto south east of Verona which controlled the crossings of the Po and passed through the hands of a number of senior condottieri in the fifteenth century.

Enfeudation was in fact a way of tying the condottiere to the state both physically and by moral bonds of allegiance. It satisfied to a large extent the common condottiere need for an independent base, but within the framework of the coalescing political system. A wide variety of jurisdictions are encountered amongst the condottiere fiefs, depending no doubt not only on the seniority of the condottiere and the extent to which he was to be rewarded, but also on the remoteness or otherwise of the fief. In both Venice and Milan even when the most complete jurisdiction of *merum et mistum imperium* was granted, the state tended to retain the control of the salt monopolies in the fief and to expect some token of homage like the offering of wax candles to the Basilica of St. Mark in Venice. What was clearly not expected as a price of feudal investiture was any form of feudal military service. The condottiere feudatories were not expected to serve by virtue of their new feudal status, and still continued to fight on the basis of a separate contractual system.

In the Papal States while the giving of fiefs was not unknown, there was the more prestigious alternative of conferring a vicariate on a senior condottiere. Small towns were placed under the control of a condottiere who had complete authority as representative of the pope, and paid an annual census to the pope for the privilege. Florence, which clearly lagged behind the other major states in the creation of a permanent army and seemed slower to resolve the problems of relations between the state and the condottieri, was on the whole more reluctant to encourage soldiers to settle within her frontiers. She had a deeply inbred fear of the pretensions of the old Tuscan feudal nobility whose power she had largely destroyed in the thirteenth and fourteenth centuries and did not wish now to add to their numbers. After the early success in persuading Hawkwood to accept a degree of permanence in his relationship with the Republic, Florence very rarely offered territorial rewards to her subsequent commanders.

Another type of reward which the Italian states could employ to win the permanent services of condottieri was the offer of citizenship or even a palace in the capital city. Citizenship, a seat on the governing council, and in the case of Venice enrolment in the Venetian nobility, were in a sense something of formalities. Out of 40 foreigners elected to the Venetian Great Council between 1404 and 1454, thirteen were condottieri in Venetian service, but few made anything more than formal appearances in the Doge's Palace. The Visconti (and the Aragonese royal house in Naples) found an alternative honour when they invited condottieri to become honorary members of the ducal family and take the Visconti name. This custom seems to have been discontinued by Francesco Sforza whose family, both legitimate and illegitimate, was already perhaps large enough.

The granting of a palace was less common as it could involve considerable expenditure to the state. Carmagnola was given the palace of the Broletto in Milan by Filippo Maria Visconti, and then when he joined Venetian service and after his victory at Maclodio (1427), he was given a palace in Venice on the Grand Canal near San Stae. This palace had formerly been bought for Pandolfo Malatesta after his successes against the Hungarians in 1412 and had cost the state 6,000 ducats. Gianfrancesco Gonzaga and Gattamelata were also given palaces in Venice, the former being bought from the Giustinian family for 6,500 ducats; and later in the century the Sanseverino clan of condottieri had a palace in the city. The three or four palaces in Venice which were normally in the hands of condottieri were used, during their long absences, for the reception of important state visitors.

Finally there were two forms of reward which, being usually posthumous, were calculated less to please the actual recipient than to encourage his colleagues. One was the state funeral often given to a senior condottiere who had died in service. Florence was surprisingly generous with these, perhaps because there was almost an element of rejoicing at the demise of a troublesome employee. The other was the memorial portrait or statue. Few of the expensive condottiere memorials were created entirely on the initiative of the state, being usually financed largely by the condottiere's family, like the equestrian statues of Gattamelata and Colleoni. But the memorial frescoes of Hawkwood and Niccolò da Tolentino in the Duomo in Florence were commissioned by public authorities, and an even better example was the fresco of Niccolò Piccinino painted on a wall in Lucca in gratitude for his services in saving the city from the Florentines in 1430. The equestrian statue of Paolo Savelli in the Frari in Venice was probably erected with public funds (but in wood), and the Doge attended the state funeral of this much prized Venetian commander.

The public painting of the portrait of a condottiere was not always intended to honour him. It was more commonly used to defame him for some act of treachery about which the state could take no further immediate action, as he had deserted. The Renaissance defamation picture was not of course confined entirely to unfaithful condottieri, but they did enjoy the doubtful privilege of being the objects of many such works. In Florence the caricatures painted on the walls of the Palazzo della Signoria of condottieri hanging upside down in chains were not uncommon sights. Niccolò Piccinino was the object of such a painting in 1428, and the element of ridicule involved no doubt contributed to his permanent enmity towards Florence. In Venice it was not the Doge's Palace which was chosen for such gestures, but the walls of the public brothel at the Rialto where Evangelista Savelli was defamed for betraying Cerreto to the Milanese in 1452.

But of course the punishment of treacherous and dangerous condottieri usually took more effective forms than just defamatory paintings. Enormous rewards were offered for the capture dead or alive of Evangelista Savelli, and Venetian diplomatic agents all over Italy published the details of his treachery in the hope that no other state would risk employing him. Certainly by the middle of the fifteenth century, when most condottieri were becoming accustomed to conditions of permanent employment, a reputation for infidelity was not to be risked lightly. Jacopo Piccinino when he left Venetian service in 1454 went to great lengths to try and ensure that no such slur was attached to his move, and, although he was one of the last condottieri to seek to establish an independent state for himself, he was at the same time very concerned to protect his reputation.

Jacopo Piccinino eventually met his end strangled by a Moorish slave in a Neapolitan prison on the orders of King Ferrante of Naples, and obscure murder or public execution was to be the fate of a number of leading condottieri. Rarely was it because of any particular crime which could be imputed to them, but rather because a suspicion of treachery made it difficult to treat them in any other way. If released after arrest, then it was likely that the indignity of the arrest would add fuel to their resentments and make treachery and desertion inevitable; if kept in prison, they would be a constant problem for their captors and a possible focus of attack. The speed with which action against potential deserters, both great and small, was taken was an indication of how seriously the states took such threats; at the same time the relatively small number of condottieri executed in the fifteenth century shows perhaps that major infidelities were less common than we imagine. Carmagnola was the only leading condottiere executed by the Venetians in the fifteenth century, although they did also hang Scaramuccia da Lucera, a lesser figure, in Brescia in 1439, and imprisoned Antonello da Corneto in the 1460's. The outstanding cases which spring to mind of Milanese action against condottieri were the murders of Niccolò da Tolentino, Tiberto Brandolini, and Donato del Conte, all in prison in somewhat obscure circumstances. Niccolò da Tolentino, who had been captured in battle, was clearly done away with as punishment for deserting Milan a few years earlier. Tiberto Brandolini met his end in 1462 after an elaborate but by no means trustworthy confession had been extracted from his chancellor under torture. The confession set out in unlikely detail a series of indiscretions and treacherous negotiations which Tiberto was supposed to have conducted over a period of ten years in Milanese service. He, like Carmagnola, only actually deserted once in his life, but there is no doubt that he was a more restless figure than most of his colleagues in the 1460's. Donato del Conte, on the other hand, was the epitome of the faithful soldier having served the Sforzas as an infantry commander all his life. His death was the result of his becoming involved in the political battle which ensued in Milan after the murder of Galeazzo Maria Sforza in 1476. Political indiscretions were probably also the main cause of the dramatic murder and defenestration of Baldaccio d'Anghiari by the Florentines in 1441. He was thought to have been too close to the anti-Medicean Capponi faction for the comfort of the Medicean government. The fact that he had also recently signed a *condotta* with the pope was unlikely to have been too disturbing to the Florentines, as Eugenius IV was supposedly their ally.

One can add to this list of 'executions' but certainly not indefinitely. The main charge, at least on the surface, in all the cases was desertion or the threat of desertion. There was clearly the feeling that it was better to eliminate a powerful condottiere than to have him join the enemy, although there was always the danger that a government that acquired a reputation for executing condottieri was unlikely to find it easy to recruit new ones.

Execution and murder were only the most drastic ways of punishing and disciplining soldiers; the normal methods were by fines and dismissal. Fining soldiers for minor breaches of contract, for not keeping their companies up to strength, or for permitting their troops to get out of hand, was a standard feature of the military organisation. Pay was often so far in arrears that retentions of pay for specific offences had only a limited impact and rarely caused much offence or resentment. Dismissal was less common, and it took a confident government to sack a leading condottiere in the way the Venetians did to Micheletto Attendolo after the defeat at Caravaggio in 1448. Micheletto was deprived of his command and exiled to his estates, but this was less because he had lost the battle than because his troops had got out of hand in the retreat and ravaged Venetian territory. However the dismissal of minor condottieri for inefficiency and lack of discipline was not unusual, particularly in the Venetian army where control was fairly tight by 1450.

What emerges from an enquiry into the relations between condottieri and their employers is that inevitably attention has been fixed on the affairs of a few major condottieri. Just as we tend to generalise from the great concessions and rewards given to Francesco Sforza or Federigo da Montefeltro, so we tend to draw conclusions from the fates of Carmagnola and Jacopo Piccinino. It is the remaining 99 per cent of the military profession who deserve more attention, and here it is important to look in a more general way at the areas of conflict between mercenaries and their masters.

In fact the Carmagnola affair is instructive if one looks closely at the whole background to it, and the long running battle which Carmagnola conducted with the Venetian authorities during his period of Venetian service from 1426 to 1432. One of the major areas of conflict was the maintenance of the army in the field, and the moment at which it was reasonable to disperse to quarters. Naturally enough, the government wished to keep the army active and united for as long as possible so that it got the best value for money and was safe from attack. However, it was traditional in Italian warfare, and particularly in the south, to campaign for two relatively short seasons each year. The spring and early summer, and the autumn were the normal campaigning seasons. Soldiers were always reluctant to take the field in the height of summer, because of the heat and because of the difficulties of getting supplies and fodder at the moment just before the harvest. The time had largely passed when soldiers returned home to help with the harvest, but this older militia custom also contributed to the tradition of the summer break. In each year of his service with Venice as captain general, Carmagnola argued with the government about dispersing the army to quarters in August. The Venetian fear was that not only would she be left defenceless, when there was no guarantee that the Milanese enemy would do the same, but also that it would be difficult to get the army together again for the autumn campaign. Carmagnola pointed out the difficulties of campaigning in high summer and that it was standard practice in Naples to disperse the army to quarters in that season. Naturally the Venetian response was that Lombardy and Naples were different. The result of the arguments tended to be inconclusive; the army normally remained in the field grumbling and inactive, and then took the first opportunity to claim the necessity of retiring to winter quarters. The quarters issue, how early in the spring the army could be moved out into the field and how long it should remain there, was a continuous one in all Italian armies. Carmagnola seemed to fight it more strenuously than most condottieri, just as he fought more strenuously the issue of inspections.

The practice of insisting on inspections in the field was considered most unreasonable by the condottieri. They preferred to postpone making up any losses of men, horses and equipment until they returned to quarters. This was not just in order to pocket the money due to missing men themselves, but in order to be able to buy horses and equipment at more stable prices and recruit at greater leisure. The longer the army remained in the field the more urgent became the necessity to carry out inspections and the more the condottieri resented this process. The thing was to some extent a vicious circle and, while his captains resorted to all sorts of tricks to deceive the inspectors, Carmagnola clashed head on with the Venetian government over the issue.

Closely connected to these issues was that of the replacement of dead horses. In fourteenth-century warfare it had been customary for the employing state to compensate condottieri for horses lost on active service. By the fifteenth century governments had succeeded in evading this responsibility and indeed in many fifteenth-century contracts it was specifically stated that condottieri could not claim compensation for lost horses. This was an important issue given the cost of horses and the increasing losses which the warfare of the time inflicted. In the 1420's the change was still very much resented by the condottieri, and it was not unusual for governments to be forced to make unofficial piecemeal concessions to individual condottieri in the forlorn hope that these could be kept secret from the others.

The treatment of prisoners was another question on which governments and their condottieri tended not to see eye to eye. The division of valuable prisoners was always laid down in the contracts, and while this produced occasional arguments the system on the whole worked. But it was the condottiere habit of releasing the rank and file prisoners, having taken away their arms and horses, which irked governments. In fact the condottieri had every right to do this; the contracts specifically laid down that such prisoners were theirs, and there was really no practical alternative to releasing them. But when Carmagnola released all his prisoners after his victory at Maclodio in 1427, he brought down on his head a storm of abuse from the Venetian government.

Here then was a whole range of specific, practical issues on which condottieri and employers found it difficult to agree. Closely related to them were the problems of ill-disciplined troops and bad pay. Rarely was an Italian army paid punctually, and this was one of the principal reasons for condottiere discontent and military ill-discipline. That shortage of pay led to bad discipline, as troops unable to buy their food took to stealing it, was evident to all intelligent politicians, and few governments could be accused of deliberately underpaying their condottieri. But, nevertheless, heavy state indebtedness to its condottieri was a standard feature, although some states found it more difficult to produce the money than others. The difficulties of Florence in this respect are very clear in the middle of the century. In 1450 Federigo da Montefeltro was owed over 25,000 florins, and over the final four years of the Lombard wars in which the Florentine army reached almost unprecedented size the problem became more acute. In 1454, after the Peace of Lodi, Florence found herself so heavily in debt to her condottieri that she was forced to offer long term peacetime contracts to some of them because there was no hope of paying them off. It was this factor which seems to have been more important than any inherent realisation of the need for a permanent army, in making Florence fall into line with the other Italian states and accept the standing army commitments of the Italian League. Even then, when these contracts ran out in 1457, Florence owed over 63,000 florins to her three senior condottieri alone. Alessandro Sforza, who was not one of those given extended contracts in 1454, spent the month of October in Florence trying to get his arrears of pay. He wrote to his brother Francesco's secretary in the following terms: 'They have decided to rob me of 20,000 florins and I don't even know if I shall be able to pay my bills here. I doubt if the barbarians would have treated me like this.' His response was to seize a Florentine merchant caravan passing through Parma and recoup himself in this way. Some years later, in 1479, another Florentine condottiere, Bernardino da Todi, who had served Florence faithfully for twelve years, protested to Lorenzo de' Medici that his troops could not afford to shoe their horses and were without shoes and stockings themselves, because their pay was so far in arrears. He left Florentine service in the next year ostensibly for these reasons.

One of the reasons why troops were so reluctant to leave their quarters was because, by refusing to take the field, an army could put pressure on its employer to produce arrears of pay. This was an absolutely basic problem and one of the principal explanations for many of the defects of the condottiere system; the Italian states of the fifteenth century lacked at first both the administrative machinery and the fiscal resources to pay properly the large armies they felt bound to employ. As the century progressed the military administrations improved steadily in most states, but actual shortage of money was always a problem.

Behind all these conflicts, however, there lay the basic difference of attitude towards the conduct of war. The state wanted quick and inexpensive victories; the condottieri wanted to make their living and save their skins. The two were mutually incompatible as long as employment was short and temporary; they became less so as contracts became longer and employment more permanent. Carmagnola was the last Venetian captain general to quarrel continuously with his government; after him relations steadily improved as the system became more organised. It was not the individual infidelities which are important in this question of the relations between soldiers and the state, but the more basic and practical conflicts which lay behind many of the infidelities, and the gradual resolution of these in the fifteenth century made the infidelities less common.

Furthermore these conflicts were not only the background to the desertions of condottieri but also to the exaggerated care with which governments handled senior condottieri. This could also stem from particular factors; the soldier prince, the man who was both condottiere and independent ruler, always posed special problems of control. His *condotta* tended to be less formal and allowed him more discretion; it tended to take on the form of a political alliance as much as a military contract. He usually expected some form of reciprocal guarantee that the employing state would protect his state, and that he would be free to take appropriate action if his state were threatened. Most of these men by the fifteenth century were not the original creators of the little states over which they ruled. By the third or fourth generation, some of these soldier princes were not really soldiers at all. They controlled companies which they rarely commanded personally but which earned a useful income for themselves and their states. These were in a sense the entrepreneurs of late fifteenth-century Italian warfare, and it was even occasionally the case that the *condotta* would be held by the widow of a deceased Romagna ruler in the name of her infant son.

7 (a) *The Taking of Pisa in 1406.* Panel of a mid-fifteenth-century *cassone* (wedding chest) of the Florentine School.

(b) *The Battle of Anghiari, 1440.* This is the other panel on the same chest. There has been a good deal of controversy about the attribution of these panels, but it seems likely that they were painted for a wedding in the Capponi family as members of the family were closely involved in both these Florentine victories.

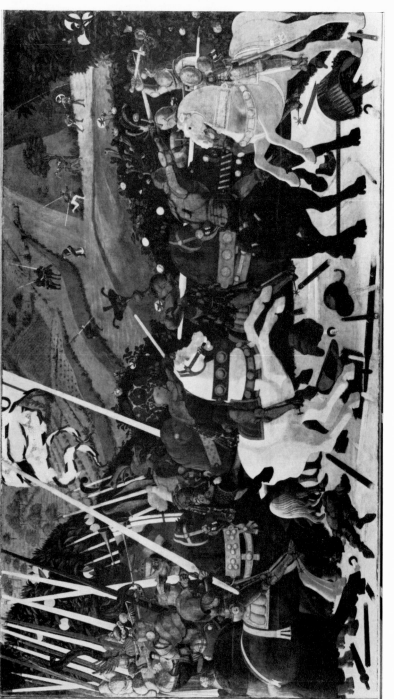

8 *The Battle of San Romano* (1432). Paolo Uccello painted three scenes from this battle for the Medici Palace in the 1450's. For details of the battle, which was described in his diary by the Florentine commissary, Luca di Maso degli

Another situation which demanded very careful handling was when condottieri developed fierce personal rivalries. These were not uncommon and states had sometimes to bear in mind when hiring condottieri that some men would not fight in the same army, let alone obey each other's orders. The constant bitter feud between Federigo da Montefeltro and Sigismondo Malatesta not only made it impossible for them to serve together, but would affect the policies of the states which they were serving. Naples in the late 1450's was partly influenced into attacking Sigismondo by the pressures from Federigo, who was her captain general. On the other hand the reverse could also be the case; close friendships and family ties between condottieri in opposing armies could have an extremely embarrassing effect. Micheletto Attendolo after he had become Florence's captain general in 1431 was ordered to move to Lombardy to join up with the Venetian army against the Milanese under Francesco Sforza. He refused to do this for a number of reasons, of which the most cogent was that, although he personally would 'fight against his own father if Florence commanded it', many of his troops had relatives and friends in his cousin Francesco Sforza's company and would be unlikely to fight well against it.

Therefore delicacy of touch was essential in dealing with condottieri. Instructions were usually presented in the form of possible alternatives rather than mandatory commands; requests tended to look like petitions, and rebukes rarely contained more than a mild note of remonstrance. This was more true of the republics than the princedoms, where the prince himself was usually in quite close touch with his soldiers. Filippo Maria Visconti, the last Visconti duke of Milan, was the most unwarlike of men and treated his condottieri with a suspicion that verged on pettiness, but his Sforza successors were mostly men with military experience. Alfonso I, King of Naples, although he was no great general, spent the long years in which he was campaigning to capture the crown frequently in the field with the army, and his grandson, the Duke of Calabria, was titular commander of the army throughout the next reign. Although none of the popes of the fifteenth century led their armies like Julius II, several of them took a keen interest in military affairs, and even Pius II, whose general opinion of mercenaries was low, had a great respect for Federigo da Montefeltro. Furthermore papal armies tended to be under the eye of one of the more militant cardinals, who gave an air of immediacy and reality to the relations between armies and the rulers they served.

The image of the condottiere had certainly changed by the middle of the fifteenth century, at least as far as the political leaders were concerned. Again the contrast between Federigo da Montefeltro and Sigismondo Malatesta is revealing. Both men were independent rulers of states and therefore had access to secure recruiting grounds and wealth; but whereas Sigismondo was an unpredictable, violent character with a high degree of military genius, Federigo was cautious, calcu-lating, and above all safe. By the 1450's it was Federigo who was the most sought after even though employers recognised that Sigismondo was the better soldier. A reputation for fidelity, a well organised and securely based company, and at least a record for not losing too often—these things meant more to an employer than the more traditional military virtues of bravery, technical skill, or even outstanding success.

One of the epitaphs on Colleoni, who died in 1475 after being Venetian captain general for twenty years, suggested that 'he who serves a republic serves no one'. This was a common reference to the vacillating quality of leadership in the Italian republics, and it has been suggested that condotti-eri preferred to serve under princes where they knew with whom they were dealing. While this was probably true of

Florence where a deeply rooted suspicion of soldiers was added to the normal oscillations of republican government, it certainly was not true of Venice whose service was eagerly sought by condottieri. It was part of the early myth of Venice that her policies were not directed by individuals but by some sort of corporate awareness of the eternal needs of the Republic. Niccolò Piccinino is said to have remarked on one occasion that he would like to serve Venice 'because while princes are mortal, the Republic will never die'. Again, however, it was not so much sycophantic reflections of this sort which really counted but the fact that Venice developed an efficient military administration and offered a better chance of permanent service than most of the other Italian states, and certainly better than her rival republic, Florence.

Filippo Maria Visconti's famous outburst in 1441 against Piccinino, who had demanded to be invested with Piacenza as a fief before he would attack Francesco Sforza's Venetian army, has often been taken as the epitome of relations between condottieri and their employers:

> 'These condottieri have now reached the stage when if they are defeated we pay for their failures, and if victors we must satisfy their demands and throw ourselves at their feet—even more than if they were our enemies. Must the Duke of Milan bargain for the victory of his own troops, and strip himself to receive favours from them.'

But this is only one side of the picture. It must also be remembered that Piccinino by this time had given Milan fifteen years of faithful service; that his pay was probably years in arrears; that he was dealing with an employer who was notorious for his treachery towards his soldiers.

The condottiere system had many defects and most of them sprang from the wider social, political and economic framework in which it was born and within which it operated.

Perhaps its greatest defect was the atmosphere of distrust which tended to exist between condottieri and employers: between soldiers and politicians; but this is after all a problem which is always with us.

———◁▷———

CHAPTER FIVE

THE ORGANISATION OF WAR

The company of a condottiere can be compared, in some respects, both with a feudal retinue and with a commercial company. Many of the followers of a condottiere would be linked to him by ties of family or personal loyalty, many more were linked to him by contract and by mutual participation in a sort of business venture. It is here at the lowest level that a consideration of military organisation must start.

A large condottiere company was divided into a number of squadrons. The largest of these was the '*casa*' or household of the leader of the company. In this would be placed not only his most experienced and faithful men-at-arms but also his chancellors, grooms, trumpeters, and various attendants. In the *casa* of a condottiere prince like Sigismondo Malatesta, many of the men-at-arms were scions of the noble families of the city over which he ruled, in his case Rimini. The idea of this was partly to give the condottiere an honourable following; but more importantly to provide hostages for the good behaviour of those families while their prince was away. The other squadrons of the company would be commanded by *squadrieri*, all of whom would hold contracts from the leader and would themselves issue contracts to their leading followers.

Micheletto Attendolo's company in 1441 numbered 561 lances, and for administrative purposes these were organised in 87 units, most of them of less than five lances. However, for battle, squadrons of about 25 lances were formed and led by the senior condottieri, most of whom had been with Micheletto for many years. Piero Gianpaolo Orsini in papal service in 1437 had 800 cavalry and 200 infantry. His company was divided into six squadrons, including his own, and two of the squadron leaders were also members of the Orsini family. Tiberto Brandolini in 1460 had 400 lances and 300 infantry. His *casa* was composed of 34 men-at-arms and 32 light horsemen, and included his master of horse, his marshal, a chaplain, two cooks, six chancellors, trumpeters, a billeting officer and a munitions officer. There were then seven squadrons of cavalry, three of them led by members of his family, and eight companies of infantry, including 20 hand-gun men and 50 crossbowmen.

In a sense this unit of the company was self-sufficient and indeed at first it had to be. However, by the fifteenth century military organisation was beginning to mean something more than the rudimentary structure of the companies themselves.

The famous army reforms of Charles VII in France in 1439 and 1445 are often thought to have laid the foundations of Europe's first standing army in modern times. They established fifteen *compagnies d'ordonnance* of 100 six-man lances each, commanded by captains appointed by the Crown. At the same time they forbade the raising of troops by any other subjects. They also created a selected conscript infantry force; these men were mainly equipped with crossbows and were exempt from taxation, hence their name—*francs archers*. That these arrangements were either a novelty for France or unique in Europe is now very much questioned by historians, but they do help us to define what is meant by a standing army. First, such an army is organised on a permanent, professional footing; secondly it consists of companies of equal size, uniformly armed according to an overall plan; thirdly the officers and soldiers are directly employed by the state and totally responsible to the state. Such an army does not have to be national; the emphasis which has been placed on Charles VII's regulations is mistaken in this respect, as they covered only part of the army. The French army, particularly at the end of the fifteenth century, contained large numbers of foreign mercenaries in addition to the national elements.

The French chronicler Philippe de Commynes commented on the French army reforms that Charles VII was imitating the princes of Italy, and the major Italian states, wealthy and highly organised, were certainly not unaware of the importance of having permanent, well-trained and loyal armies. The armies of these states were becoming increasingly permanent in the fifteenth century; they were by no means the miscellaneous collections of hurriedly employed mercenary companies which have often been described. The standing forces agreed to by the Italian states in the Italian League of 1455 far outnumbered the standing army of France at that time, and the Italian League was only one in a long series of treaties and alliances which had imposed commitments for standing forces on various Italian states. These permanent forces created new and considerable administrative problems, and all the states found themselves faced with the need to create a permanent military organisation. They also had to face the problems of paying for the permanent armies on which about half the annual budgets of Italian states were spent even in times of peace.

An Italian army of the fifteenth century was organised in two parts: on the one side there were the mercenary companies of the condottieri and the constables, on the other a growing number of troops of all categories employed as individuals directly by the state. The evidence of lengthening contracts, peacetime service, and increasing fidelity of mercenary captains has already been discussed. The domestication of the condottieri was not only a part of state policy, but also a result of the individual initiative of the captains themselves. But it is only one side of the creation of permanent armies in Italy; we must now look at the other, even more permanent, types of troops and the administrations which were growing up to deal with both these and the companies.

The first permanent troops in Italy were, as one might expect, garrison troops. Garrisons and city guards were formed either by employing infantry constables with long term contracts or by employing troops, mostly infantrymen, individually. Such men were called, from an early date, *provisionati* because they received a *provisione*, a regular wage, from the state. But in the mid-fourteenth century *provisionati* was being used to describe the first documented cavalry bodyguard set up in Italy. These were the *provisionati* recruited by Bernabò Visconti from amongst Milanese noble families in 1369. These men were selected by local officials and received a fixed wage even in peacetime. They were normally expected to serve in rotation for two months of the year, and wore a uniform of red cloaks and tunics with silver accoutrements.

The Visconti cavalry *provisionati* seem to have been a fairly short-lived experiment, but in the 1420's Filippo Maria Visconti, the Duke of Milan, had an equivalent force known as the *familiares ad arma* or later the *famiglia ducale*. At first these consisted of 700 cavalry enrolled from amongst those who had served for at least five years in the Milanese army, and in 1439 the *famiglia* was reckoned as an integral part of the army by the Venetian chronicler Sanuto, and estimated at 600 strong. That this group was something more than a bodyguard becomes clear in the Sforza period when its size steadily increased and it was both billeted and campaigning well away from the Duke's person. In 1467 eleven squadrons of the *famiglia*, amounting to about 2,000 cavalry, took part in the Molinella campaign. In 1472 the strength of the *famiglia* was fully described in the army lists which the administration of Duke Galeazzo Maria Sforza drew up with such care. Each squadron had two commanders among whom at this stage were Giampietro Bergamino and Gian Jacopo Trivulzio, men who were to become leading Milanese commanders during the next twenty years. Trivulzio in fact, who eventually deserted to the French and led the French army during many of the battles of the Italian Wars, was scarcely a condottiere in the true sense of the word; he passed all his period of Milanese service as a commander either in the *famiglia ducale* or later in the other force of permanent cavalry, the so-called *lanze spezzate*. Also apparent from the 1472 army lists is that only one squadron of the *famiglia* was specifically called the 'squadron of the guard'. In 1497 the *famiglia ducale*, which still numbered about 2,000 men, was clearly divided between the *famiglia di casa* and the *famiglia fuori casa*. Besides the elements of the *famiglia* which served as a bodyguard for the Sforza dukes, they also had a guard of 300 mounted crossbowmen.

The Neapolitan demesnial cavalry organised by Alfonso V after his occupation of the Neapolitan throne in 1442 must have been rather similar to the Milanese *famiglia*. In a state which was still strongly feudal the demesnial cavalry were presumably in theory raised from the royal demesne or estates, and numbered 1,000 men in the 1440's and 1450's. It seems that financial stringency made it difficult for the Aragonese kings to maintain the whole force in being, but in 1467, in response to Florentine pleas for assistance against the aggressive intentions of Bartolomeo Colleoni, Alfonso d'Avalos led 20 squadrons of the demesnial cavalry northwards.

The popes also had an old-established bodyguard, but this

was largely composed of infantry. In the fifteenth century one of the senior papal infantry constables was given a long term contract to provide the papal guard of about 300 men, and these were sometimes used on active campaigns with the papal army. But although some popes did accompany their armies to war, it was not considered necessary to create a large, prestigious and permanent cavalry force to fight with them.

However, by the mid-fifteenth century, all Italian states were using another type of cavalry force known as the *lanze spezzate*. The name means broken lances and clearly the origins of such troops were individual cavalrymen who for various reasons had become detached from condottiere companies and their traditional lance formation, and had taken service directly with a state. Inevitably the companies of *lanze spezzate* tended to be organised into lances as were all heavy cavalry of the day, but the principle of direct dependence on the state was maintained. Some men presumably enrolled in *lanze spezzate* as a gesture of independence, but on the whole these troops were made up of deserters from other armies, and particularly of groups of soldiers whose condottiere had been killed. A standard way in which a state could retain the services of a good company whose commander had died, was to enrol them as *lanze spezzate*, appoint a new commander of its choice, and thus build up a nucleus of permanent cavalry. The papal *lanze spezzate* in the 1460's were mostly men from the Patrimony of St. Peter (southern Tuscany and northern Lazio) and the district of Rome, and were presumably remnants of the companies of the Anguillara family who had been defeated and driven into exile by Paul II in 1465.

Pandolfo Malatesta, the Lord of Brescia, had a squadron of *lanze spezzate* in the early fifteenth century, but no doubt it is possible to trace their origins further back than that.

In the 1420's the Milanese army contained 700 *lanze spezzate* who were mostly remnants of Braccio da Montone's troops who had been left leaderless after the battle of Aquila. In 1427 the Venetians had about 400 men enrolled as *lanze spezzate*, and the Florentines 150. In 1434 an independent assessment of the Milanese and Venetian armies showed that 1,200 out of 7,550 Milanese cavalry were *lanze spezzate*. Also in the 1430's a squadron were enrolled in the papal army. By the 1440's the Venetians were building up a considerable force of such troops, as the first generation of their faithful condottieri began to die off. In 1441 the company of the Cremonese condottiere, Cavalcabò de' Cavalcabò, were enrolled as *lanze spezzate* after his death, and in 1476 a large proportion of the Venetian army was made up of the companies of long dead condottieri like Gattamelata, Roberto da Montalboddo and Antonello da Corneto, which had been kept in being as *lanze spezzate*. The status of such troops is clearly indicated in the papal cameral accounts where they were paid individually and commanded by officers appointed by the Camera Apostolica. In 1472 there were 4,000 men enrolled in the Milanese *lanze spezzate*, and they were commanded by four governors appointed by the Duke. This made the force double the size of the *famiglia*, and in the 1480's the two groups made up two-thirds of the Milanese cavalry.

Finally what of permanent infantry forces? Traditionally infantry were raised in the same way as cavalry by issuing *condotte* to constables for set periods and set numbers of men. But again beside the *condotta* system there is evidence of increasing numbers of *provisionati* employed directly by the state for service in the field. Milan had 1,000 *provisionati* in the 1420's, and soon afterwards we find references to the *provisionati di San Marco* in Venetian service. The infantry of the papal army after 1450 was clearly divided between companies of the constables and the *provisionati*, who were paid individually and commanded by corporals appointed by the Camera Apostolica. By 1476 Milan had 10,000 permanent infantry, including 2,000 hand-gun men, and the commander Donato del Conte, who had been one of Francesco Sforza's leading infantry commanders thirty years earlier, was one of the most influential men in the state. At this point, however, it is clear that the word *provisionato* was being used in a new context. Both Milan and Venice began a system of selective conscription to produce a sort of superior militia. The men selected were fully armed and commanded by professional infantry constables. They could be called out for full-time service in an emergency and otherwise for periodic training sessions. The system somewhat resembled that of the *francs archers* in France and probably accounts for the 10,000 *provisionati* in Milanese pay in 1476. Certainly it is about then that one becomes aware of Venice raising troops in large numbers in this way for service against the Turks in Friuli, and they are clearly quite distinct from the ordinary militia.

All these, then, were permanent forces in the most complete sense of the word. By the middle of the fifteenth century the Milanese, Venetian and papal armies, and to a lesser extent the Neapolitan army, were filled with growing numbers of professional soldiers who were not part of the *condotta* system. There is little indication that Florence had much of a standing force of this type, and here once again we are faced with an impression of Florentine backwardness in military developments during the Renaissance period.

To judge the significance of these permanent forces and the extent of the administrative organisation which their presence demanded, it is necessary to put together some overall view of the size and composition of the main armies of Renaissance Italy. The estimation of numbers in war is always a snare for the historian as he seeks to counterbalance the exaggerations of contemporary rumour and propaganda. Nor are administrative documents, army lists, muster rolls, *condotte*, etc., necessarily a reliable guide. In all medieval and Renaissance armies, one is faced with the problem of distinguishing between fighting men and non-combatants in a host, although for administrative purposes the total number of an army in the field is still a significant figure.

There are three ways of thinking of an army: first there is the total force recruited by a state; secondly the army in the field; thirdly the army in a particular battle. For the total forces recruited by Italian states we have some quite useful statistics; at certain moments one can be reasonably sure that records have survived of all the *condotte* issued by a state, and these are often a better guide to numbers than is thought. In a well organised Renaissance army condottieri were expected to keep their companies up to strength, and frequently there are clear indications that they were doing so. There are also occasional attempts in contemporary documents to assess the total strength available to a state. The Milanese administration of Galeazzo Maria Sforza was particularly given to making estimates of this nature, but these tended to be optimistic assessments of the total number of men who could be called out rather than realistic appraisals of the actual numbers under arms. One always has to bear in mind that total numbers and actual fighting strength have to be distinguished in the figures available, and that many of the non-combatants, who accompanied armies and often had to be paid, never appear in most official records. This confuses the issue particularly when one tries to assess the size of armies in the field when the numbers of auxiliaries, pioneers, and even lightly armed militia, are rarely given more than approximately. On the other hand even when the strength of a state was concentrated on one front and apparently in one army, there was inevitably a great difference between its total recruited force and the size of the army in the field. Estimates of field army strength are more rarely found in administrative documents than those of total strength, and estimates of the troops actually engaged in any given battle are even more rare. For these one is left to rely on the contemporary narrative and chronicle accounts, which can again be more useful than is often supposed. Occasionally one comes across wild distortion as in the papal campaign in Corsica in 1445–6, when chroniclers put the papal forces at 16,000, while a study of papal financial records, which are unusually complete, shows that the fighting strength of the papal army in Corsica cannot have been much above 1,000 men. But there are other occasions when chroniclers' figures can be checked and found far less inaccurate, and when there are several independent accounts of the same battle or campaign a reasonably clear picture can be built up.

Very rarely in the fifteenth century did a field army exceed a total strength of 20,000 men, but in the wars in Lombardy between 1425 and 1454 both the Milanese and Venetian armies approached this strength. At the beginning of the century Giangaleazzo Visconti was reputed to have 20,000 cavalry and 20,000 infantry under arms. It is not an impossible figure as Milan was often fighting on two fronts, and the surprisingly large proportion of infantry clearly includes auxiliaries. The Milanese army at that time was certainly larger than at any other period in the century. Venice in 1404–5 when attacking Verona and Padua certainly had 9,000 cavalry in the field, and probably her army reached the same sort of size in the war against the Hungarians in 1411–12. Ladislas of Naples, at the time of his death in 1416, is said to have assembled about 16,000 cavalry, and judging by the number of leading condottieri in his service this is again not an unbelievable figure. In the late 1420's the Venetian and Milanese field armies in Lombardy probably numbered 10,000 to 12,000; the Florentine army was more dispersed and rather smaller; the papal army numbered about 4,000. In the 1430's the sizes of the Milanese and Venetian armies grew rapidly. In 1432 total Venetian field strength was about 18,000, and in 1439 when the Venetian chronicler Sanuto attempted to assess the cavalry strengths of all the Italian armies he gave the Milanese 19,750 cavalry, the Venetians 16,100 and the Aragonese 17,800. The papal and Florentine armies were much smaller. Sanuto listed the condottieri serving in these armies with the sizes of their individual companies, and for Venice and Milan his estimates seem to be reasonably accurate. Venice always had more infantry than Milan so one could assess the total strength of these two armies at this time at about 25,000. Sanuto's figures for the Aragonese army in Naples rely to some extent on the paper commitments of feudal barons and seem inflated; the estimate of the overall size of the Florentine and papal armies (3–4,000 cavalry) is reasonable, although his details of the breakdown into component companies are often inaccurate.

Throughout the 1440's and up to 1454 the Milanese and Venetian armies continued to number about 20,000. The Florentines, fighting active campaigns in southern Tuscany in the last years of the wars (1448–1454), considerably increased their forces to 10–12,000, but a part of these troops were lent by Milan. The Neapolitan army operating against the Florentine in these years was about the same size. The papal army also increased in size in the 1450's and maintained a strength of 8–10,000 throughout the minor campaigns conducted by Paul II in the 1460's. This was a considerably larger army than that imposed on the papacy by the Italian League of 1455, and all the major states seem to have more than fulfilled their commitments for permanent forces in these years.

In 1456 the Milanese ambassador in France advised Charles VII that Milan had 12,000 cavalry under arms in peacetime; this was a much larger force than the French permanent *compagnies d'ordonnance*. By 1472 the administration of Galeazzo Maria Sforza in Milan was drawing up details for the mobilisation of an army of nearly 43,000 men. This was an ambitious and optimistic assessment, and an army of this size certainly never took the field at this time; but it was based on a greater degree of reality than is sometimes thought. All the commanders were named and were divided into categories. First there were the senior condottieri who had long term contracts to maintain certain forces in readiness in peacetime and to increase those to war time levels when called upon. Some of these were condottiere princes who were not normally resident in Milan; others were more immediately available. They included Ludovico Gonzaga, Marquis of Mantua, who was lieutenant general and kept 1,300 cavalry on standby, and was expected to increase them to 3,000 in war time. Other princes were the Marquis of Montferrat, Pino Ordelaffi of Forlì, Costanzo Sforza of Pesaro and Giovanni Bentivoglio of Bologna; together with these were Roberto da Sanseverino, the senior of the resident condottieri, and Donato del Conte, the commander of the permanent infantry who also had a large cavalry *condotta*. These seven men were expected to produce 10,700 cavalry in war time; they were all under contract and were continuously paid for their peacetime forces. The next category were the condottieri 'ad discretionem' whose commitments were more nominal. They were the feudatories of the Sforza dukes and seem to have received no pay in peacetime. However, they clearly maintained certain forces on their estates, and their commitments to serve in war on a contractual basis were laid out. Amongst these men were the Sforza brothers and halfbrothers of the Duke each of whom maintained a considerable entourage of permanent cavalry. The war time strength of this group was about 6,500 cavalry. Then came the permanent ducal forces, the *famiglia* and the *lanze spezzate* which were maintained at a high degree of readiness and numbered a further 6,000 cavalry. Most of the infantry forces, which numbered about 18,000, were also permanent *provisionati*. Thus the Duke of Milan at this time was paying a permanent army of well over 20,000 men, and his hopes of increasing these to over 40,000 if needed were reasonably well-founded.

Venice was maintaining a much smaller army in the 1470's —probably little more than 10,000 men—but she was able to raise this quickly to about 20,000 for the War of Ferrara. A large proportion of this army were *lanze spezzate*, including the companies of the ex-Venetian commander in chief, Bartolomeo Colleoni; and most of the condottieri were either nobles of the Terraferma cities, men like Alessandro and Annibale da Martinengo from Bergamo, and Luigi Avogadro from Brescia, or they were feudatory condottieri like the Brandolini, Ranuccio di Antonio da Marsciano and Bernardino Fortebracci. The Venetian infantry were particularly strong, and the army had the support of a larger and better trained militia than that of any other Italian state. Finally by 1483 there were six squadrons of stradiots, the dreaded Albanian light cavalry which Venice was introducing into Italy.

The strong papal army which Paul II had built up in the 1460's was allowed to run down in the early years of Sixtus IV's pontificate, but began to grow again for the Pazzi War (1478–9) and the War of Ferrara (1482–4). Once again the tendency to use native or 'naturalised' commanders was strong by this time and for the papacy this meant the Roman barons. In Paul II's army the leaders were Napoleone Orsini, Braccio Baglioni, Giovanni Conti, Mariano Savelli and men of that type. The commander of the papal army was usually a papal nephew carrying the title of Gonfalonier of the

Church. While nepotism had its advantages in giving power to men who could be relied on to be faithful to the pope, it had clear military drawbacks. The papal nephews were rarely experienced soldiers and this, together with the tendency to give them unusually large *condotte*, created both animosities and imbalance in the papal army. The predominance of Girolamo Riario, the nephew of Sixtus IV, who not only commanded the army in 1483 but also had about 3,000 cavalry in his own company, tended to impede the growth of a natural leadership in the papal army and forced some leading soldiers from the baronial families to take service elsewhere.

Neapolitan barons were specifically forbidden from serving other Italian states, and it was they who increasingly provided the leadership of the Neapolitan army. Throughout the long reign of Ferrante I (1458–92) continuity of reasonably effective leadership was provided by his son Alfonso, Duke of Calabria, and he, for much of the period, had the experienced Federigo da Montefeltro at his side to assist him. But there was a danger in relying too much on a native nobility to officer the army, as was shown in 1485–6 when a baronial political revolt shattered the strength and morale of the army. However, by the 1490's the Neapolitan army was thought to be the strongest army in Italy, although scant evidence of its numerical strength has yet come to light.

Florence took little part in this trend towards native or 'naturalised' leadership of an increasingly permanent army. Before 1454 her contracts had been shorter than those of other states; her armies much more temporary. She distrusted a native nobility and refused to create a nucleus of condottiere feudatories. She accepted the provisions of the Italian League for maintaining a standing army with ill grace and allowed the few commanders whom she kept on after 1454 to go unpaid and dissatisfied. As a result in 1478, to oppose the invasion of the papal and Neapolitan armies, she had to turn to her allies, Milan and Venice, not only to send large contingents under their own banners, but also to lend her condottieri whom she paid. Eventually the links forged by Lorenzo de' Medici with the Orsini family provided some permanent leadership for the Florentine army and it was Niccolò Orsini, Count of Pitigliano, who led the Florentine contingent to the War of Ferrara. But the real interests of the Orsini lay in the Papal States and Naples, and the employment of them by Florence was scarcely a satisfactory solution to the problems of reliable military leadership.

The command of these quite sizeable fifteenth-century armies was a real problem for the Italian states. It was soon recognised that the coherent direction of armies and the maintenance of good discipline required that one of the condottieri be elevated above the others and given special powers and authority. The actual title to be conferred, the extent of the powers, and particularly the choice of the individual, were problems which aroused great debate and produced a variety of subtly varied solutions. In most states the rank of captain general implied supreme command over all troops with wide jurisdictional powers over them, the right to issue safe conducts, and the right to negotiate with the enemy and thus participate in political activity. A less common and more indefinable title was that of lieutenant general. In Milan the lieutenant general was the deputy of the duke and exercised very wide powers over civilians as well as soldiers; he seems to have presided over the whole military organisation in which considerable civilian involvement was necessary, and to have been superior to the captain general who commanded the army in the field. Venice seemed to come round to a similar arrangement by the end of the century when the lieutenant general was recognised as the senior appointment; but in the early part of the century the lieutenant general was subordinate to the captain general and commanded a detached army. Thus during the Milanese wars the Venetian army in Lombardy was commanded by the captain general, while the smaller army in the Romagna was commanded by the lieutenant general 'beyond the Po'. A further rank often used was that of governor general which was clearly subordinate and implied military command of a small army, often without jurisdictional powers. The governor general did not receive the baton which was the symbol of authority conferred with great ceremony on the captain general by the government of the employing state.

The Italian republics, Florence and Venice, were often loth to give sweeping powers to a soldier. It meant paying a high salary as well as running the risks of a military coup. There was a lingering belief that it was better to employ all the good condottieri available and hope that they would seek to excel each other, even if cooperation between them was likely to be difficult. However the size and permanence of mid-fifteenth-century armies made the choice of a prestigious and increasingly permanent captain general essential. Thus the second half of the century was dominated by a small group of commanders who, for various reasons not necessarily connected with military prowess, had emerged as the captain generals. The leagues of the period also created the new need for men who not only commanded armies but commanded allied armies, and in 1484 after the War of Ferrara, in a brief moment of apparent amity amongst the states, Roberto da Sanseverino demanded the title of captain general of all Italy. What he was demanding, however, was the prestige and wealth of a supreme commander in an organised military system, and this was very different from the sort of independent political power which some of the great condottieri of the early fifteenth century were seeking.

Beneath the captain general there was only slow progress

towards the creation of an officer hierarchy within the armies of Italy. The size of his company continued to be the main yardstick by which the prestige and rank of a condottiere was assessed. All armies had a council of senior condottieri who advised the captain general; some of these men were given the rank of marshal in the army, but this implied more administrative and organisational responsibilities than superior military command. More and more, however, the rapidly growing tasks of administration were being taken over by professional officials, and it is to this side of organisation that one must now turn.

The growth of standing armies in fifteenth-century Italy brought about a steady change in methods of military administration. As long as field armies were employed and assembled on a very temporary basis the administrative structure required was both limited and temporary. Special officials were needed to recruit soldiers and draw up contracts, and civilian commissaries were appointed to accompany the army in the field and supervise the support services needed for a short campaign. In both cases the task was a short-lived one and the posts were filled either by chancery officials detached for the purpose, or by members of the ruling class of the state elected or appointed for the necessary length of time. In the fifteenth century, however, the numbers and categories of such officials steadily grew, and the need for continuity of experienced and professional administration became acute. The temporary commissary or *provveditore* was still appointed to act as the main link between the employing government and the army, but his role was increasingly confined to that of supervising the actions of the commanders, and transmitting orders and advice. At a lower level, and only very indirectly presided over by the commissaries, were emerging a host of permanent officials responsible for various aspects of military administration. Paymasters, provisioners, quartermasters, inspectors and transport officers were all needed to provide for the needs of the army as a whole, while each condottiere company continued to have its own chancellors and treasurer. But perhaps the most significant and powerful of the new officials was the *collaterale* who began to assume an overall responsibility for the administration of the army. He drew up and signed the contracts, supervised inspections and pay, detected deserters and controlled demobilisation, and oversaw all the support services. He enforced the series of regulations which each state used for the organisation and discipline of its army. The *collaterale* in fact took his place alongside the captain general and the commissary as one of the most important figures in a fifteenth-century army.

Collaterali had appeared at an early stage in Milanese military organisation. They are to be found in the fourteenth century resident in some of the main Lombard cities and responsible for recruiting and the organisation of local garrisons. There was a *collaterale generale* in Milan who controlled the local administrators, but how far these men had a responsibility for the army in the field is not clear. What is clear in the fifteenth century is that, as field armies increased in size and remained in being longer, both condottiere independence and supervision by temporary officials gave way to a permanent professional administration. In Milan the moment when Francesco Sforza became Duke was rather important in this process as he brought with him the administration of his condottiere company which was by far the largest in Italy, numbering 4–5,000 men. Many of the men who were the administrators of the Milanese army in the 1450's and 1460's, and also frequently the diplomatic representatives of the Milanese state, had served Francesco Sforza as soldiers and administrators before his final rise to power. A typical figure was the Tuscan Orfeo de' Cenni da Ricavo from a country middle class family who took service in the ranks of Francesco Sforza's company about 1440. At what stage he transformed himself from being a soldier into being an administrator and diplomat is not certain, but by 1454 he was representing Francesco on diplomatic missions in Florence, and later Ferrara. However, his principal role in the Duchy was as a military administrator. He accompanied the Milanese contingent to the Angevin wars in Naples in 1460, and inspected the expeditionary force which was sent to France in 1465. He was a great favourite of Galeazzo Maria Sforza and figured prominently in all the military ventures and plans of his dukedom. It is highly likely that he was largely responsible for the elaborate military dispositions set out on paper in 1472, and in that year he was depicted in a fresco on the walls of the Castello Sforzesco giving instructions to troops. He was a ducal councillor and commissary for the army through the 1470's until in 1479 he was imprisoned by Ludovico Sforza for his loyalty to the Duchess Bona after the murder of Galeazzo Maria. However, he was released in 1481 on the intercession of Lorenzo de' Medici and retired to exile in Arezzo where he died the next year. Orfeo da Ricavo was given estates in Cremona by Francesco Sforza and founded the noble family of the Orfei of Cremona. It is an interesting career and by no means unique. The Milanese army in the 1460's and 1470's had a mass of permanent officials responsible for all aspects of its administration. Domenico Guiscardo was for many years the commissary responsible for the *famiglia ducale*; Bartolomeo da Cremona was chief munitions officer; others presided over provisioning, the acquisition of horses, pay, billeting, etc.

Venice in the early years of the fifteenth century, when she first began to tackle the problem of a large land army, relied on the normal method of filling government posts by election in the Great Council. Venetian nobles and middle class citizens took turns to fill a variety of administrative posts in the camp. The first *collaterali* to appear were Venetian nobles. But alongside them were soon to be found military advisers who were usually experienced soldiers and often natives of the Terraferma cities which were falling under Venetian control. Gradually such men began to occupy permanent positions as inspectors and recruiting officers as well as advising on specific projects. In the 1420's an interesting figure emerged who was to dominate the administration of the Venetian army for the next thirty years. This was Belpetro Manelmi, who came from a prominent family of Vicenza. Manelmi was made *collaterale* in Verona in 1416, but nothing is yet known of his prior experience. His duties in Verona were largely concerned with inspecting and paying the garrison of the city and local fortresses, and he was clearly a man of considerable local influence. He was a friend of the prominent Veronese humanist, Guarino, and his reports on local military arrangements and his criticisms even of Venetian officials were taken seriously in Venice. In about 1427 he was made *collaterale generale* of the Venetian army and from that moment onwards references to his activities multiply. He assumed overall responsibility for the maintenance of the strength and efficiency of the whole army. He negotiated and drew up *condotte*, supervised infantry recruiting, inspected companies, organised the frequent mobilisations and demobilisations of troops, and generally presided over the whole military administration. He was frequently associated with the captain general and the *provveditori* in plans for reorganisation and redeployment of Venetian forces. He was described in 1432 as hated by the soldiers, which was probably a good indication of the efficiency with which he carried out his duties because it certainly made no difference to his standing with Venice. Manelmi's place was normally beside the captain general in the field, but he was also often to be found in Brescia which was the main headquarters of the Venetian army in Lombardy and where he had a house allotted to him. Under him were five *vice-collaterali*, each based on one of the main Terraferma cities, and these men received their remuneration by retaining a small proportion of the first month's salary of every soldier they signed on. These *vice-collaterali* also were a very permanent group and at least two of them were also from Vicenza; one of them, Evangelista, may have been the Evangelista Manelmi who was present at the siege of Brescia in 1438-9 and wrote an account of it; the other, Chierighino Chiericati, came of a good Vicentine family and was associated with Belpetro from at least 1434.

Belpetro Manelmi finally died in 1455. His death left the Venetian army in confusion, and it was clear that during the very long time which he had held his position the organisation over which he presided had become very much dependent on him. In 1455, therefore, Venice decided, in view of the long period of peace which it was hoped would follow the signing of the Italian League, to establish a closer control over her army organisation. Manelmi's *vice-collaterali* were dismissed and replaced by five Venetian nobles elected for three years. This unusually long period of office for elected officials indi-cated an awareness of the need for some permanence in army organisation, combined with a desire to avoid the officials becoming as independent as Manelmi had been. However by the 1470's professional permanent *collaterali* were once more in charge of the military administration.

An interesting postscript to the story of Belpetro Manelmi comes ten years later in Rome. Paul II, the recently elected Venetian pope, was preparing to launch his army against the troublesome Anguillara family. A number of Venetian clerics were already established in the papal financial organisation, but the man to whom Paul turned to organise his army was

Chierighino Chiericati, Manelmi's former secretary and assistant. Paul knew Chiericati from the time when he was Bishop of Vicenza and was obviously aware of his qualifications and experience for such a task. Chierighino was a notary by training, but from at least 1434 he was attached to Belpetro Manelmi's administration. In 1441 he was *vice-collaterale* with Francesco Sforza's army in Venetian service, and in 1445–6 he was responsible for the inspections and pay of Micheletto Attendolo's company. In 1452 he led a force of 4,000 Veronese militia in an attack on Mantuan troops which proved disastrous for the militia. In 1455 he lost his job along with the other *vice-collaterali* and spent some years in Milanese service. Then in 1465 he went south to take up his appointment as commissary and inspector of the papal army, a post which he held throughout the pontificate of Paul II.

Prior to the appointment of Chierighino, the administration of the papal army seems to have been very much in the hands of officials of the Camera who drew up the contracts and paid the troops. This gave some continuity to the organisation but not the sort of professionalism that was increasingly needed, although clerical status was by no means a bar to military efficiency as was shown by the energy and ability of some of the cardinal commissaries with the papal army. Another device which seemed to be peculiar to the papal military administration was to settle administrative posts on families and allow them to become hereditary. The Ponziani family held posts as inspectors of troops and horses for most of the fifteenth century, and this was once again a characteristic which provided continuity but not necessarily efficiency.

Our knowledge of the administration of the Neapolitan army is limited to the figure of Diomede Carafa who took over its control in 1458 and was still an active figure in military affairs nearly thirty years later. Carafa was first and foremost a soldier, but he was also a man of considerable intellectual ability and a patron of repute. His surviving writings, which all took the form of advisory homilies on various subjects, reveal a man for whom discipline and efficiency were important. There is no doubt from his remarks on military affairs that he thought in terms of standing armies and he constantly stressed the need for paying troops well and regularly, and preserving good discipline. As Neapolitan military records for the period do not survive we can only assume that he in his influential position did something to put these precepts into practice.

When we turn to Florence we are in a rather different world. Here there survived an emphasis on equity rather than efficiency; all responsible executive and administrative positions were filled by drawing lots amongst the Florentine ruling class, and this lack of continuity, when combined with a deep suspicion of soldiers, tended to produce an erratic military administration. The predominant figure in Florentine military organisation throughout the fifteenth century was still the temporary commissary. The role of Luca di Maso degli Albizzi, attached to the army of Niccolò da Tolentino in 1432, admirably illustrates this point. Albizzi was sent primarily to carry instructions to Niccolò and to act as political adviser, but he found himself chivvying troops out of their beds to get on the road, issuing instructions to local officials about producing pioneers and provisions, and planning the formation of an artillery train, as well as participating actively in the councils of war. At one stage when Niccolò da Tolentino went ahead with a small force to reconnoitre the enemy's position at Montopoli, it was Albizzi who was left in charge of the army. On this mission Albizzi was only with the army for three weeks before returning to Florence exhausted, no doubt to be replaced by another temporary administrative coordinator.

Early in the 1430's another insight into the poor

administrative state of the Florentine army is given to us by Belpetro Manelmi himself. A contingent of Florentine infantry had been sent to join the Venetian army in Lombardy, and Manelmi protested bitterly about their condition. They had come with no muster rolls, so that no meaningful inspection could be made of them; the Florentines had sent insufficient money to pay them and they were greatly deficient in arms. Manelmi commented graphically that the Florentines might as well have sent them straight to join the enemy, the Milanese, as to send them in this condition when they were bound to desert. Here in fact was the root of the whole problem of the infidelity of mercenary soldiers; an army that was properly and systematically controlled and paid would remain faithful and efficient, and most of the Italian states were beginning to realise this and act accordingly.

The Florentines, however, even as late as the Pazzi War, were still relying on temporary officials, and the result was that the Milanese and Venetian troops, who were sent to Tuscany to support them, complained bitterly about the administration of the combined army. Gian Jacopo Trivulzio, at this time a commander in the Milanese *lanze spezzate*, wrote a graphic account of the chaos to which he was clearly not accustomed:

'these Florentine troops are so badly organised that it disgusts me; the men-at-arms are spread out in confusion, often with squadrons mixed up together in a way which seems to conform to no plan, and squadrons as much as half a mile apart. The soldiers are billeted all over the place without any provision for pioneers or other essential auxiliaries; there are very few infantry, about 700, of which 150 only are properly armed although I have made constant protests about this. . . . . These Florentine officials sell victuals at the dearest price possible without any concern for the regulation of prices and quality; the money is debased so that it buys very little; and if provisions are sent from Lombardy or elsewhere these Florentines make us pay duty on them, or even keep them for themselves.'

These strictures were repeated by other Milanese condottieri who complained about inadequate provisions, debased currency, and rat and plague infested billets. However, despite these Florentine shortcomings, Philippe de Commynes who visited both armies during the Pazzi War remarked: 'As for the provision of food supplies and other things necessary for maintaining an army in the field, they (the Italians) do it much better than we do.' This from a man who knew the French and Burgundian armies well was significant praise indeed.

The first task of a military administrator was to recruit soldiers. This, for a large proportion of the armies, meant recruiting condottieri, although of course the choice of condottieri involved a consideration not only of the skills of the leader, but also of the quality of the company which he commanded. All the Italian states received reports from their diplomatic representatives and from spies on the quality of troops available, and all sent out special officials to assess recruiting possibilities in various areas and to hire specific captains. All the states also had recruiting offices established in their main cities. The Florentine *Ufficio delle Condotte* was one of the earliest of such organisations, although it was always staffed by rotating officials. In Venice and Milan, recruiting was increasingly controlled by the *collaterali*, and the activities of the recruiting officers intensified as more troops were hired individually in the fifteenth century.

Once contracts were signed or individuals hired, the next task of the military administration was to compile the muster rolls with detailed descriptions of every fighting man and horse. The conscientiousness with which this task was done and the efficiency and consistency with which the lists were subsequently used in inspections, were the keys to the discipline and effectiveness of the army. Meaningful inspections and accurate pay were impossible without the muster rolls. How far they in fact followed from the muster rolls which we know were made is another matter, and one of the hardest problems in any administrative study. The muster rolls which survive show clearly the intentions of the administrators; the place of origin and the physical characteristics of each man-at-arms or infantryman were described so that substitution at inspections was more difficult. Horses were branded and any markings noted. Furthermore regular reviews were still expected in all Italian armies, at least during war time. Certain very senior condottieri were able to gain dispensation from reviews, and it became common to allow more flexibility in peacetime standing armies, but on the whole the principle was still insisted on. How far was the practice carried out? This is difficult to say, but all the evidence suggests that far from the states becoming more lax about this, as many historians have suggested, the muster and review system became more efficient for the average condottieri and soldiers. The appearance of permanent military officials would certainly imply this, and there is plenty of evidence of condottieri being fined for defects discovered at review in the second half of the fifteenth century. In 1468 Chierighino Chiericati reported the deficiencies that he had found in the papal army; 18 condottieri and constables were fined for failing to keep their companies up to scratch out of the 50 or so who were in papal employ; of these the most flagrant offenders were Giovanni Conti who was short 13 horses out of a total of 200, and Niccolò da Bologna who had only 38 infantry instead of 50. This would suggest that in this period the real strength and organisation of the papal army did not fall far short of what appeared on paper.

Certainly a preoccupation with military discipline and morale was not a sudden realisation of Guicciardini and Machiavelli after the defeats of 1494. Fifteenth-century writers and soldiers were aware of the importance of these factors; Alberti stressed them in the preface to the *Della Famiglia*, and the military writers Orso Orsini and Diomede Carafa constantly discuss them. One of the major tasks of the *collaterali* and their assistants was to prevent desertions, desertions which when they occurred were more often the result of bad faith or bad pay on the part of the employer than better offers being made by the enemy. It was certainly common practice to seek to weaken one's enemy by persuading his troops to desert, but at the same time suspected deserters were treated with increasing promptitude and savagery in Italian armies. Successful deserters were denounced with all the publicity and propaganda facilities available to a state, and this could have a considerable effect on the career possibilities of the deserter.

Regularity of pay was at the root of all problems of discipline and fidelity. Governments were well aware of this and rarely deliberately refused to pay troops. Irregular pay resulted from political ambitions or defensive needs outrunning the limited and overstretched fiscal resources of the state. Military ill-discipline was inextricably linked with the wider bureaucratic and administrative problems of the fifteenth-century state. There were certainly cases of soldiers suddenly demanding more money than they had been promised, and there were no doubt many cases of corrupt officials holding back funds destined for the army. The main emphasis of the pay system towards paying troops through their captains and condottieri made it difficult to ensure that the men received all that was due to them. But these were all matters of detail;

the root of the problem usually lay with the failure of governments to produce enough money at the right time. But as
this study can scarcely concern itself with the overall problems of fifteenth-century fiscal policy it must content itself with
what details of the military pay structure can be observed.

For the condottiere companies there were two methods by
which pay was assessed. One was the *provisione* or total lump
sum payment to the condottiere or constable. This was usually related to the size of company contracted for, but was
sometimes entirely arbitrary and implied for the condottiere
the obligation to employ a force of 'suitable' size. Payment
by *provisione* was a growing practice in the second half of the
fifteenth century, but this was not an indication of the growing independence of the condottiere as has sometimes been
suggested. In a situation of lengthening permanent service
and the distribution of armies into winter quarters, it became
less practicable to maintain close supervision over the monthly
pay of troops. It was also a period in which the condottieri
themselves were becoming regarded more as permanent and
faithful captains who could be trusted. Finally it was a period
in which the paymasters were becoming directly responsible
for the pay of large numbers of troops and auxiliaries directly
employed by the state, and thus tended to leave the payment
of condottiere troops entirely to their own captains.

The other method of assessing pay of condottiere troops
was based on detailed rates of pay for each type of soldier
laid down in the original contracts. To the monthly sum thus
arrived at were added bonuses for the captain and his officers
expressed in various forms. An early form of bonus was the
caposoldo—an additional ducat per lance per month to be
divided up amongst the officers. Another form which became
increasingly popular was the *paga morta*, or what in the
English system of the sixteenth century was described as the
blynde speare. This meant payment for lances or infantry who

9   *A Camp at Night*. Manuscript illumination by Giovanni Bettini da Fano for the *Esperide* of Basinio da Parma (c.1458). This poem was dedicated to Sigismondo Malatesta and described his relief of Piombino in 1448. This scene portrays the camp of the besieging army of Alfonso of Aragon.

Ec minuſ interea diuu pater atq; uiroruiu
Culmine procelſo uaſti ſublimiſ olympi
Magnanimu alloquitur ſedato pectore matre
Sic uerum extinctor belli uiolenta poteſtaſ

10　*The Siege of Piombino*. Another illumination from a different manuscript of the same work as plate 9 in which Malatesta's relieving Florentine army is shown attacking the Neapolitans in the rear as they tried to storm the city in 1448.

were not in fact enrolled. The *paga morta* was always granted according to a set proportion and was both a recognition of the natural tendency of condottieri not to employ the full numbers contracted for, and also a way for a state in financial difficulties to avoid having to find the necessary bonuses. Senior captains also expected a personal *provisione* over and above the *caposoldo* to maintain their own suite and to pay the overheads of a large company. This system which was the more common one for most of the fifteenth century implied a tighter control over the pay system by the paymasters, but evidence of paymasters actually paying condottiere troops individually is rare. It seems likely that the end product of this detailed assessment of the pay due to a company was still usually a lump sum to the captain. It is clear, however, particularly in the Venetian army, that the monthly payment to the captain was based on the actual strength of his company verified in the *collaterale*'s inspection, and not on the contract strength.

Besides the condottiere troops there were the increasing numbers of permanent troops who were paid directly and individually by the paymasters; the household troops, *lanze spezzate, provisionati,* gunners, engineers, etc. That by the sixteenth century even the remaining condottiere troops were paid in this way is suggested by the fact that the practice of giving a lump sum to the captain was described as '*modo francese*' and had clearly become rather exceptional in Italian armies.

The next point to consider is the actual rates of pay offered to fifteenth-century soldiers. It has been argued that there was a marked drop in pay rates in the early years of the century from those which the mercenaries of the fourteenth-century companies had been offered, and that this was part of a long term process of reduction both in the bargaining power and in the status of soldiers. That the bargaining power of mercenaries was reduced by the growing permanence of armies is true, but an analysis of the rates of pay over the whole century does not support the idea that the status of soldiers steadily fell. There are many factors which explain the differences between the average rates of pay of cavalry in the fourteenth and fifteenth centuries. In the fourteenth century rates of pay of up to 20 florins a month for a three-man lance were not uncommon; in the fifteenth century the average was about ten florins with relatively little variation between states and little evidence of any steady fall in rates during the century.* It is clear that intense competition for the very temporary service of highly prized non-Italian troops created very different bargaining conditions to the more static and permanent situation of the fifteenth century. Troops employed for three months inevitably had to be paid more than troops in permanent service. Their expenses of moving from one service to another had to be taken into account, together with the possibility of long periods of unemployment. The end of the emphasis on the need for non-Italian troops made a considerable difference to the amount of suitable manpower available. A further point is that the lump sum payments to companies were invariably assessed in gold florins or ducats, whereas the actual payments to individual soldiers were usually made in silver currency. During the late fourteenth and fifteenth centuries the ratio of silver to gold changed rapidly, and the purchasing power of gold increased considerably. Thus smaller payments in gold to the companies did not necessarily imply a decline in the actual rewards to soldiers.

* The problem of trying to estimate the value in modern monetary terms of Renaissance currencies is a difficult one. The best that can be done is to indicate a few examples of contemporary wages and prices to give the reader some idea. In Florence, around 1400, the lowest paid manual workers received the equivalent of 20–25 florins a year, while a skilled artisan would get about twice that. A florin would buy two barrels of red wine or 50 kilos of meat. A florin and a ducat were of roughly equal value.

A detailed look at pay scales in the fifteenth century bears out the impression of a relatively stable picture, after a dramatic and rapid decline round the beginning of the century, but it also reveals some interesting minor comparisons. In the very earliest years the decline from fourteenth-century rates was clear; in 1404–5 papal and Venetian troops were still getting 15 ducats per lance. By 1414 it was 12–13 ducats and in the 1420's ten. At this stage some comparison between the states is possible. The highest rates tended to be paid by Florence whose army was always the least permanent and least well organised. Throughout the wars between 1424 and 1454 Florence paid 11–12 florins per lance. At the same time the normal rate in the papal army was 9–10 florins per lance, while in the Milanese and Venetian armies 8 florins was more common. There were sometimes local variations depending on the cost of living and forage, but on the whole it seems clear that the more a state had progressed towards creating a standing army the lower the rates of pay it was able to impose. In the second half of the century it became increasingly common to quote pay rates as annual rather than monthly figures, and 80 florins a year in ten monthly payments became a very standard figure for the three man lance. Throughout this period, and indeed back into the fourteenth century, there had been very little variation in infantry pay. Three florins per month for a single infantry man was very standard, with a tendency to descend to two and a half or two by the middle of the fifteenth century.

These estimates of rates of pay are all drawn from contractual evidence and are the rates agreed between captains and governments. What was actually given to the soldiers is far less easy to evaluate. It was a very common custom to pay a part of the wages in cloth, and in most companies it was the practice for the captain to provide food and drink, and dock his troops' pay accordingly. Thus a man-at-arms in the company of Galeotto da Sanseverino in 1465 in Milanese pay received 2–2½ ducats a month together with clothing, food and drink for himself and his two followers.

A further point to be considered is that all states levied taxes on their troops. These took the form of standard retentions of pay in the order of about 5 per cent and were often devoted to specific purposes. The *Onoranza di San Marco* was levied by the Venetians and in the 1440's was as much as 10 per cent; the *Onoranza della Camera Apostolica* was retained by the papacy. Troops employed by Bologna contributed to the building of S. Petronio, and those hired by Florence paid the *onoranza* towards the building of the cathedral. These were all retentions on basic pay which were quite separate from arrangements which were usually made for a division of booty. In Venice it was common practice for one-tenth of the booty taken by the army to go to the state.

Besides their pay, troops could expect occasional special remuneration. An additional month's pay for storming a city was a well established custom and was indeed the very least that soldiers expected for exposing themselves to the particular dangers which storming and street fighting involved. Individual acts of bravery were often rewarded by cash payments, particularly in the context of storming fortresses when the first man over the walls would be offered large cash rewards. The Venetians offered 300 ducats to the first man to enter Rovigo in the war of Ferrara, plus a pension for life if he was an ordinary soldier. In fact pensions for retiring or disabled soldiers were becoming increasingly common in the fifteenth century, particularly in the Venetian army where long service can be first noted. The infantry corporal, Ferrando da Spagna, was one of a number of relatively low ranking soldiers who were offered pensions by Venice in the 1440's. His right arm was shot off by a bombard at the crossing of the Adda late in 1446, and he was offered a pension of six *lire* a month for life. Ferrando however, who had already served for 18 years in the Venetian army, refused to retire and demanded to be allowed to continue to serve the Republic with his left arm, so the pension was changed to a gift of 40 ducats. This may of course have been calculated avarice rather than fortitude or devotion, but it was one of many instances of the beginning of a pension system.

After pay, provisioning was the next most important aspect of military organisation and the two were to some extent linked. Pay was sometimes given in kind, both grain and clothing, and the principle was clearly established in Italian warfare that troops paid for their provisions when operating in friendly territory. Italian states had no system of purveyance to help with the problem of actually assembling enough supplies for a large army, but their subjects were normally obliged to sell supplies to the troops at fair prices. The troops were also guaranteed fair prices in their contracts and so the state inevitably had to concern itself with the problem of collecting supplies. There were three basic ways in which this could be done. First, supplies could be collected in bulk at a base and moved up to the army by the provisioners. Given the mobility of Italian warfare with its dependence on rapid manoeuvre, and the difficulty of much of the terrain over which armies fought, this was rarely a possibility in a field campaign. Besieging armies could be supplied in this way and indeed frequently had to be as the immediate countryside was stripped of provisions. But it could be argued that one of the factors in dictating the mobility of Italian armies was the tendency for them to live off supplies collected locally, and the speed with which such supplies were exhausted. Thus the second method of supply was for local officials and army provisioners to collect stocks in the area in which the army was operating. Thirdly, and this method was always complementary to the other two, markets were established in or close to the camp, and local farmers and merchants were encouraged to come and sell direct to the troops. Some of the most specific clauses in camp orders issued to Italian armies always concerned safe-conducts for such merchants, and the Florentines, in the fourteenth century at least, not only had officials in Florence responsible for collecting supplies for the army, but also three elected *Signori del mercato dell'esercito* who regulated the market in the camp.

Once the army had passed into enemy territory, its obligation to pay for its food ceased and it was expected to live off the land in the true sense of the word; nevertheless, some method of organised supply continued to be necessary. Individual foraging was usually discouraged as being bad for discipline, and each company would detach squadrons specifically for this purpose to supplement the activities of the provisioners.

The problems of supply, of course, affected clothing, arms and horses as well as food, and as armies grew in the fifteenth century, central responsibility for these also increased. Cloth was often issued in lieu of pay, particularly in the spring at the start of a campaign, and from an early date we find quartermasters and munitions officers responsible for supplying expendable munitions like crossbow bolts, gunpowder, balls, etc. Milan, with the great reputation and resources of the armourers of the city, was probably the first to organise comprehensive munitions supplies to the army. In 1427 after the defeat by the Venetians at Maclodio which resulted in the entire Milanese army being stripped of its arms, Milan was able to re-equip her troops from her warehouses in a few days. Two armourers alone provided arms and equipment for 4,000 cavalry and 2,000 infantry. The arsenal in Venice had always concerned itself with the production of arms for the galleys, and now in the fifteenth century began increasingly to provide for the army as well. It became one of the largest manufacturers of gunpowder, supplying not only the Venetian army but also the papal army in the Romagna and the Marches. In the Papal States Spoleto had developed a considerable arms industry and supplied cross-bow bolts, shields and lances to the army. At the lowest level condottieri and constables were still responsible for maintaining their companies properly armed, but increasingly army quartermasters were helping them to do this.

The question of the supply of horses is an obscure one and it is often difficult to imagine how Italy could supply not only the 70,000 mounts needed in 1439 by Italian cavalry, according to the estimates of Sanuto, but also the immense numbers of replacements which warfare of the period demanded. That the shortage was severe is indicated by the price of horses which normally cost at least 30 florins—or the equivalent of an infantryman's wages for a year—and could cost up to 150 or 200 florins. Horse dealers were prominent among the merchants who haunted the army camps, but where the large numbers of horses required were reared is far from clear. Some of the condottieri went in for horse breeding, particularly the Gonzaga family; but of large scale imports there is little trace, although the majority of the horse dealers associated with the Venetian army in the second half of the century were Germans. The concern for branding and inspection of horses by employers, and the claims for replacement of horses by soldiers, both indicate the difficulties which the maintenance of supplies presented. By the fifteenth century all governments had begun to resist claims from their troops that replacement of horses lost in battle was the employer's responsibility. The Venetians in order to ensure that the quality and number of horses was maintained insisted that not only should lost horses be replaced within ten days, but that the skins of dead horses should be shown to Venetian officials to prove that the originally approved horse had in fact been killed and not sold.

The billeting of troops was a complex problem of military organisation which could, like provisioning, be resolved in a number of ways. The possibilities ranged from the large, fortified, but essentially temporary, encampments of the field armies, to the barracks specially built by Caterina Sforza for her troops in Forlì. The latter were commissioned in 1491 and were something of a novelty in that they were specifically designed for soldiers. Caterina ordered 70 houses to be built in two rows, with each row divided into five terraces of seven houses. They were to be built of wood and were to include stabling and storage space for fodder as well as rooms for the soldiers and their families. Such facilities certainly seem to have been exceptional, although it is very hard to decide what the winter-quarters of troops did consist of. The Duke of Calabria when preparing winter quarters for his army in the Maremma in 1447 built wooden huts, and it seems likely that the permanent encampments outside the main Venetian cities, the so-called *serragli*, must have contained similar lodgings. The *serraglio* was a well-established tradition in Lombardy; it was an area outside the walls of a town which was provided with natural defences of ditches and ramparts, and in which quite sizeable forces could be encamped for long periods.

In Florence in the fourteenth century troops were normally billeted in the Borgo S. Lorenzo, the northwest quarter of the city, within the walls. Here houses were allotted to them, and the life of that part of the city was very much dominated by them. But normally, large numbers of troops were not billeted in Italian cities. In sieges, of course, it was necessary, and when on the march contingents of the army would sometimes be billeted in small towns and villages. For this purpose a captain general or army commander normally kept close to him a special squadron, made up of representatives of all the companies, which went ahead of the army on the march to divide up the billets. The responsibility of allocating billets for winter-quarters was usually in the hands of permanent officials by the end of the fifteenth century; in Milan there were special commissaries of lodgings who carried out this task.

Normally, however, in the field the armies encamped. This was an increasingly elaborate process demanding the erection of various types of tent ranging from the captain general's pavilion to the primitive shelters built by the ordinary soldiers. The stradiots, indeed, were accustomed to sleeping under their horses with just their cloaks thrown over the backs of the animals and hanging down on either side to give some protection. Fortification of the camp was also an increasingly elaborate process in the fifteenth century, but this is a point to be taken up elsewhere.

The setting up of camps and discipline within the camps was still, however, a matter very much for the soldiers themselves; the civilian officials had little role to play in this aspect of military life. They did, however, come back into the picture in the final aspect of military organisation which has to be considered—demobilisation. Here it was once more the *collaterali* who had to enforce the unpopular decision to pay off some of the companies at the end of the war, or dismiss inefficient ones during hostilities. The problem of getting rid of soldiers at the end of their contracts was one of the factors which was pushing Italian states towards maintaining permanent armies in the early fifteenth century. With some of the states, of course, it was a problem of finding the money to pay them off in the first place, and when this could not be done it seemed easier just to renew their contracts and thus mollify them with promises of future payment. But even if the money was available and the companies had been fully paid, there were always problems in getting them to leave the state at a time when they had ceased to feel any obligation towards that state. Venice was confronted with this problem in 1405 as she proposed to demobilise part of the considerable army which she had assembled for the siege of Padua. The instructions to her *provveditori* and officials set out various ways in which the difficulty could be tackled. One was to issue *condotte in aspetto*—i.e. promise a continuation of part-time payments if the companies would leave Venetian territory and remain on call elsewhere. Another was to take hostages from the companies which were to be demobilised and not give them their final pay until they had moved beyond the frontiers. A third form of coercion was to cut off supplies to them. Finally, and here was the real answer, the officials were instructed to rehire the best troops, and if necessary use them to drive out the inferior companies which were being demobilised.

Once the principle of large standing forces had been accepted, the problems of demobilisation became less acute. What had been a major issue for Venice in 1405 was never to become so again. But there was always the problem of dismissing the occasional inefficient company, or getting rid of the company of a disgraced condottiere. A large company like that which Bartolomeo Colleoni left when he fled from Venetian service in 1452 could present great problems. In this case part of the troops were massacred in an assault organised against them by the *provveditori*; part were paid off; and part were rehired either in the *lanze spezzate* or in the companies of other Venetian condottieri. It was the *collaterali* who, from their knowledge of the worth not only of the companies but also of individual soldiers, had to sort out who was to be kept and who discharged on these occasions.

Much of the discussion of the organisation of war in fifteenth-century Italy has revolved around the question of the avail-

ability and distribution of money. This was not just because of the increased use of mercenaries; soldiers had been
paid for centuries, and the 'foreign' mercenaries employed
by fifteenth-century Italian states were uncontrollably rapa-
cious. While the size of armies increased, the rates of pay
tended to drop. But pay was by no means the only expenditure. Money was needed to buy munitions and equipment on an increasing scale, to pay vast contingents of non-
combatant pioneers and engineers, to reward spies and
informers, and to finance the whole structure of administrative services which has been described. How this money
was raised and the impact of raising such sums on contemporary government and society are topics which go rather
beyond the scope of this study, but no discussion of warfare
can be complete without at least raising the issues.

————◁▷————

CHAPTER SIX

THE ART OF WAR

One of the principal complaints of those who have deplored the Italian military scene in the fifteenth century has been that an anachronistic type of heavy cavalry continued to predominate in Italian armies, and that current developments outside Italy in the use of artillery and infantry were ignored; in short that the art of war made no progress. To examine this comprehensive verdict must be the ultimate and overall aim of this chapter, but first it is necessary to look in detail at the various components of Italian armies and the methods which they employed.

It is true that both in terms of numbers and particularly in terms of prestige, heavy cavalry did tend to predominate in Italian fifteenth-century armies. The numerical predominance was certainly declining by the middle of the century and in certain armies was even reversed. Much depended on the purpose for which an army had been assembled. For major sieges a predominance of infantry was always necessary; in 1469 the papal army besieging Rimini was probably made up of about 5,000 cavalry and 5,000 infantry, and in 1472, when Florence summoned up her strength for the subjugation of Volterra, the army consisted of about 10,000 infantry and 2,000 cavalry. By this time most field armies contained roughly equal proportions of cavalry and infantry, and one should not be misled by the appearance of the average condottiere company. These were still the core of the heavy cavalry, although they themselves tended to contain increasing numbers of light cavalry and infantry. But armies in the second half of the fifteenth century consisted of much more than condottiere companies. There were the companies of the infantry constables employed on a contract basis, the squadrons of permanent *lanze spezzate* and *provisionati*, a few detachments of light cavalry, the gunners, and thousands of lightly armed or unarmed militia and pioneers. The numbers of this last element were usually entirely approximate and should perhaps be excluded from estimates of the size and proportions of an army, but it must also be remembered that the lances of the condottiere companies contained a proportion of lightly-armed support troops. Thus in terms of overall numbers, although it is true that the heavy cavalry still tended to predominate in the century as a whole, this predominance was by no means clear-cut in the second half of the century. The growth in the use of field fortifications, which was the most significant development in Italian fifteenth-century warfare, made it essential for all armies to employ growing numbers of infantry. At the same time the core of the French standing army was still the heavy cavalry of the *compagnies d'ordonnance*, and the vaunted French army in 1494 still had more than half its strength made up of heavy cavalry.

What is perhaps of more significance than actual numbers is that the prestigious arm was still clearly the heavy cavalry, although this also was a declining factor. A number of the leading infantry commanders of the latter half of the century were of noble blood, and as the infantry companies grew in size and in quality, so the prestige of their leaders grew. But it is scarcely surprising that the peculiar status of the cavalryman should remain, in a society which was as status conscious as that of Renaissance Italy. However, one often has to avoid confusing the personal status and prestige of cavalry leaders with the military significance of the troops they commanded, and this was already true in late fifteenth-century Italy.

Cavalry

In the early years of the fifteenth century, Italian warfare was certainly affected by the absence of any large bodies of highly trained infantry. There was no lasting equivalent to the English archers or later the Swiss pike squares in Italian warfare. Thus there was no pressure on Italian cavalry commanders to dismount their men-at-arms or otherwise adapt their methods. The basic unit of Italian cavalry forces remained until about 1450 the three-man lance. This was not an all-round fighting unit of the type that the French and Burgundian lances became, in which archers and crossbowmen supported the man-at-arms. The Italian lance remained fundamentally a cavalry unit and, in a certain sense, had a social as well as a military justification. In the early fifteenth century the type of three-man lance attributed to Hawkwood, in which two similarly armed men-at-arms were accompanied by a page, was still common. But this had developed in the context of men-at-arms fighting on foot and as this became less common so the lance tended to change to a structure of one man-at-arms with a less well armoured sergeant and a page. Increasingly the main task of both the followers was to 'service' the leader of the lance, to groom, hold and lead his horses, maintain his arms and armour, provide his food and carry his messages. As long as the needs of the man-at-arms varied little, the size of his entourage remained static.

But after 1450 the three-man lance was no longer the rule, particularly when armies were put on a war footing. At first the changes were informal, and the only indication of them comes from contracts which laid down the minimum number of men-at-arms in a given body of cavalry. Increas-

ingly this number represented less than one-third, and the
references to such men as 'true men-at-arms' (*armigeri veri*)
or 'helmets' (*elmetti*) would suggest that fighting men other
than the traditional heavily armed man-at-arms were appearing amongst the lances. That it also meant an increase in the
size of the lance is clear from specific references to four-man
lances in Florentine and Milanese contracts in the 1470's, and
to the five-man *corazza* in papal contracts in the 1460's.

The *corazza* was clearly a development from the lance,
and the fact that it was first used in the papal army about
1464 suggests that perhaps the recent presence of Angevin
troops in Naples, organised into six-man lances, may have
influenced this Italian innovation. However, whether the new
formation in fact imitated the French lance in including
crossbowmen and transforming itself into an all-round fighting unit seems unlikely. No evidence has yet come to light
of the exact composition of the *corazza* or the enlarged lance,
but it seems most probable that it differed little in function
from the old three-man lance. The needs of the man-at-arms
were changing by this time; the growing weight of armour
of both man and horse meant that war-horses tired more
quickly and a man-at-arms had to change mounts frequently
during a battle. This meant more horses and more attendants
to look after them and lead them. At the same time there
was a tendency, as men-at-arms became more heavily armoured, for their opponents to strike at their mounts. This
had been considered 'bad war' in the early fifteenth century,
but by the later years was accepted practice. The result of
this also was to increase the number of horses and attendants
needed by each man-at-arms. There were therefore clear
reasons for the expansion of the Italian lance without it necessarily changing its nature, and, given the fact that supporting
light cavalry and infantry units were developing outside
the traditional framework of the lance, it seems likely

that the lance or *corazza* continued to serve the same function.

As well as the changes which were taking place in the lance around the middle of the century, there was also a move to standardise the larger units in Italian cavalry forces. The squadron of 25 lances had always been a rough guide-line for cavalry organisation, and the larger condottiere companies had tended to be organised roughly on this basis. But in the days of the greater independence of the companies around the beginning of the fifteenth century, it was the company itself which had been the normal battle unit. Given the immense differences in size of the companies, this was too untidy a system for the more highly organised and integrated armies of the later years. So not only were the *condotte* themselves becoming increasingly standardised, particularly at 50 or 100 lances, but also the squadron of 20–25 was becoming more accepted as a standard unit. By the later years of the century, armies were being assessed in numbers of squadrons rather than numbers of lances. With the increased size of the lance, this meant that the total strength of a squadron was increasing, and squadrons of the 1460's and 1470's would number up to 150 men. But the actual fighting strength remained much the same, around 25 men-at-arms commanded by a *caposquadra* or *squadriere*.

Another feature of the emerging organisation was the appearance of larger units known as columns. Even in the fourteenth- and early fifteenth-century armies, a number of senior condottieri had been named as 'marshals', and this had implied a certain subdivision of the army. But it was only in the second half of the fifteenth century that a clearly defined larger unit began to emerge and a senior condottiere was sometimes described as a *colonello*. The size of the column varied greatly depending on the overall size of the army, but it is clear that in the armies of this period, groups

11 A group of knights fighting. The great fresco and *sinopia* by Pisanello, of which this is a detail of the *sinopia*, were recently uncovered in the Ducal Palace in Mantua. They were executed between 1447 and 1455 for Gianfrancesco and Ludovico Gonzaga, and probably represent a tournament rather than a battle scene.

12 (a) This is a detail from Pisanello's fresco described below Plate 11. The very ornate and cumbersome plume of the knight's helmet suggests that the scene is a tournament as battle armour was normally a good deal less extravagant.

(b) *Federigo da Montefeltro in his Library.* Justus of Ghent, who painted this work, was one of many artists employed by Federigo, Duke of Urbino, and this portrait of Federigo as scholar, bibliophile, and successful captain sums up the qualities which made him so admired in his day.

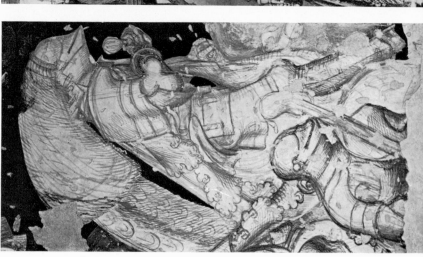

of eight to ten cavalry squadrons were being organised together, regardless of the condottiere companies of which they
formed a part. Sometimes a company would be split between
two columns, although this was still probably exceptional.

Apart from these developments in organisation and formation, the role and methods of heavy cavalry changed little
in the fifteenth century. Greater emphasis on squadron units
allowed for greater flexibility and discipline in battle, and
it is certainly a misconception to think of the mass frontal
cavalry charge as being the main tactical manoeuvre of
Italian heavy cavalry. But they remained basically heavily
armoured lancers. This does not mean that they were the
cumbersome, robot-like figures, beloved of epic film makers,
who had to be lowered on to their horses by primitive cranes.
The most sophisticated armour in Europe was produced in
Italy, providing a maximum of protection compatible with
freedom of movement. A suit of battle armour was fitted
and articulated, and weighed little more than 20–25 kilos,
while the accompanying helmet would have weighed about
two kilos. The inconvenience of such armour stemmed more
from lack of ventilation than weight and led to the very considerable problems of campaigning and fighting in the heat
of an Italian summer.

The fact remained, however, that heavy cavalry was an
inflexible component of all fifteenth-century armies, and it
was inevitable that there should be attempts to develop
types of light cavalry for the variety of tasks created by more
sophisticated methods of warfare. In a certain sense the
lightly armed, mounted followers of the men-at-arms could
be described as light cavalry, and the number of these was
increasing. But this would be misleading, as these were not
fighting men, and the definition of cavalry must be men who
fight on horseback. However, such a definition does create
the problem of how to classify those who moved to battle

and campaigned on horseback but dismounted to fight. Clearly such troops were as mobile as cavalry, and this was the point of mounting them, but in battle they became infantry and were controlled and organised as such. Here one is thinking particularly of the mounted crossbowmen, and later mounted hand-gun men and arquebusiers, who appeared in ever increasing numbers in Italian armies. Such men did not form part of the lances but were organised in units of their own. From 1430 onwards, however, a number of condottiere companies included groups of mounted crossbowmen, and entirely separate companies of them were also being formed. While it is probably true that such troops normally dismounted to fight, their mounted potential was clearly important, quite apart from just getting them to the scene of a battle. Scouting, foraging, and pursuit were the essential tasks of light cavalry, and these could all be performed by mounted crossbowmen, who were equipped with sword and dagger as well as their bows.

However, an even more distinctive and effective type of light cavalry emerged in Italy with the introduction by Venice of Albanian stradiots recruited in her overseas empire. Venice had always made considerable use of such troops in the empire and in her wars with the Turks, and it was during and following the long war of 1463–79 with the Turks that stradiots began to appear in Italian armies. They were mounted on light, unarmoured horses and equipped sometimes with crossbows but more commonly with light lances and javelins. Their armour was limited to breastplate and shield. Clearly the possession of organised units of such troops gave an army much greater manoeuvrability and flexibility in battle, and a number of the leading condottieri of the later years of the century perceived these possibilities. It is true, on the other hand, that the Albanians had a reputation for ill discipline and, as one of their prime functions was to carry

out wide encircling movements aimed at an enemy's rear
and his baggage train, this was a defect of no little conse-
quence. However, both in the mounted crossbowmen and
the stradiot units, the Italians had seen the way forward in
cavalry development, and the light horse were to become
increasingly significant during the Italian Wars.

Infantry

It is a commonly held view that disciplined and effective infantry largely disappeared from the Italian military scene in
the second half of the fourteenth and in the fifteenth centuries. Indeed even the great masses of ill-trained levies,
which provided the numbers of thirteenth-century armies,
seemed to play little part in fifteenth-century warfare. However, the emergence of smaller groups of more professional,
more specialised, infantry was an early development, and,
although there was perhaps a period when such troops were
still relatively few and the mass levy was either discarded
or clearly recognised as a separate auxiliary force, this period
was short, and throughout the fifteenth century the number
of genuine and effective infantry in Italian armies was growing.

At the beginning of the fifteenth century the effective infantry were still divided into three groups: the infantry
lances, the shield bearers, and the crossbowmen. An infantry
company was usually made up of equal proportions of each,
and, although only the larger condottiere companies contained infantry, there were many wholly infantry companies
available. It is true that the role of such infantry was largely
defensive; the lancers and the shield bearers with their long
cumbersome shields could form a wall behind which cavalry
could reform. The other main role for such infantry was in
siege warfare, when both the defence of the besieging en-
campment against sorties and the actual assault were entrusted to them.

Although the crossbow was the main missile weapon of Italian infantry and had been since the early thirteenth century, there were still some companies of English archers to be found in Italy as late as 1430. Thirty archers under John Clement and Godfrey Reynolds were in Florentine service in that year, and in 1431 Walter of England was employed by Venice with 90 archers. The pay of these men was rather better than that of the average Italian infantryman, but this was perhaps because they were still mounted in the tradition of Hawkwood and his archers, rather than because their services as infantry were particularly prized. There was still a slight predominance of Genoese amongst the crossbowmen but, on the whole, ability to use the crossbow was widespread. Venetians all learnt to fire a crossbow as part of their civic obligations, and it was the standard weapon of garrison troops and town guards.

Infantry units maintained this threefold division until around the middle of the century, although the prestige of infantry was certainly growing. Both Sforza and Braccio attached particular importance to their infantry. Francesco Sforza developed a highly disciplined infantry force, commanded by such men as Pietro Brunoro and Donato del Conte, in which crossbowmen, and later hand-gun men, predominated. In this emphasis one can see an intention to use infantry in a more offensive role, and Braccio had the same ideas, as he developed a lighter type of infantry armed with sword and round shield which took part in the assault on Perugia in 1416. By the 1440's the leading infantry commanders were men of considerable reputation and were regarded as the equals of the best of the cavalry leaders. Diotisalvi Lupi, who commanded the Venetian infantry for many years in the 1430's and 1440's, was a close associate of Carmagnola and Colleoni, received large estates and rewards, and was knighted by the Republic in 1447. His successor, Matteo Griffoni, had commanded the Florentine infantry in the 1440's and was brought to Venice about 1447. He still commanded the Venetian infantry in 1470. He also was knighted for his services and was second only to Colleoni in the military hierarchy of the Republic. He commanded a company of 500 infantry of his own as well as his overall command of the Venetian infantry.

The emergence of men such as these, and the Venetians were by no means exceptional, is indicative of the way in which the wars in Lombardy between 1425 and 1454 changed the nature of Italian warfare. The central Lombard plain, the area of the subsequently famous Quadrilateral, was ideal country for campaigning. It is open and flat and yet intersected with several rivers and many canals. Here increasingly large armies could be deployed, and there was room to manoeuvre large bodies of cavalry. At the same time the natural barriers could be readily converted into massive field fortifications, and there was plenty of peasant manpower available for digging. This development brought the infantry to the fore, while the new size of armies and their subsequently retarded speed of manoeuvre enabled infantry to participate much more fully in the campaigns.

It was to combat the new emphasis on field fortifications that a new type of infantry became popular in Italian armies. This was the so-called 'sword and buckler' infantry, first experimented with by Braccio. They were lightly armed, agile, and equipped for hand-to-hand offensive fighting. The type had already been developed in Spain in fighting with the Moors, and the establishment of the Aragonese in Naples in the 1440's clearly had something to do with their appearance in Italy at this time. But the best infantry forces appeared in Lombardy and were clearly a development from the special conditions of Lombard warfare. Florence, for example, retained the traditional types of infantry well into the 1470's, and, despite its Spanish antecedents, there is no indication of a particularly effective Neapolitan infantry growing up. After Milan and Venice, it was the papal army which had the best infantry in the middle of the century. This was partly a matter of having some of the best recruiting grounds in the mountain valleys of Umbria, the Romagna, and the Abruzzi, but it also in part perhaps reflected the Spanish influence of Calixtus III and his entourage. A number of the leading infantry captains in the papal army in the 1450's were Spaniards.

It was at about the same moment that the other major development in Italian infantry took place—the large scale introduction of hand firearms. The earliest hand firearm was the *schioppetto* or hand-gun, and the introduction of these has been postulated as early as the late thirteenth century. By the second half of the fourteenth century there is a good deal of sporadic evidence of their use but almost entirely in the defence of towns. The primitive hand-gun was three or four feet long, rather cumbersome and shapeless and had to be fired with a match. It cannot have been an easy weapon to use in the field or without a rest. However, by the 1430's there was growing evidence of groups of specialist hand-gun men in the field armies. The emperor Sigismond had 500 in his following on his visit to Rome in 1430, but these were clearly intended for display and their presence does not indicate that the hand-gun had arrived as an infantry battle weapon. But the presence of *schioppettieri* companies in the Milanese and Venetian armies in the next two decades, and descriptions of their activities, clearly do indicate just such an initiative. Both Francesco Sforza and his cousin Micheletto Attendolo, who commanded the Venetian army between 1441 and 1448, had hand-gun contingents in their companies, and Colleoni and the Venetian infantry commander, Dioti-salvi Lupi, were others who were associated with the new weapon in this period. In the 1440's the Venetian senate was alarmed by reports that the Milanese army had superior numbers of hand-gun men and that these were causing considerable casualties in the Venetian army. In 1448 at the battle of Caravaggio, Francesco Sforza had so many hand-gun men firing that they could not see each other for the smoke from their guns. In the next year when the short-lived Ambrosian Republic of Milan sought to oppose Francesco Sforza, it was claimed that it could put 20,000 Milanese citizens into the field equipped with hand-guns. This was clearly pure propaganda intended to frighten Sforza off, but the very fact that such a claim could be made and thought to be efficacious indicates the extent to which the hand-gun had arrived by this time. Certainly hand-gun men captured in the battles of the 1440's received short shrift and were usually executed on the spot; this was a tribute to their effectiveness rather than a sign of abhorrence for their unchivalrous weapon.

In the years following the Peace of Lodi in 1454 hand-gun companies became a part of all the Italian standing armies. As in so many of the military developments of the period, Florence seemed to be behind in the use of the new weapon, but hand-gun men appeared in the papal army from at least the mid-1450's. At the siege of Rimini in 1469, the papal army had a company of 77 hand-gun men led by a German commander, and by this time a number of Germans appeared in this role in Italian armies. But there is no evidence that hand-gun development was exclusively a preserve of Germans. In 1476 one-fifth of the Milanese infantry, 2,000 men, were equipped with hand-guns, and in 1482, in the preparations for the War of Ferrara, the Milanese contingent was issued with 1,250 hand-guns, 352 arquebuses, but only 233 crossbows. By this time in fact the old hand-gun was beginning to be superseded by the arquebus, a more sophisticated weapon, perhaps heavier, but fitted with a trigger. The Milanese hand-gun man was equipped with a steel skull-cap and breastplate, and in addition to his gun and powder he carried a sword and a halberd. By the 1490's mounted hand-gun men and arquebusiers were being used by Camillo Vitelli and Cesare Borgia, and thus a new dimension was added to the light cavalry as well as the infantry forces.

It has been usually thought that the hand-gun was a largely ineffective and despised weapon before 1500, but both the evidence of its growing use in Italian armies and of the growing numbers of casualties inflicted by hand-gun men would suggest differently. No serious comparison of the range, firepower or practicability of the hand-gun and the crossbow has yet been attempted, but it is clear that the former was steadily replacing the latter as the principal infantry missile weapon from a fairly early moment in the fifteenth century. This was to some extent because the hand-gun and its ammunition were cheaper to produce and easier to use than the crossbow, rather than because of its superiority as a weapon. At the same time the stage had not yet been reached when trained and disciplined bodies of hand-gun men could swing the course of a battle by controlled and concentrated fire. The hand-gun was still used, as the crossbow had been used, to harass the enemy and protect the flanks of an army in the field and even more effectively, both by besiegers and besieged, in siege warfare.

Infantry forces, therefore, formed a significant part of fifteenth-century Italian armies. It is true that there was no disciplined pike infantry of the Swiss type, which was enjoying brief, but lastingly significant success beyond the Alps. It is also true that, because of the nature of the Italian mercenary system, the companies tended to be small and unused to operating *en masse*. But large numbers of specialist and well-trained infantry were available and played an increasing part in the warfare. Only infantry and light artillery could deal with the field fortifications, which were so much in vogue, and the decisive victory won by Roberto Malatesta over the Duke of Calabria at Campomorto in 1482 was won by an infantry assault over marshy ground on a fortified camp.

As we have seen, permanent infantry forces in the pay of Italian states were appearing beside the companies of the mercenary constables. The increased status of the infantry-man was indicated by the fact that the organisation of professional infantry was beginning to resemble that of the cavalry lance, with an infantryman attended by two or three followers who looked after his equipment and supported him in battle. This improvement in status was also evident amongst the infantry leaders, who were more often than not drawn from noble families in the later fifteenth century. Finally the ranks of the infantry companies were more filled with foreigners than were those of the cavalry, and this was a factor in ensuring professionalism and progressive developments. Corsicans were particularly prominent both as constables and in the ranks, and there were increasing numbers of Spaniards, Germans and Albanians. Of the eighteen commanders in the Milanese regular infantry in 1467, three were Spaniards, three Corsicans and one Albanian. These men did not command integrated companies of their own nationals, and it seems to be true that the proportion of foreigners amongst the leaders was higher than amongst the rank and file. All this, however, was a world apart from the untrained militia and country levies who certainly played their part in Renaissance warfare, but in different capacities to those so far described.

Artillery
One of the capacities in which country levies were employed was as pioneers to prepare emplacements for artillery and move it into position, and one of the categories of infantry which have not yet been discussed were the gunners. Cannon

were, of course, no new sight in the fifteenth century. The exact moment of their invention is still a matter of dispute, but throughout the fourteenth century there is plenty of evidence of their use in Italy. Florence was already making cannon which fired iron balls in 1326, and the papal army in the fourteenth century was one of the best equipped in this respect.

But throughout the fourteenth century there is little indication that artillery was yet used on the battlefield. The brief, fast-moving campaigns of the period gave little scope to the deployment of cumbersome, heavy weapons of doubtful value. The one example which is clearly authenticated of the use of artillery in a fourteenth-century battle is at Castagnaro in 1387. Here John Hawkwood, leading the Paduan army, prepared an ambush in which he posted both crossbowmen and cannon, and then succeeded in drawing the Veronese army into it. The result was a complete victory in which the entire Veronese army surrendered, but it was a victory achieved by successful tactics, and the addition of cannon to other missile weapons contributed little to it.

In the fifteenth century, cannon appeared with greater frequency on the battlefield, and many of the condottieri were associated with their use. Carmagnola used artillery to take Bergamo in 1419, and Bartolomeo Colleoni was a great advocate of guns in battle. At Caravaggio artillery did great slaughter and at Molinella (1467), a battle fought at the end of an exceptionally mobile campaign, Colleoni used his guns to such effect that he gained the false reputation of being the first to use them on the battlefield.

Once again it was the development of field fortifications which hastened this transfer of cannon from ramparts and siege emplacements to the battlefield. Both the preparation of static fieldworks and the overcoming of them gave time and scope for the use of artillery, and by the middle of the century such artillery was becoming much more mobile as wheeled gun carriages were introduced and the trunnion was developed, which enabled guns to be elevated and depressed quickly. Some of the condottiere companies had their own artillery; this applied not only to major figures like Francesco Sforza and Colleoni, but also to medium-sized companies like that of Tiberto Brandolini in the service of Milan in the late 1450's. Brandolini had 400 lances, and he was able to support them with two bombards and two smaller pieces. But the major artillery trains were owned by the states; the manufacture or purchase of guns and of the materials needed to use them, and the administrative and organisational problems of moving them, were enterprises that only states could afford on any large scale. This is scarcely surprising when we consider that the Milanese artillery train in 1472 consisted of sixteen guns which, together with spare lances, hand-guns, and powder, required 227 carts and 522 pairs of oxen to transport. The ox was the standard Italian draught animal of the period, although the papal army made considerable use of buffaloes to pull its guns. Both were very slow, particularly on bad roads. Many of the larger guns had to be dismantled for transportation, and the carriage of the great stone cannon balls caused almost as many problems as those of moving the guns themselves. Iron and lead balls were not unknown in Italy, indeed some of the first cannon in the fourteenth century had fired them, but only of small calibre. The heavy guns of the fifteenth century all fired stone balls which either had to be transported with the guns, or cut on the spot by stonemasons, who were an essential part of an artillery train. Such balls could weigh up to 150 kilos, so clearly the problem of creating mobile and effective artillery was not just one of guns. Girolamo Riario, when conducting the siege of Cave, was sent 400 travertine balls by Sixtus IV which had been cut from the stone of a dismantled Roman bridge and sent many miles across country to supply the papal guns.

Here we are in the realm of siege warfare, and it was only in this context that heavy guns were used. Of the eight varieties of cannon developed in Italy in the fifteenth century, only the lighter ones, firing shot of two or three pounds, were used on the battlefield. The ponderous heavy guns could take weeks to get into position and prepare for action. Even then their rate of fire was exceptionally slow and their bombardment by no means accurate. They and their gunners had to be protected from counter-bombardment and enemy sortie. All these factors have to be borne in mind in assessing the impact of the introduction of artillery on warfare and in particular on siege warfare. It is strangely true that artillery contributed perhaps more to the defence of cities and fortresses than it did to their assault. Guns permanently mounted on the walls of a city could be supplied much more efficiently and used much more speedily and effectively than the guns of besiegers hauled up into temporary emplacements from many miles away. It was for these reasons that, as we shall see, the art of fortification changed relatively slowly in response to the new threat. What did happen quickly was that all fortified places acquired massive collections of artillery with which to defend themselves. As early as 1381 Bologna had 35 pieces of artillery on its walls, and throughout the fifteenth century one finds evidence of the great quantities of artillery sited in the defences of Italian cities; artillery for which mobility and rate of fire were no problem. Even small papal fortresses like Soriano had twelve guns in 1449, and Ostia had eleven in 1455. Castel Sant'Angelo in Rome had one monster weighing four and a half tons, and in 1470 was defended by a total of 16 guns. The castle at Imola in 1473 had 33 guns, and in 1496 when the Venetians took over Brindisi they found no fewer than 98 pieces of artillery sited in its defences. This was all at a time when besiegers were still using a multitude of traditional siege engines in addition to the guns which took so long to get into action. It seems probably true that in most Italian sieges of the fifteenth century, artillery was used on only a limited scale by the besiegers. The slowness with which siege pieces were moved into position was balanced, however, by the speed with which a heavy gun, once ready to fire, could breach the medieval fortifications of most Italian cities and castles. Thus if a siege lasted more than a few weeks, the chances were that the besieged would then quickly be forced to sue for terms, as shortages of supplies and breaches in their walls made defence difficult. In the siege of Zagarolo, which lasted six weeks in the spring of 1439, the papal artillery seemed to have used only about six tons of powder; and even in the siege of Rimini, which lasted for two or three months in the summer of 1469, the same artillery was supplied with only just over twelve tons of powder. This has to be compared with the 20,000 balls fired at Verona in 1516 by the French and Venetian artillery, and the 32 tons of powder a day used by Henry VIII's army in siege operations in 1513 in northern France.

It has recently been very rightly observed by John Hale that 'cannon revolutionised the conduct but not the outcome of war'. This revolution was taking place on only a very limited scale in Italy in the fifteenth century. Guns appealed to the imagination of the Renaissance as a most appropriate symbol of war, but symbols to some extent they remained. They were gradually influencing the art of fortification, they were contributing to the development of heavier armour, they were slowing down armies in the field and greatly adding to the administrative problems, they offered certain new tactical possibilities in the field, they inflicted unexpected casualties and introduced a new atmosphere of uncertainty and fear into warfare, but they won no battles as yet and took surprisingly few cities. They accelerated the costs of war out of all proportion to their effectiveness, and thus their greatest impact lay in the wider context of war rather than in the practice and art of warfare.

Fortifications and Engineering

Whatever one may think of the slow and cumbersome operations of Italian siege artillery, the guns once installed certainly made a difference to siege warfare and the art of fortification. Furthermore, the delays in transforming fortifications to meet the new threat, and Italian backwardness in these developments, have been very much exaggerated. Too often the success of the French army of Charles VIII in 1494 with its formidable artillery has been seen as a condemnation of Italian methods of fortification, whereas in fact very few Italian fortresses were actually assaulted by the French. At the same time the survival of many Italian medieval castles contrasts with the natural disappearance of many of the transitional and often intentionally temporary examples of early gunpowder fortification, to give a false impression of developments in Italian fortification. The Italians themselves have tended to fix their eyes on the great geniuses who interested themselves in military architecture in the two decades before and after 1500, Francesco di Giorgio Martini, Leonardo da Vinci and Michelangelo, and neglect the practising military architects, whose innovations were appearing at least from the middle of the fifteenth century onwards.

The crucial feature in the changes in fortifications produced by the use of gunpowder lay not in preparing walls which could withstand battering by artillery, but in using artillery to defend those walls, to hold the enemy at a distance and strike at his siegeworks. Hence it is on the bastion, the solid low tower, either round or angled, on which heavy guns could be mounted to fire outwards, that attention must be concentrated. In this field earlier writers have tended to look in France and at the new fortifications of Rhodes in the early sixteenth century for the earliest examples, remembering perhaps that it was the Frenchman, Vauban, who finally perfected the art of the new fortification in the late seventeenth century. But many of the earliest predecessors of Vauban were working in Italy in the fifteenth century, and one does not have to look very far to see the Italian fortresses which bear out this claim.

Apart from the development of artillery, it was the political conditions of fifteenth-century Italy which made it a natural breeding ground for improvements in castle and fortification building. The uneasy atmosphere of continual warfare followed by balance of power, the preoccupations of expanding territorial states with frontiers and newly-won lands and cities, the availability of large public treasuries and prestigious artists and architects deeply involved in the problems of military architecture, all produced a preoccupation with fortification which the activities of the armies of the day did nothing to dispel. The objects of military aggressors were devastation and the capture of small, isolated strongholds, and these were countered by strengthening the strongholds and providing refuges for the populations of the ravaged countryside.

The initial reactions of defenders to the threat of artillery were to thicken their walls and to scarp them so that the cannon shot would be deflected upwards. At the same time the cannon which soon appeared in the defences were used primarily to strengthen the crossfire from the towers and thus impede the assault. Gunports were cut in the sides of the towers at ground level, and the guns were sited, often on fixed lines firing through small round apertures. The parapet walks and wooden floors of the medieval fortifications were not strong enough to bear artillery firing outwards from the defences. Evidence of innovations of these limited types can be found going back into the fourteenth century, but at that time the pressure for change was not great enough nor the resources for dramatic rebuilding available to bring about major developments.

It was in the middle years of the fifteenth century that a number of fortresses were completely rebuilt according to new principles. The emphasis was on the small fortress rather than on extended city walls, as it would always inevitably be in a period of transition and innovation. It was the castles that lay at the heart of the defences of Italian cities which underwent transformation. The bastions of the fortresses of Fano, Cesena, Imola, and Pesaro in the Romagna and Marches bear witness to the preoccupation of the papacy and its local vicars with the new problems of fortification. In the lands of the great condottiere Federigo da Montefeltro, Francesco di Giorgio Martini worked on reorganising many of the castles. In the rest of the Papal States and particularly on the approaches to Rome, Baccio Pontelli and the Sangallo family led the way in new fortifications in Civitavecchia, Ostia, Civita Castellana, and Tivoli. The Sienese refortified Talamone, Orbetello and Sarteano with the help of the master architect, Vecchietta; and the Florentines rebuilt many of their frontier fortresses, particularly on the southern approaches to the state at Brolio, Castellina and Poggio Imperiale. All this was the work of the period between 1450 and 1494, and all the Italian states were spending heavily on fortifications.

Some of the leading artists of the Renaissance spent much of their time working on fortifications. The new problems of ballistics and angles of fire appealed strongly to the experimental and enquiring minds of Renaissance artists; war was a major preoccupation of society, and in the fifteenth century the artist who wanted government or princely patronage was bound to find himself employed on fortifications. Andrea

Pisano and Orcagna worked on the walls of Florence in the fourteenth century, and Brunelleschi devoted a large amount of his time to assisting in siege operations, designing new fortresses at Pisa and Vico Pisano, and advising government officials on the modernisation and repair of castles all over the Florentine state. Alberti and Filarete both devoted large sections of their architectural treatises to military architecture, and all this was well before we come to the more familiar names in the field in the later years of the fifteenth century.

Nor was the creativity of artists and architects confined entirely to fortifications in the military sphere. Siege engines were a problem which fascinated some of these men. Brunelleschi designed them for Florence in the siege of Lucca in 1429–30; Francesco di Giorgio Martini and Leonardo da Vinci devoted much time to such devices, which were by no means obsolete by the end of the fifteenth century. Similarly the mining of fortresses with explosives was an area in which architects and engineers played their part. The ease with which counter-bombardment and new fortifications kept pace with the development of siege artillery, turned men's eyes to other methods of overcoming fortresses. Francesco di Giorgio Martini is often credited with being the first successfully to mine a fortress when he organised the mining of Castelnuovo in Naples in 1495. But there were certainly earlier precedents, notably when the Florentines mined Sarzanella in 1487, and at the siege of Andria in 1462. There seems to be an even earlier example of this technique when Domenico da Firenze mined the Paduan-held fortress of Castelcarro for the Venetians in 1405.

Domenico da Firenze was a typical example of the early Renaissance military engineer and architect. His work included the diversion of rivers for military purposes, firing the Florentine fortified bridge across the Po at Borgoforte with fireboats in 1397, mining and siegework, as well as building both permanent and field fortifications. For the building of permanent fortifications for cities and castles is by no means the only area of military engineering which needs to be discussed in the context of developments in the art of war in the fifteenth century. Even in siege warfare the growing artillery potential of the defence was forcing the besiegers to take greater care for their own protection. Their guns had to be protected, and above all, trenches and ramparts had to be dug around the beleaguered city to enable the besiegers to resist sorties and move in close under the hail of fire, now supplemented by firearms, from the walls. Carmagnola, when besieging Brescia in 1426, dug a five-mile trench around the city, and this was to be the pattern for all fifteenth-century sieges.

Field fortifications were the most crucial area of development in Italian warfare. However, they have to be seen not only from the tactical point of view, that is the fortified camps and earthworks for protecting troops on the battle-field, but even more importantly as part of developments in strategy and outlooks on war as a whole. The major states in Italy in the fifteenth century were no longer city states: they were territorial states. Their interests in defence were no longer confined to the walls of their capital cities and the castles of their rulers. The Italian fifteenth-century state was concerned with defence at the furthest point possible from the centre, with defensible frontiers and frontier fortresses. Within the state it was anxious not so much to protect the populations of its subject cities, but to maintain a defensive stronghold within those cities and to provide protection for increasingly permanent armies in fortified encampments. Finally such a state now had infinitely greater reserves of conscript labour to call on for the preparation of the new defences.

In 1513 Michele Sanmicheli, the Veronese architect, was

invited by Venice to make an inspection of the defences of Friuli and advise on how they could be improved and modernised. In his report he made three main points. First in regard to the chief city of Friuli, Udine, he argued that the important thing was to have a good castle; to hold the site for Venice was more important than to defend its inhabitants. Subsequently the walls of the city could be strengthened, but this was of lesser importance. Secondly the mountain passes and the ports through which artillery could enter the area must be blocked by good fortresses. Thirdly both to defend Friuli from the west, and more importantly to defend the rest of the Venetian state from an enemy who had broken into Friuli, the line of the river Livenza was a natural defence which should be improved and exploited. Sanmicheli was not saying anything new on the question of fortresses in subject cities or on frontiers, and these were clearly the principles on which all fifteenth-century thinking was based. Nor in fact was he saying anything new about the line of the Livenza and the importance of adapting natural barriers as defensive works. In 1411 when Venice had been attacked by the Hungarians, it was along the line of the upper reaches of the Livenza for twenty-two miles that a ditch was dug and a rampart was thrown up. The turning point in the war came when the Hungarians tried to force the line at Motta and were thrown back by Malatesta Malatesta. Country folk from all over the Veneto had been called in to dig this ditch, and special barracks had been built to house them while the work was in progress.

The Livenza line was only one of many such major defences created during the fifteenth century. Venetian expansion in the period was always geared to the use of the major rivers, which flow across the Lombard plain, as frontiers. In 1451 it was the line of the Adda which was being fortified to resist the Milanese. Venice, in fact, seems to have concentrated more than the other Italian states on the use of natural obstacles strengthened by field fortifications for her defence, and to have devoted less attention in the fifteenth century to the permanent fortifications of her cities. It is not in Venetian territories that one finds the early bastions; it was only in 1508–9, when threatened by forces which were likely to over-run her frontier defences, that Venice turned hurriedly to the refortification of Vicenza and Padua.

So once again it was in Lombardy, and particularly during the years before the middle of the century, that we find the most important developments appearing. The Milanese as much as the Venetians relied on major works of field forti-fication to supplement the natural obstacles of the river systems in a period of almost continuous and large-scale war. Both armies were accompanied by thousands of conscripted pioneers, who were employed in the major works and on the defences for each night's camp and the siegeworks for every major siege. In 1438 Niccolò Piccinino had a ditch five miles long dug in a single night between the Soave and the Adige to impede the march of Francesco Sforza's army northwards. In 1448 it was the strength of Sforza's fortified camp at Cara-vaggio which held the Venetian assault and gave time for his cavalry to deploy on the flanks and encircle the enemy. The fortified camp was an essential ingredient of Renaissance warfare. It was not usually the square, symmetrical camp of the Roman legions which Renaissance theorists cited as the ideal example, but a more temporary defensive work taking full advantage of natural obstacles and only using the ditch and rampart on the sides from which a cavalry charge might be expected. Field fortifications such as this were not a con-scious imitation of classical example, an extension of the con-cept of 'renaissance' into military life, but a practical tactical development devised largely by the soldiers and employed extensively in particular wars in a particular theatre—

Lombardy—long before the best known treatises of men like Diomede Carafa and Orso Orsini, not to mention Machiavelli, were written. In 1465 the Milanese ambassador in Paris reported that the city was being fortified against the rebel forces with elaborate field fortifications 'in the Italian style'.

Carafa in his *Memoriale* to the Duke of Calabria written in 1478 suggested that not only the pioneers but every soldier should be able to handle a spade, and it was not only for fortifications that this skill was needed. The diversion of rivers from their natural courses was a favourite device in fifteenth-century warfare. The objects of such immensely laborious undertakings were several. Flooding an enemy's camp or a besieged city could be achieved by diverting a river. Brunelleschi in 1429 tried to flood Lucca by diverting the river Serchio into a canal dug towards the city. But the Lucchese in a sortie broke the banks of the canal and flooded the Florentine encampments instead. Cutting off a besieged city from its natural supply route was another aim of such operations; here the best example was Leonardo da Vinci's attempt to divert the Arno away from Pisa in 1505. Again given that rivers provided natural defences, the successful diversion of rivers could expose weak points in the enemy's defences. Domenico da Firenze tried to achieve this in the Milanese siege of Mantua in 1393. Mantua, in a bend of the river Mincio, is surrounded on three sides by water, and a diversion of the river could leave it defenceless. Again the attempt failed as the dams burst after unexpected rains. Finally with the importance of river warfare in the Lombard plain, diversion of a river could upset the enemy's plans for supporting his army with a river fleet.

Another task for the engineers and pioneers was to build roads in unexpected places and thus enable armies with their artillery to take the enemy by surprise. In 1482 the Venetian commander, Roberto da Sanseverino, had a road built on a rampart and bridges right across the marshes of the Polesine between the Adige and the Po in order to make a surprise attack on Ferrara. The road was over five miles long and was constructed in two days and two nights. It enabled Sanseverino to penetrate into the heart of the Ferrarese defences. But the Marquis of Mantua, who led the Ferrarese, was equal to the occasion, and by swiftly damming the Tartaro, a tributary of the Po, he was able to flood the area, sweep away the road, and cut Sanseverino off.

In all this discussion of the contribution of engineers and engineering to Renaissance warfare one must not forget the soldiers themselves. Many of the condottieri were the instigators of these new forms of warfare and were the leading builders of advanced fortifications. The comments of leading soldiers were always invited on fortification projects, and of course in the area of field fortifications and tactical engineering the condottieri played a major part. A number—men like Federigo da Montefeltro, Francesco Sforza, Sigismondo Malatesta and Napoleone Orsini—were directly responsible for major fortresses. All had a good deal of experience in siege warfare and the engineering problems involved. In this respect, as in many others, it is clear that leadership in Renaissance warfare was not a preserve of bone-headed cavalry commanders.

River warfare
Before summing up this review of the various components of Italian warfare in the fifteenth century, it is necessary to look briefly at one final aspect—river warfare. It is not my intention to consider naval warfare as a whole in this book, but the use of sizeable fleets on Italian rivers and lakes in conjunction with armies was an essential feature of land warfare and one which has been almost entirely ignored by military historians.

Once again for obvious geographical reasons it was the rivers of Lombardy which were particularly suited to co-operation between fleets and armies, and it was in the period 1425–54 when this cooperation can be best observed. That the Venetians as the dominant seapower in Italy should, when they became committed to creating a state on the mainland and hence involved in extensive land warfare, seek to utilise their naval strength in the struggle is scarcely surprising. Although Venetian nobles played a considerable part in the land warfare as *provveditori*, administrators and even occasionally as leaders, it was as commanders of river fleets that they could make their most natural contribution. Furthermore in an area where wide, usually slow-flowing rivers were both natural defences and the natural communications, it was but an extension of the widening concept of warfare to make direct use of them. River fleets could both control the communications, and either strengthen or surmount the effectiveness of rivers as natural obstacles.

Not surprisingly the Venetians had a natural advantage in this type of warfare. The Venetian arsenal was the largest shipyard in Europe, and Venice controlled the mouths of the Po and the Adige through which large ships could be introduced into the Lombardy river system. But even Venice built a considerable number of the smaller craft used in river warfare in her inland cities, particularly Verona, and Milan, who quickly developed a powerful river fleet, was able to do the same in the river ports of Cremona, Piacenza and Pavia. Nor did the engineers of the time hesitate to move quite large ships overland if direct water communications were not available. The main components of river fleets were full-sized seagoing war galleys and the smaller galeots, a class of ships specifically designed for river service called 'galleons', and armed *barche* which must have been little more than rowing boats. The Venetian *barcha* had a crew of five, two

173

crossbowmen and three oarsmen, and it was equipped with a small bombard. In a fleet of *barche*, a Venetian noble commanded every ten boats, and in 1404 Venice had a fleet of 150 such boats operating in the Polesine to prevent Ferrarese forces moving north to assist Padua.

The role of these fleets was partly to win control of the rivers from each other, and battles between them were not uncommon. Fireships were a frequent device employed not only against the enemy but also against bridges which were often themselves bridges of boats constructed to create a temporary crossing point. But it was the cooperation between these fleets and land forces which is the most interesting aspect of this warfare. Venice always had fleets on the Po and the Adige; from the Po detachments could be sent up the Adda, Oglio and Mincio when required. The Mincio, however, was controlled by Mantua, and the Gonzaga rulers of Mantua had their own fleet which was by no means always at the disposal of Venice. Milan concentrated its river fleet on the Po and its tributaries.

One of the earliest successful river ventures of Venice was the fleet which assisted in guarding the line of the Livenza against the Hungarians in 1411–12. Pietro Loredan, one of the most skilled Venetian naval commanders of the first half of the fifteenth century, commanded this fleet and gave considerable assistance to Malatesta Malatesta in his victory over the Hungarians at Motta. Indeed Venetian chroniclers tended to attribute the victory entirely to Loredan, and there was always a very close involvement in Venice with the activities of the river fleets. The destruction of the Po fleet in 1431 by the Milanese, and Carmagnola's apparent refusal to go to its assistance, contributed considerably to the condottiere's fall from grace and execution. Mutual support of fleet and army was clearly expected, and Carmagnola had overall command of both. After the fleet's defeat it was considered impossible for Carmagnola to cross the Adda which was the last line of defence before Milan, and the whole campaign was disrupted. A few years earlier in 1426 the Po fleet had consisted of ten galleys, 40 galleons and 20 *barche*, and was commanded by Francesco Bembo.

Perhaps the most famous example of this sort of warfare was the fleet which Venice put on Lake Garda in 1438–9 and the fighting which ensued. The idea of having ships on Lake Garda was by no means a new one, and a number of the towns on the lake had small harbours. But with Brescia besieged in 1438, it was decided to operate a large fleet on the lake, including war galleys, and to supply Brescia by water. The galleys and some of the smaller ships had to be brought up the Adige and then carried over a short stretch of rough country before being launched in the lake. The whole project has been often associated with Gattamelata, who was certainly responsible for protecting the operation during its most vulnerable phase, the portage from the Adige to the lake. But the planning was done in Venice and the engineer in charge was the Cretan, Niccolò Sorbolo. The fleet was successfully assembled on the lake but was defeated and largely destroyed by Biagio da Assereto, who commanded the Milanese fleet on the lake. Biagio was a Genoese naval commander of considerable repute, who had won the battle of Ponza against the Aragonese in 1435, and so it is interesting to find the old rivalry between Venetians and Genoese being renewed in this remote field of naval warfare.

The War of Ferrara in 1482–4 was another campaign in which river fleets played a major role, but outside Lombardy there is little evidence of their use. The rivers of central and southern Italy were not suited to the continuous passage of even small boats. There was some naval activity on Lake Trasimene, and in 1496 the papal forces attacking the Orsini tried to put a galley on Lake Bracciano to cut off supplies to the Orsini stronghold at Bracciano. But the galley was burnt by Orsini troops as it was being carried to the lake. There can be few things more vulnerable than a ship on land!

Tactics and strategy

When seeking to sum up the developments in the art of war in fifteenth-century Italy we must face a fundamental Renaissance problem. How important was classical example in dictating the course of military affairs? Or to put the question in a wider form: was example more important than experience to the Italian soldier? Both the fourteenth and fifteenth centuries produced their share of military theorists and military treatises. How far were these, or the classical sources on which they relied heavily, read and studied by soldiers? That most of the leaders of Italian armies were literate can be taken for granted; that some of them, men like Federigo da Montefeltro, Gian Jacopo Trivulzio, and Antonio, Count of Marsciano, had important and relevant libraries is an established fact. But there is little evidence to show that the practice of war in the fifteenth century was much affected either by classical writings or contemporary theorists. The military treatises of the fifteenth century were mostly written by men of great practical experience in war; they reflected the preoccupations of the time, concern for the discipline and organisation of armies, and prudence and calculation in campaigns; they help to show us what warfare was like. But they do not proclaim any startling innovations. The fifteenth-century captain learnt the art of war as an apprentice to an established condottiere, not from books. He may have been gratified to learn from one of the humanists in his entourage that his tactics resembled those of Caesar in Gaul, but it is unlikely that he consciously intended it to be so. It was not a study of the Roman republican army which produced a revived interest in infantry but the practical necessities of fifteenth-century warfare.

The treatises of Diomede Carafa and Orso Orsini tell us much about the basic concepts of contemporary warfare. They both emphasise the need for prudence and caution, the need to avoid battles except in favourable circumstances. They were both admirers of the Sforzesco school of soldiers and to this extent they do not reflect all the spirit of Italian warfare. The Braccieschi placed more emphasis on speed, mobility and the decisive blow, but in fact the two schools were working within the same framework. The basic concept of Italian warfare was defensive–counter offensive; that the counter offensive tended to be too long delayed because of over-caution was sometimes true, but not always. The first essential for an Italian commander in war was a firm and secure base; the fortress or field fortification in which he could not be surprised. From this he could strike out to ravage or destroy, thus weakening the enemy state and perhaps provoking its army into a false move. By superior knowledge both of the enemy, through spies, and of the terrain, he hoped to be able to catch his opponent at a disadvantage. Then by the speed of his movements and the mobility and discipline of his troops, he hoped to seize his advantage. This was the basic theory; it was a military world in which the spy and the informant, stratagem and deceit, field fortifications and exhausting forced marches all had a part to play.

At the same time, obviously, it was not so ordered a world as the theorists made out. Mistakes were made, or there would have been fewer battles than there were. Battles sometimes developed accidentally as a skirmish gradually escalated and whole armies were drawn in. But this itself could be a carefully planned ruse; scouting parties were often sent ahead with just the intention of drawing a well entrenched army into the open. Battles were often fought at the end of a campaigning season as a result of political pressures, as each side sought to win some advantage from the year's expenditure. Caution would be thrown aside for a few short weeks, and soldiers took risks which, left to themselves, they might well have preferred to avoid.

The battles themselves could be both brilliant set pieces and unholy shambles. Many of the condottieri and their companies were highly professional soldiers, who could achieve the coordination in battle necessary to carry out highly complicated tactical manoeuvres. Outflanking moves, feints, and above all the tactical use of reserves were all common ploys. But things could go very wrong; desertions at the height of a battle, the death of a commander, the realisation of some unexpected quirk of the terrain, could all throw an army into complete confusion. It was little wonder that the condottiere faced battles with misgivings. If he lost he probably would live to fight another day, and so would most of his men. But he risked imprisonment and having to find a heavy ransom to free himself; he risked a loss of reputation and possibly loss of his contract; perhaps above all he risked losing all his horses and arms to a victorious enemy, and the cost of replacing these would be enormous.

All this can perhaps be best illustrated and summed up by looking at one of the most significant battles of the fifteenth century, the battle of Caravaggio fought in 1448. Caravaggio is a small town south of Bergamo and was at this time held by the Venetians. Francesco Sforza, commander of the Milanese army, was besieging it and had built himself a strong fortified camp to protect his bivouacked army. Caravaggio was unlikely to hold out long against Sforza's artillery, and Micheletto Attendolo led the main Venetian army to relieve it. The Venetians camped a few miles to the east of the Milanese and took stock of the situation. Sforza's army was strong and appeared to be well defended; Caravaggio was not really important enough to risk a defeat to relieve it. But on the other hand the campaigning season was drawing to a close; Francesco Sforza's army was all that stood between the Venetians and the tottering Ambrosian Republic in Milan. A decisive victory now could mean the end of the Milanese state, so the Venetian *provveditori*, on instructions from Venice, were pressing for an attack. Micheletto Attendolo was a tried and experienced condottiere, he had fought all over Italy and had been amongst the leading Italian captains for twenty-five years. He was also a cousin of Francesco Sforza. This last consideration probably did not weigh too much with him as they had been on opposite sides before, but all the characteristic caution of the condottiere told him that an attack on the Milanese camp was dangerous. He was supported by some of his senior advisers, but a number of the Venetian condottieri saw things in a different light. Bartolomeo Colleoni and Tiberto Brandolini had reconnoitred the Milanese position thoroughly in disguise and had discovered that on one side Sforza had relied largely on the protection of a marshy wood which seemed to be impassable to cavalry. Colleoni and Brandolini thought otherwise and urged that it was possible to launch an attack on this flank. Their advice together with the political considerations carried the day and the decision was taken to attack.

Francesco Sforza learnt of the decision through his spies within hours of it being taken, but he still could not believe that the main Venetian assault would come in from such an unfavourable direction. So the element of surprise was not completely lost. The Venetians supported by Colleoni's guns broke into the Milanese camp at its weak point and for a moment the fate of Milan hung in the balance. But Sforza, partly forewarned, reacted exceptionally quickly. He not only himself rallied the wing of his army which was wavering before the Venetian attack, but he dispatched strong cavalry forces out on to both flanks to encircle the enemy. These, moving quickly in the open, closed on the Venetian rear before their army could extract itself from the now treacherous wood. Some of the Venetians managed to fight their way out, but a large part of the army was taken prisoner.

Many of the main features of Italian Renaissance warfare are clearly depicted in this battle. The role of field fortifications, the complexities of military decision making, the use of ground and of spies, the use of artillery and the coordination of arms. Caravaggio was not a bloody battle, but it was a decisive one. The Venetian army did not recover fully for some years; Micheletto Attendolo was sacked and exiled to his estates. The independence of Milan was saved, but Francesco Sforza moved one step nearer to taking over the rule of it. As Duke in the following years he was to do little more fighting, but many of the men who were to lead Italian armies for the next twenty years fought under him or under Attendolo at Caravaggio.

CHAPTER SEVEN

THE PRACTICE OF WAR

The battle of Caravaggio and the other battles which have been described in these pages were the set pieces of Italian warfare. Such battles were relatively rare, although it was naturally on these that the chroniclers concentrated. The administrative documents of military life rarely mention the battles except as an aside to explain casualties and losses of equipment. In this they are more realistic and more informative than the chronicles, but neither succeed in telling us what military life was really like. Fifteenth-century military diaries have yet to be discovered, but still an attempt must be made to get below the surface and look at the realities of military practice, the day-to-day activities of Italian soldiers.

One man who was a conscientious writer of diaries, at least during his official missions, was the Florentine Luca di Maso degli Albizzi. He was the brother of Rinaldo degli Albizzi, the leading Florentine statesman who was overthrown and exiled by the Medici in 1434. Luca, like many Florentines of his class, spent much of his life on missions as representative of the Florentine Republic, and in May 1432 he was dispatched as special envoy to the camp of the Florentine captain general, Niccolò da Tolentino, near Arezzo. For about three weeks he was with the army and his account of those days is an interesting insight which is worth looking at in some detail.

Luca degli Albizzi left Florence on 18 May with a junior assistant, Bernardetto de' Medici, and fifteen followers. He spent the first night at Castel S. Giovanni in the upper Arno valley where he was met by the civilian commissary with the army and a group of condottieri who were also on their way to join the captain general. The 200 men of these condottieri were billeted some miles further on in Montevarchi, and it was agreed that Luca would pick them up there the next morning and they would all go on together to the camp. Luca was an early riser and the next morning he arrived at Montevarchi to find the soldiers still in bed. They were clearly billeted in houses all over the town, and it took until mid-day to get the squadrons assembled and on the road. They arrived at the camp in mid-afternoon to find that Niccolò da Tolentino had gone out the previous evening with a force of 700 men to try and catch the Sienese under Francesco Piccinino in a night ambush. As he was not yet back, Luca waited for a couple of hours and then rode to Arezzo to spend the night in comfort. Niccolò had in fact failed to catch the Sienese who had received warning of his intentions, but he had ridden all the way to Montepulciano which was being besieged by the Sienese and had sent supplies and more troops into the town before returning. This itself meant that Niccolò da Tolentino had ridden over 50 miles in the 24 hours, but this was not considered in any way extraordinary.

On the 20th Luca returned to the camp and spent six hours with the captain general and his senior officers. They drew up written plans for the campaign, and Niccolò outlined his immediate needs. The troops needed pay, but even more important he wanted 60 mules to carry provisions behind the army as he planned to move fast and did not want to waste time collecting food. He also wanted two or three bombards and some stonemasons to make balls for them. He thought that a few hundred militia auxiliaries would be useful, including 50 pioneers with spades and axes. Luca got off a messenger immediately to Florence with these require-

13 (a) *An army breaking camp.* Another of the illustrations by Giovanni Bettini. The army is that of Sigismondo Malatesta operating in Tuscany about 1449.

(b) *Sigismondo Malatesta.* A portrait medal by Pisanello. Sigismondo was the great rival of Federigo da Montefeltro in the arts both of war and peace.

(c) The reverse of Pisanello's medal which depicts a mid-fifteenth-century suit of armour.

14 (a) *Sigismondo Malate[sta's] castle at Rimini.* This early [medal] (c.1446) by Matteo de' Pas[ti of] the famous castle shows cle[arly] that it was not the major [step] forward in gunpowder fo[rtifi]cation which has someti[mes] been suggested.

(b) The fortress of Volterra built by Francione for the Florentines after the revolt of 1472 had been suppressed. It was one of the first examples in Tuscany of the new styles of fortification which spread through Italy in the second half of the fifteenth century.

ments, and he himself began to ride round collecting the militia.

The strategic position which Luca and Niccolò da Tolentino faced was that a number of contingents of allied Sienese and Milanese troops were operating in southern Tuscany occupying castles and towns and damaging crops. Another Florentine army was camped near Pisa under Micheletto Attendolo, but the needs of the campaign were speed rather than great strength, so it was decided not to try and link up with Attendolo. Niccolò da Tolentino was very anxious to get on with it and declined an offer from Luca that he should postpone operations until the normal ceremony for handing him the baton as captain general had been arranged. News had come that the Sienese were besieging Linari and Gambassi in the Valdelsa, and speed was vital if these towns were to be saved. However, it was bound to take three or four days to collect what was needed and break camp.

After three days of intense activity, the militia, provisions, and munitions had been assembled, and at dawn on 24 May Niccolò da Tolentino moved off with his army of about 4,000 men. He had about 50 miles of difficult country to cover to reach the besieged towns, and as half of the force was made up of infantry and militia it could not move very fast. A messenger met them on the first day with the news that Linari had surrendered, but that the enemy forces were still divided into two camps, one commanded by Francesco Piccinino and the other by Bernardino della Carda. On the evening of the 26th the army reached Poggibonsi and there heard that the Sienese had united, taken Gambassi, and were now moving to meet Niccolò's army. The night was one full of alarms and false alarms, in one of which Niccolò's eldest son, Baldovino, was shot in the leg by a jumpy Florentine archer. Luca marvelled at the Captain's self control when he heard of this incident.

The next day, Tuesday, Niccolò da Tolentino detached some of his infantry and militia north-westwards to begin the siege of Linari, and he himself went southwest to try and cut off an enemy march towards Siena. But again either he had received false information or the Sienese got word of his movements, and they doubled back and headed towards the Arno valley taking Pontedera on the way. This left Niccolò with the task of retaking Linari before he could move on in pursuit. He tried negotiations with the defenders, threatening to hang them all if he had to take the town by storm, but this proved useless. There were only 100 Milanese and Sienese infantry defending it, but it had good walls and they believed that Niccolò would not waste time over them. Indeed he did not plan to waste time; he wanted to get on and bring the enemy to battle, but he was determined to deal with Linari first. He only had small bombards and the weather was blazing hot, but nevertheless he ordered an assault at dawn on the morning of the 30th. Four breaches were made in the walls and Niccolò's dismounted men-at-arms surged into the assault. After three hours of bitter fighting the town was taken and sacked. There were a number of casualties; all the professional infantry in the defence were held as prisoners, but the local defenders were allowed to go free; a number of women were also taken by the Florentines. Finally the walls of Linari were pulled down and half the town burnt. Linari was a Florentine town; the treatment of it was harsh but effective; this was partly a reflection of basic Florentine attitudes towards the subject towns, partly a matter of military necessity. The place had to be made useless to the Sienese otherwise this sort of warfare could go on indefinitely.

The next day Niccolò da Tolentino turned northwards to join up with Micheletto Attendolo and seek out the enemy in the Arno valley. By now the militia had melted away; they were getting far from their homes near Arezzo and the few days' campaigning had been tough. On 1 June the army came out into the Arno plain. It was a Sunday and normally in Italian warfare this was regarded as a day of rest when little activity was expected. It was perhaps for this reason that Niccolò da Tolentino succeeded at last in catching the enemy. The Sienese had begun to besiege Montopoli, and Niccolò, moving rapidly now that his troops were out in the open country, came up on them fast. He and Luca went ahead with 30 cavalry and Luca who knew the area well pointed out the lie of the land. Niccolò felt however that he still did not have a clear enough idea of the enemy's dispositions and so, while Luca stayed with the main body and gave an oration to the troops, he went on further ahead with a few men and thoroughly explored the enemy position. Then without further delay he launched his attack. The battle was short but hard fought, and Luca commented on the useful role of the infantry. The arrival of Micheletto Attendolo from the other direction completed what appears to have been a thoroughly well-planned and organised operation. The Sienese were completely routed, a number of captains and 150 men captured and 600 horses taken. Some of the prisoners escaped the next day as they were being escorted to Empoli, but were quickly rounded up. This battle, described by Luca degli Albizzi, was in fact the Rout of S. Romano later made famous by the series of paintings executed by Paolo Uccello for the Medici palace. Luca's eye-witness account is somewhat different to traditional descriptions of the battle, which suggest that Niccolò da Tolentino was surprised with a handful of men and held out against enormous odds for eight hours until Attendolo arrived. No doubt a desire to glorify Niccolò's achievement played some part in the distortions which have crept into the story, but Luca's account of Niccolò leading a carefully planned attack does the condottiere no less credit in a different way.

The Florentine army got its rest day on Monday and then began to besiege Pontedera. This was, however, a more formidable task than the siege of Linari and without good artillery was likely to take some time. After a fortnight's intense activity, during which the army had covered many miles of difficult country, taken a town by assault, and won an important victory, there was inevitably a lull. Luca degli Albizzi returned to Florence on the 6th to urge on the provision of supplies and artillery. He confessed that he felt completely exhausted.

This is an instructive glimpse into the life of an army and one which is all too rare in the fifteenth century. The mobility of Niccolò da Tolentino's force, although half its strength consisted of infantry, is indicative of one of the major features of the warfare of the period. Luca degli Albizzi remarked at one point that only 300 of the 2,000 infantry in the army were concentrated together in one column and the rest were divided up amongst the cavalry squadrons. Does this perhaps mean that many of these infantry rode behind the men-at-arms on their horses when on the march? This could well be the explanation of the speed with which small armies could move. Niccolò da Tolentino's army of course had very limited artillery and apparently no carts in the baggage train, but it did have 60 mules with provisions and was not living off the country. A larger army, and particularly later in the century, would inevitably have been much more encumbered with munitions and baggage. But it was usually the case that the heavy baggage was detached from the fighting elements of an army and moved on different routes in the rear.

We can get an impression of the activities of the other Florentine army in 1432 under Micheletto Attendolo from the letters written by Micheletto and his attendant commissaries to Florence. It had moved out of its winter quarters outside Pisa in late March and did not return to these quarters finally until mid-December. During the nine months, the army marched all over the Arno valley and deep into the hills on either side; it conducted at least four sieges and numerous skirmishes, but fought no major battle other than its tardy intervention at S. Romano. In 1440 Baldaccio d'Anghiari marched with a small force from Lucca to Piombino in two days—a distance of over 100 miles.

However, some of the most striking evidence for the mobility of mid-fifteenth-century armies comes from the campaigns of 1438-9 in Lombardy. The march of Gattamelata around Lake Garda in the autumn of 1438, when he escaped with his Venetian army from Brescia, became almost legendary in the annals of Italian warfare. Brescia was being closely besieged by the Milanese under Niccolò Piccinino and the direct route eastwards was well blocked. But it was essential to extricate Gattamelata's main army, both because its size was creating serious provisioning problems in the beleaguered city and because without it the defence of the rest of the Venetian state, and particularly Verona, was dangerously weak. The only feasible escape route was over the mountains around the north of Lake Garda. It was a route which had never been used by large bodies of troops and was therefore thinly guarded by the Milanese. It was over this route that Gattamelata marched his army of 3,000 cavalry and 2,000 infantry, brushing aside the Milanese opposition and reaching Verona in five days. Piccinino was astonished by the feat, but he himself in the next year almost equalled it. Brescia was still being besieged and Gattamelata and Francesco Sforza marched to relieve it by the same route through the mountains. Piccinino moved north from Brescia to meet them and was badly beaten at Tenno. It was said that he escaped from the town, as the Venetian troops swarmed into it, carried in a sack on the back of a German soldier. However, he quickly rallied his forces and marched them around the south shore of the lake to attack Verona, while the Venetian army was still in the mountains. His forced march took Verona completely by surprise, and he occupied the city, although failing to take its two fortresses. Anxious messengers rode through the night to carry the news to Gattamelata and Sforza, and they, again acting with remarkable speed, marched back over the by then familiar road. It was once again the turn of Piccinino to be surprised; thinking that the Venetian army was still on the other side of the lake, his troops were contentedly looting Verona when Sforza and Gattamelata arrived outside the walls. Once more they had done the long march through the mountains in unbelievable time and the Milanese were in no position to defend their new possession. Piccinino and his men were bundled unceremoniously out of Verona having been its masters for less than three days.

The mobility of these armies around Lake Garda was the result of military necessity, but often the errant characteristics of Italian armies were dictated by the search for provisions. Particularly in the first half of the century, it was rare for camp to be pitched in the same place for more than two or three nights, even when the army was on the defensive. After 1450 the growing use of field fortifications and the improvement in provisioning organisation made camps much more permanent affairs. In 1479 the camp established by the Florentines and their allies at Poggio Imperiale was the base for the combined army throughout the summer.

It was Gattamelata and Sforza in 1439 who issued one of the best known sets of army regulations for this period. It was probably normal practice from early in the fifteenth century for a captain general to lay down regulations for the conduct of his army, particularly when in camp, but very few have survived. Such regulations were fairly stereotyped and clearly there were conventions about such things which soldiers accepted without question. In fact Italian army regulations differ little from those which have survived from English military administration of the same period. Gattamelata and Sforza were in a slightly unusual position in that they commanded a joint army; Gattamelata as Venetian captain general commanded the Venetian forces, Sforza was captain general of the League and commanded his own very large company and a certain number of Florentine-employed troops. Their regulations therefore had some peculiar features when they laid down the order of march; the two armies took turns day by day to lead and to be responsible for the defence of the marching column. Otherwise the regulations were conventional in their emphasis on not breaking ranks, on all provisioning companies being properly protected by cavalry, on the formation of a special billeting squadron consisting of representatives of each company, on the role of camp marshals, and on the procedure in the event of a sudden attack on the camp.

The one major omission from these regulations as compared with contemporary English ones was any reference to women in the camps. This was a distinction often noted by observers: Italian armies were encumbered (or perhaps inspired?) by the presence of large numbers of female camp followers. Niccolò da Tolentino's army in 1432 took women from Linari after the assault and presumably added them to its following. But English regulations were quite specific that no women should be kept in the camp. Anyone finding a harlot about the camp could take all her money, break her arm, and drive her from the army. Niccolò de' Favri, a member of the Venetian embassy in London, reported on Henry VIII's 1513 expedition: 'They did not take wenches with them and they were not profane swearers like our soldiers. Indeed there were few who failed daily to recite the office and Our Lady's rosary.' The second distinction observed by the

Venetian seems to place the English army in a somewhat unreal light, although it is true that Italian army regulations were less concerned about blasphemy than contemporary maritime regulations. However, the distinction on the role of women in the camps was a true one, but one which reflected totally different social attitudes. Prostitution was an accepted feature of Italian society and so was the military brothel; the Florentines licensed brothels outside the walls of Pisa and used the proceeds from the taxes on them to repair the walls. The 211 prostitutes captured by the Paduans in the defeat of the Veronese army at the Brentelle in 1386 were escorted with great honour to Padua and entertained at the Lord of Padua's table.

Given the seasonal nature of Italian warfare, camp life was only a part of the soldier's life. The side about which we know even less is the conditions of troops in winter quarters. The Borgo S. Marco outside the walls of Pisa was often the winter quarters of Florentine armies and there Micheletto Attendolo spent the winter of 1431–2. It served the same purpose as the *serragli* of the Venetian cities, but one suspects that in the Borgo S. Marco troops were billeted in private houses, whereas in the *serragli* there were probably some form of permanent encampments. The bulk of the troops of a condottiere prince like Federigo da Montefeltro probably returned to their homes in and around Urbino in the winter, parading perhaps at infrequent intervals to receive pay. Even in the Venetian cities, where the companies had the same winter quarters for years on end, it seems likely that many of the soldiers had their families to which they returned when the campaigning season was over. But certainly, as the century advanced, there is increasing evidence that armies were held together and paid, at least in a rudimentary fashion, in the winter. Nor indeed was it always the case that campaigning stopped in the winter, and the winter break could certainly be very short; December and March were months in which there was often plenty of military activity. The summer break, still common in the first half of the century, was becoming less standard after 1450, although the Venetian army in the sixteenth century still held its manoeuvres in peacetime in spring and autumn.

The emphasis on active campaigning in spring and early summer, and again in the autumn, was not only the result of these being the more clement seasons for military operations. They were also the seasons when armies could do the most damage to crops, and this was always one of the prime aims of Italian warfare. Devastation and organised looting was economic warfare of a most effective kind; if carried out systematically it could have a much greater impact on a small Italian state than the defeat of its army in the field. The conscript pioneers attached to Italian armies were known as *guastatori* (devastators); their first function was breaking down and burning crops, and only subsequently did they become increasingly important as diggers of field fortifications and other constructive work.

Devastation and looting were therefore by no means necessarily to be linked with ill-discipline, although they were operations which could easily lead to loss of control and bad discipline. There were in fact two totally different sides to this problem. When an army was operating on friendly soil there was of course no question of systematic devastation. All provisions were in theory bought and, as far as possible, troops were kept under control. There were inevitably clashes between troops and civilians, but the condottieri were responsible for the discipline of their men and could be fined if these men inflicted damage on civilian property. The behaviour of troops in this situation was often the subject of complaints from the local populations, but the volume of individual complaints which have survived is not such as to suggest that the increasingly permanent armies were a positive scourge to their own civilians. After a defeat, when an army was in retreat, was the most dangerous time, and it was not uncommon for serious damage to be inflicted on the friendly local population. The other situation was that of an army operating in hostile territory when the whole outlook was totally different. Such armies lived as far as possible off the land and were committed to a policy of devastation. Both the collection of supplies and the ravaging were organised, and there were usually instructions that the property of the Church was to be spared. The condottieri were still concerned to see that their men did not get out of hand and that booty was divided up fairly.

Francesco Guicciardini, who was certainly no friend of the Italian mercenary system, remarked: 'Ever since the times of antiquity in which military discipline was severely exercised, the soldiery had always been licentious and burdensome to the people, yet they never gave themselves loose to all manners of disorders, but lived for the most part on their pay, and their licentiousness was restrained within tolerable bounds. But the Spaniards in Italy were the first that presumed to maintain themselves wholly on the substance of the people.' After 1494 the large French and Spanish armies in Italy were living permanently on hostile soil and behaved accordingly. The average Italian army of the fifteenth century spent most of its time billeted or camped on friendly soil, and this was when its 'licentiousness was restrained within tolerable bounds'. Discipline depends to a large extent on long service under respected and responsible leaders; the peculiar and increasingly permanent *condotta* system of the fifteenth century provided these conditions to a greater extent than we sometimes imagine. It is significant that Luca degli Albizzi in the three weeks he was with the army in 1432 said not a word about bad discipline except to report that all the militia had deserted. Linari was sacked, but the impression given is that this was a calculated affair, a reprisal for resistance.

The possibilities of booty and at the same time a break-down of discipline were always at their greatest when a town surrendered or was stormed after a siege. As in northern Europe, it was accepted practice in Italy that a town was formally summoned to surrender before a siege started. It was at this moment that a town could expect to secure the best terms before time, patience and lives had been lost in a siege. However, the terms of a surrender were by no means necessarily related to the length of the siege or the effort involved in it, nor indeed were the terms agreed necessarily honoured once the gates had been opened to a besieging army.

One of the commonest features of any surrender negoti-ation in siege warfare was the idea of a delayed surrender. A town would offer to surrender after a certain period had elapsed if no relief had arrived. During this period the siege would not be pressed and the besieging commander would avoid subjecting his troops to the more inflammatory hard-ships of siege warfare; above all he could look forward to avoiding the most dangerous exercise of all—storming a well fortified city. The defenders could not only hope for relief but could have time to prepare themselves for the entry of the enemy troops by hiding their possessions.

There were, broadly speaking, four levels of surrender terms. A wealthy city could offer a cash ransom to avoid sack. This was often acceptable before a siege started and before the besieging troops had become psychologically pre-pared to plunder the city. However, there was always the danger that the offer of a ransom would only encourage a besieging army to think that there was much more to be gained by stripping a city bare. Surrender could also be nego-tiated on the terms of the inhabitants being free to leave with as much of their possessions as they could carry. However, the commonest terms were those which spared the lives of the defenders but left their possessions and all moveable property in the city entirely at the mercy of the besieging army. Finally a city might be forced to surrender itself entirely to the mercy of the enemy commander without terms, in which case its position in theory was no better than if it had been taken by storm, although it might reasonably hope that the enemy would have more mercy, and more control over his troops, if actual assault had been avoided. There are in fact very few examples in fifteenth-century Italian warfare of cities being treated entirely ruthlessly even after assault. A slaughtered civilian population and a destroyed city ceased to be a valuable prize.

Once a surrender had been negotiated, the besieging commander had to decide how he was going to use his opportunity. It was very common practice for him to divide the city up amongst his companies and allot a section to each, reserving to himself the major share of the booty. This was a system which could lead to fracas between the companies and ill feeling against the commander, and Francesco Sforza developed a different method in his campaigns which was subsequently used by Milanese troops in Piedmont in 1476. This was to order his besieging troops to lay down their arms and to enter the city at a given moment through one gate. It was then a question of every man for himself with a strong Sforza provost guard to keep some semblance of order.

The most dangerous situation for a besieged city was if entry was gained by stealth, or as a result of the treachery of some of its own troops. Then a sack could start without any surrender terms having been negotiated and without any prior organisation. This seems to have been partly the trouble at the famous sack of Volterra by the Florentines in 1472. In this case the rebel Volterrans had surrendered on very favourable terms, but before the negotiations were complete some of the Volterran mercenaries opened the gates and themselves invited the Florentine army to a sack in which they joined. Federigo da Montefeltro, the Florentine commander, and Lorenzo de' Medici were perhaps not averse to their troops seizing this unexpected opportunity, and Federigo contented himself with decreeing that the sack should last for twelve hours only. Most sacks were given a fixed duration after which the victorious commander would move in with his picked troops and restore order.

The problems of discipline and control at the end of a successful siege were always great. The besieging army had been subjected to physical hardship, boredom, and often peculiar danger outside the walls. It had been deprived of other opportunities by a period of enforced inactivity; it had often found itself trying to live off an increasingly despoiled countryside. If an assault had been necessary this would have inevitably been a good deal bloodier than normal fighting in the open field, and even the siege itself would have given opportunities for the marksmen on the walls of the town to inflict unusually high casualties on the besiegers. Condottiere troops never relished storming cities, and a majority of the condottieri who were killed or wounded in action received their wounds in siege warfare.

A large number of the battles of Italian Renaissance warfare occurred as a result of a clash between a besieging army and a relief force. These were occasions when military necessities tended to outweigh the caution of condottieri and their penchant for elaborate manoeuvre. The need to relieve the besieged city and the attractive possibilities of catching the besieging army unawares on the one side, and the reluctance to abandon a siege and the eventual possibility of booty on the other, created a situation in which armies were prepared to fight. Braccio da Montone's major battles of S. Egidio and

Aquila were both fought in these circumstances, as was the decisive battle of Caravaggio in 1448 when the Venetians were seeking to raise the siege of the town. Battles fought in these circumstances could also be peculiarly bloody, as the besiegers stood their ground determinedly and often found themselves caught between the relief army and a sally by desperate and frustrated troops from the beleaguered city. The siege of Piombino by Alfonso of Aragon's troops in 1448 was a notably bloody affair. The defender, Rinaldo Orsini, had just made himself lord of the city by marrying the D'Appiano heiress and was determined to hold out until Florentine relief arrived. His adversaries were largely Spanish troops, and this added to the general lack of regard for the normal conventions in this campaign. When Sigismondo Malatesta's relieving Florentine force arrived, the battle was fierce and the casualties heavy; the Spaniards were caught between the Florentines and the walls of the city and left over a thousand dead on the field.

Machiavelli's well-known remarks about the 'bloodless battles' of the Renaissance have been the starting point for many of the misunderstandings about Italian warfare. 'Wars were commenced without fear,' he wrote, 'continued without danger, and concluded without loss.' Ridicule was a major weapon in his attack on Italian mercenaries and the condottiere system, but it was an attack which was a compound of exaggeration and misunderstanding. Machiavelli was a Florentine whose experience of the condottieri was largely limited to the one army in Italy which had failed to achieve the permanence and professionalism of those of the other major states. He admired the army of Cesare Borgia but believed mistakenly that its strength lay in a high proportion of militia, whereas the bulk of Borgia troops were mercenaries like any other army. His humanist preoccupation with a national militia as the solution to the problem of national strength blinded him to the more realistic alternatives of the time, while his limited experience of a few notorious condottiere failings blinded him to many of the realities of warfare in fifteenth-century Italy. Machiavelli was also a political secretary; even in his official reports on contemporary battles he used the time-honoured propaganda technique of exaggerating the losses of the enemy and minimising those of his allies. It is partly the survival of reports of this nature that makes it difficult to arrive at the truth about casualties in Italian battles. But it has been established that at the battle of Anghiari in 1440 at which, according to Machiavelli, 'one man was killed and he fell off his horse and was trampled to death', the losses on both sides were about 900 dead. Similarly at Molinella in 1467 when 'some horses were wounded and some prisoners taken but no death occurred' a more careful appraisal of the losses puts them at about 600. The chronicles describing this battle say that for days afterwards the whole countryside smelt of death as the bodies rotted in the ditches. At Campomorto in 1482, one of the bloodiest battles of the century, about 1,200 dead were left on the field; and at Rimini in 1469, when the papal army besieging the city was routed by Federigo da Montefeltro, the dead collected and buried after the battle by the monks of Sta. Colca numbered 300. Rimini was remarked on as being one of the least bloody battles, and certainly the numbers engaged were rather smaller than in the others mentioned.

Certainly there is no doubt that the battles of Italian warfare in this period were not fought to the death, and casualties, particularly amongst the heavily armoured knights, were fewer than one might expect in fighting that often went on all day. The deaths occurred on the whole amongst the more lightly armed troops, the infantry and auxiliaries, whom perhaps Machiavelli discounted. If one looks only at the more senior condottieri, the number who were killed or mortally wounded in battle was very small. Of the 170 senior captains, in the fifteenth century, who commanded more than 200 lances, only a dozen died fighting; some of these were clearly the objects of particular vendettas and were, in a certain sense, murdered on the battlefield or immediately after, like Braccio da Montone, Ottobuono Terzo, Niccolò Fortebraccio and Paolo Orsini. Most of the others were killed either by artillery or hand-gun fire in sieges, or in fighting the Turks: in the first category go Taddeo d'Este, Leone Sforza, Gentile da Leonessa and Alvise dal Verme; in the second, Jacopo dal Verme, Bertoldo d'Este, and Guidantonio Acquaviva. Amongst lesser commanders and particularly infantry leaders, the casualty rate was slightly higher, but still no more than one in ten of Italian captains could expect to be killed in battle.

Two changes during the fifteenth century notably affected these casualty rates. The steady growth of the use of gunpowder clearly made siege warfare more hazardous and many condottieri were wounded at least once in their lives by firearms. Secondly the growth in the amount of fighting against the Turks increased the casualty rate particularly in the Venetian army. A surprising number of the Venetian commanders sent to the Morea in 1463 never returned, and after this Venice tended to rely on Albanian and Greek stradiots to fight the Turks. The stradiots themselves also added a new element of brutality to Italian warfare, as they were paid a ducat for each enemy head which they brought back to the Venetian paymasters. It was reported that at Fornovo in 1495 one stradiot, despairing of finding a French head, cut off the head of a local country priest and claimed on that. Similarly the intervention of other European troops in Italian warfare tended to increase the casualty rate. The case of the Spanish troops at Piombino in 1448 was an example of this, and in 1447 French troops fighting Colleoni at Alessandria were said

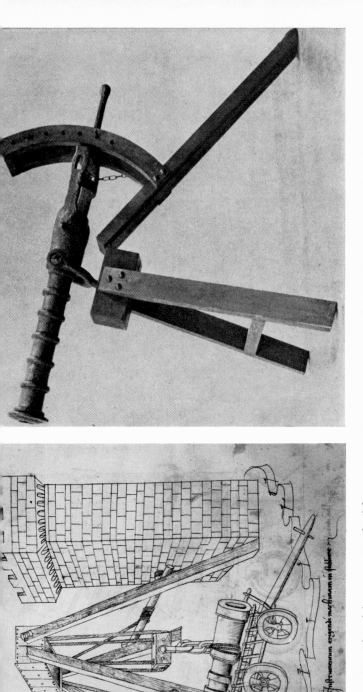

15 (a) This elaborate engine for lifting a cannon into position appeared as an illustration to Valturio's *De re militari*. Valturio's treatise is not noted for the accuracy with which it depicts contemporary warfare (c.1455), but this illustration does give an impression of the cumbersomeness of early artillery.

(b) A small mortar of the late fifteenth century with its primitive elevation mechanism.

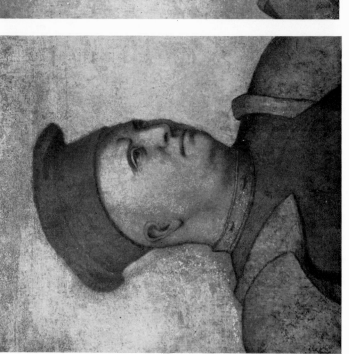

16 (a) Niccolò Orsini, Count of Pitigliano (?)

16 (b) Bartolomeo d'Alviano (?)

These two frescoes by Gerolamo Romanino were originally in the palace at Ghedi built by Pitigliano when he was Venetian captain general. There has been considerable controversy about the identification of the portraits and the left hand one was at one time thought to be of Gattamelata. However it seems more likely that they repre-

to have opened up the visors of fallen men-at-arms and dispatched them with their daggers. This was described by the Italians as not 'good war' but they themselves could be equally ruthless when faced by the 'barbarians'.

Wounds and death resulting from enemy action were by no means the only hazards which faced the Italian soldier. Brawls in the camps often led to bloodshed, and Lombardo's heroic and idealised recumbent effigy of Guidarello Guidarelli conceals the fact that he was killed in a sordid fracas with Spanish soldiers in Cesare Borgia's siege of Faenza. The drowning of Musio Attendolo Sforza while fording the Pescara was not an exceptional case; rivers usually had to be forded and this posed dangers for heavily armoured knights. Roberto da Sanseverino died in the same way when trying to cross the Adige during the battle of Calliano (1487). Camp fevers of various sorts were also common; it is probably true that more men died of fevers contracted on campaign than died in battle. Particularly common with condottieri were the various back and joint complaints; what we should nowadays call slipped discs frequently resulted both from falls in battle and from long periods of riding in heavy armour. Most condottieri spent a part of their lives taking the waters for such trouble. A period at the baths at Abano near Padua was standard sick leave for Venetian condottieri, although Gattamelata obtained permission to go all the way to Petriolo near Siena for treatment.

The medical treatment that a soldier might expect to receive for his wounds and illnesses was rudimentary but by no means non-existent. In Neapolitan armies there were military doctors who were treated on the same terms as the feudal nobility; in return for a fief from the king they were expected to serve in the army as doctors, and there is evidence that their attention was not wholly concentrated on the senior officers. Most senior condottieri would have at least a barber–surgeon in their company. When Bernardino Forte-braccio was wounded twelve times at Fornovo in 1495, he was attended by several doctors after the battle and three pieces of bone were removed from his head. He was said to have recovered completely from his wounds and to be walking about in Venice a few weeks later. An even more striking case of recovery from serious wounds was that of Giovan-antonio di Gattamelata. He was hit in the head by a ball from a hand-gun in 1452 and his life was despaired of; however, surgeons removed the ball from his brain and he survived for a further four years, although with his faculties rather impaired. In fact so surprising was his survival that there was a serious danger that the elaborate funeral arranged for him by the people of Brescia would be wasted. However, two or three months later his uncle, Gentile da Leonessa, then the commander of the Venetian army, was killed also by a hand-gun shot and a family funeral went ahead as planned.

Italian Renaissance warfare was therefore far from blood-less but rarely unnecessarily brutal. Particularly exceptional, and therefore always commented on, was brutality to prison-ers. Pippo Spano, the Florentine commander of the Hun-garians, was regarded with utter loathing by the Venetians because he cut off the right hands of his prisoners before releasing them. This was the epitome of 'bad war' by Italian standards; it represented a concept of total war, a determin-ation to ensure that the enemy did not fight again, which was largely alien to contemporary Italian attitudes to war.

By the fifteenth century there were clear conventions about the treatment of prisoners. Ordinary soldiers who had nothing but their arms and their horses could expect to be stripped of these and released. Men of standing had to ransom them-selves, and senior captains and members of ruling families had to be handed over to the employing state by their captors in return for some proportion of the ransom. According to

the conventions of 'good war', such men were not supposed
to be imprisoned but either released on parole, having given
guarantees, or detained under house arrest, having sworn not
to escape. But these conventions were both slow to emerge
and frequently ignored. In the early fourteenth century the
automatic release of prisoners was clearly not the rule. The
first inmates of the famous Stinche prison in Florence were
the captured defenders of the castle of Stinche in 1304, and
many of those detained there in later years were prisoners
of war. In the fourteenth century, negotiations and contracts
for the release of ordinary prisoners of war were not uncommon, but by the fifteenth century they seem to have
disappeared.

In 1386 when the Paduans took over 9,000 Veronese prisoners at the battle of Brentelle, Cortesia da Serego, the captured
Veronese commander, asked that the rules of 'good war' be
observed and indeed many of the rank and file were quickly
released. But Serego himself was held in prison for over a
year and died soon after his eventual release as a result of
the privations he had suffered. The prisoners taken by Niccolò
da Tolentino at the battle of S. Romano were clearly not
released immediately but escorted to Empoli, and after the
Milanese victory at Castel Bolognese in 1434 a number of
senior Venetian condottieri were held prisoner in Milan for
periods of up to six years. Astorre Manfredi who was captured
at Anghiari in 1440 was handed over to the Florentine government by his captor, Niccolò Gambacorti, and imprisoned in
the Stinche until peace was signed. Manfredi regarded both
the fact that he had been handed over and his imprisonment
as breaches of the conventions, and, although Gambacorti's
action had been entirely justified by the terms of his contract
with Florence, he found himself the object of a vendetta
which culminated in his murder in Bologna by emissaries of
Manfredi.

The hopes a condottiere might have of quick release depended very much on his wealth and influence. If he was important to his employers, they might negotiate an exchange for him, although often debiting his pay account with an amount equivalent to his ransom. If he had influential friends or ex-colleagues amongst the enemy commanders, they might stand guarantee for him. However, his final release would always be in return for an oath not to fight against his captors for a specific period, and these oaths were often observed. In the last resort he could change sides and join his captors rather than pay a ransom. But as the fifteenth century advanced, this practice, so damaging to the reputation of the condottiere, became less common.

The lot of the ordinary soldier captured in war certainly improved in the fifteenth century. But this was not so much because warfare became more humane, but because armies increased in size and tactics became more sophisticated. The well prepared ambush or the well executed encircling movement could produce mass surrenders which were an embarrassment to the victors. The prison camp played no part in fifteenth-century warfare, so there was little alternative but the wholesale release of prisoners.

What did, however, play a considerable part in warfare was treachery, deceit, and underhandedness of all types. The Italians regarded themselves as the most intelligent and highly educated people in Europe, and while it is certainly wrong to think of all Italian captains as students of the classics and devotees of the principles of classical warfare, one of the most popular of the small group of classical military writers whose work was widely read in Renaissance Italy was Frontinus. Frontinus' *Strategemata* is a casebook of military deceptions and reflections on the role of a sort of primitive psychological warfare. For Frontinus any military methods were justified by a successful result—victory, and while few Italian leaders had actually read Frontinus most would have agreed with his principles. Not only could successful 'stratagems' be justified by victory, they could also save lives—at least on one side. A very common practice in Italian warfare was to seek to poison the enemy's food supplies. This was recommended by Frontinus but it was not really carried out with sinister malevolence. It was rather an extension of scorched earth policy. To poison a well was the simplest way of denying use of it to an enemy. In fact there is remarkably little evidence that such attempts enjoyed very much success. The Sienese in 1353 tried to get rid of Fra Moriale's company which was ravaging the surrounding countryside by poisoning the food supplies with red arsenic; but in the last resort money did the job more successfully. In 1479 one of the items which appears in the accounts of Florentine expenditure for the Pazzi War was payments to men to go and poison the flour behind the enemy lines in southern Tuscany. A standard practice in siege warfare was to catapult the corpses of horses and men over the walls of a besieged city to spread both disease and despondency.

Perhaps the comparative failure of these macabre practices is a reflection on Renaissance techniques of poisoning generally, for certainly the knowledge and use of poisons was a good deal less sophisticated than we sometimes imagine. Attempts to murder, by poison or otherwise, individual enemy captains were rarely more successful, but they enjoyed widespread popularity as military techniques. After Carmagnola had fled from Milanese service in 1425 and joined the Venetians, he was pursued by a Visconti murder squad which was detected and summarily disposed of in Treviso. This failure had an effect entirely contrary to the intentions of its instigators in that both Carmagnola became more convinced of the wisdom of his decision to get away from the Visconti, and the Venetians were reassured about the sincerity of Carmagnola's intentions to join them. Filippo Maria Visconti, who had inspired this attempt on Carmagnola's life, was himself the object of numerous murder plots devised by the Council of Ten in Venice. On one occasion in 1431, the experiments being carried out on pigs by the Ten, to test the efficacy of their poisons, were not only unsuccessful but became public knowledge, and so this particular enterprise was hurriedly abandoned. Undeterred, however, the Council of Ten later launched a number of attempts to murder Francesco Sforza both when he was a Milanese general and after he became Duke. One of these involved a noxious substance which when rolled into balls and thrown on a fire gave off a lethal, sweet-smelling gas. This was tried out on a condemned prisoner in the prison of the Ten with undisclosed but apparently successful results. However, Francesco Sforza remained unaffected by these machinations as did most of his fellow targets.

A more effective method of eliminating a dangerous enemy commander was to betray him, either for actual or indeed for fabricated treachery, to his employer. Francesco Sforza brought off a brilliant coup of this nature against two of his captains who had deserted him and joined King Alfonso of Naples. Pietro Brunoro, who had been Sforza's leading infantry commander, and Troilo Orsini found themselves imprisoned for ten years in Spain by Alfonso after he had been shown letters forged by Sforza purporting to show that the two captains were planning to change sides once more and desert the Aragonese. No one will know how many of the executions of condottieri by their employers were partly the result of similar betrayals.

The most pervasive and effective element in this underworld of war were the spies and informants who operated in every court and infiltrated every army. Renaissance espionage is a subject about which we know little for obvious reasons, but it is clear that good information services were fundamental for a successful commander. These ranged from straightforward reports on the terrain and on the disposition of enemy forces to the secret information gleaned from spies close to the enemy leaders. A large part of the personal expenses of an army commander was allocated to paying for information. As one condottiere put it in a letter to Lorenzo de' Medici: 'There is no need for me to remind Your Magnificence reverently that to conceal one's own secrets and to discover those of the enemy can be held to be a most potent factor in the ultimate victory.' This particular man, Antonio, Count of Marsciano, was certainly a student of Frontinus as he had a copy in his library, but his words would have been a commonplace to any of his less erudite colleagues.

The frequent use in letters and chronicles of the period of the terms 'good war' and 'bad war' suggests that warfare in Italy, as in the north, was governed by a series of conventions or laws of arms. In a sense this was certainly true; many of the legal and military treatises which constituted the framework of a sort of international code of arms in the fifteenth century were Italian. Giovanni da Legnano, Egidio Colonna, and Bartolomeo da Saliceto were amongst the most influential writers and codifiers in the fourteenth century, although in fact, and perhaps significantly, the fifteenth century did not produce many similar treatises in Italy. Apart from Bartolomeo Cepolla, the Veronese jurist who elaborated on the work of Giovanni da Legnano, military writers of the fifteenth century in Italy tended to produce rather practical treatises in which a code of arms played relatively little part. However, conventions there certainly were, formed as in the north out of a combination of standard legal codes and long-standing military and chivalric custom. Indeed the fifteenth century saw a considerable revival in Italy of a sort of pseudo-chivalry particularly in the courts of northern Italy.

However, there is little evidence in Italy of such a code being enforced either by military courts or by duels. It was an ideal to which appeal was often made but which was never allowed to override practical considerations. The conventions governing sieges were clear cut and lip service was paid to them, but in the last resort the conduct of a siege or an assault was governed by the practical possibilities and by the problems of disciplining troops. When Micheletto Attendolo at the battle of Aquila ordered his men to go for the enemy's horses and thus cripple them, this was regarded by contemporaries as 'bad war'; but the technique became more and more common because of its effectiveness. The convention that armies did not move camp or fight on Sundays could always be overridden by practical necessities as was done by Niccolò da Tolentino in 1432. The high regard in which 'stratagems' and deception were held was essentially inimical to any serious concept of 'good war', and the protests about breaches of conventions tended to come from the losers or from unrealistic civilian commissaries.

It could be argued that this pragmatic attitude to the rules of war and of chivalry was the result of entrusting leadership in war to a group who were not exclusively drawn from the high nobility. Indeed the conventional view of the condottieri as social upstarts would support such an interpretation. However, this is too simple an explanation; most fifteenth-century condottieri did come from a noble class as we shall see, nor was the self-made soldier as rare amongst northern leaders as the contrast would imply. War in Italy was not fought according to strict rules because war rarely is; it was not a game played by professionals for their own advantage and satisfaction, but an aspect of the total life of Italian society governed by the normal considerations of practical necessity and individual self-interest.

CHAPTER EIGHT

SOLDIERS AND SOCIETY

In June 1362 the Florentines were preparing for a campaign against Pisa, a campaign which could be expected to bring great economic advantage to the whole city and which fitted admirably into the increasingly nationalistic and expansionist ideology of the self-confident city state. According to established practice the exact moment at which the expedition should set out was determined by the astrologers, who suggested mid-morning on 20 June. A great procession was organised, starting with the issuing of the standards from the Palazzo della Signoria, and culminating with the largely mercenary army marching out through the gates to the accompaniment of the cheers and best wishes of the citizens.

However, the whole ceremony took longer to organise than anticipated and there was soon a danger that the propitious moment would be overrun. The troops and the crowd began to quicken their pace, and then the astrologers decided that the route chosen through the Borgo SS. Apostoli was not after all a suitable one and should be changed. But the new route along the Via Porta Rossa had not been prepared for the passage of the standards and the mounted lances. The awnings of the shops had not been taken down and soon all was confusion. This was in turn regarded as an evil omen and the whole occasion fell rather flat. The war which ensued was, perhaps predictably for many Florentines, not a success.

The superstition characterised by this story was not peculiar to the fourteenth century. A century later Italian princes were still timing their public activities with the help of astrologers. Nor was the civilian involvement in the events a feature only of that century. War was a continual preoccupation of Renaissance society.

However, one of the main features of the military thought of Machiavelli was his emphasis on the gap which had grown up between military and political institutions as a result of the emergence of the mercenary system. He and other writers of the early sixteenth century gave the impression of an unbridgeable gulf between soldiers and civilians, between the licentious and predatory mercenaries and the decadent and effete citizens who employed them, between warfare and the other activities of society. War appears as a sort of game played by crafty and self-interested condottieri for their own satisfaction and profit; a game in which the real losers were the civilian employers, who could neither understand nor control the reprobates who took their money. Mercenaries were a race apart; a few brave but misguided men, a majority of deplorable villains who could not be expected to die for a state to which they had no natural loyalty.

This picture of the essential separateness of fifteenth-century warfare has some justifications. Machiavelli was part of a long humanist tradition of contempt for and vilification of mercenaries, and it was a tradition which had a good deal of influence on articulate civilian attitudes. Not only was the opinion of most classical authorities against the use of mercenaries, but the whole emphasis of early humanist thought on the active life and civic participation militated against a fair judgment of the activities and status of the condottieri. Petrarch launched unrestrained vituperation against mercenaries, and Coluccio Salutati, the Florentine chancellor, denounced them as 'outcasts who had entered into a perpetual conspiracy against peace and order'. Even Flavio Biondo, who unlike many humanists had direct experience of military life as the chancellor of Cardinal Vitelleschi, was irritated by the dog-latin barbarities of contemporary military terminology and the lack of order and discipline in the camps. This was the tradition which led the Florentine politician Alamanno Salviati to write: 'In general all men of his (Niccolò da Tolentino) occupation disgust me, because they are our natural enemies, and despoil all of us, and their only thought is to keep the upper hand and to drain our wealth.'

This sort of attitude to soldiers as natural enemies was both the result of and responsible for a widespread belief amongst certain groups that it was dangerous to arm subjects. The mercenaries were usually thought of as 'foreign mercenaries', and in Florence and Venice in particular there was considerable prejudice, if not actual legislation, against entrusting the command of armies to native citizens. This was the basis of the atmosphere of distrust and suspicion which often existed between soldiers and civilian employers and the very real divergence of motives in the relationship.

Furthermore, the condottieri were without doubt a rather exclusive group. The military profession in the fifteenth century was not one in which success and fortune came easily. An analysis of the 170 leading captains of the period shows that over 60 per cent of them came from thirteen families or military clans. The Sforzeschi and the Bracceschi were linked by blood ties as well as by long traditions of military service; the Roman Orsini and Colonna families each provided over a dozen of the leading condottieri of the century. The families tended to inter-marry and captains passed their companies on to their sons-in-law, thus making it very difficult for new men to make their way in the profession. They retained a monopoly of increasingly professional and recondite skills which set them apart from civilians and encouraged the sense of separation between the two groups.

However, having made these obvious points, one must also look at the ways in which the gulf between civilians and soldiers has been exaggerated. The contemporary intellectual tradition was by no means entirely hostile to soldiers. It was not on the whole motivated by any strong current of pacificism, and alongside the distrust of foreign mercenaries went a strong tendency to glorify military actions and to praise valiant men. Most of the humanists looked with approval on what they saw as the resurgence of Italian arms under Alberigo da Barbiano, and many of them were attached to one or other of the leading condottieri and wrote fulsome praises about their activities. In part these were of course paid rhetoricians saying what their patrons and masters, often the soldiers themselves, wanted to hear, but it was also a clear stream in the humanist tradition. It was the stream that made Plutarch's *Lives* one of the most popular classical works and which made a preoccupation with battles and wars one of the foundations of humanist history.

Guarino da Verona wrote in 1446: 'One must feel sorry for this generation in many ways, but amid so much that is bad, one factor above all emerges upon which we may congratulate modern times; they have had the good fortune to witness a revival of the long lost art of warfare; foreigners have for some time been dispensed with, and Italy has had a more than adequate fund of military talent of her own. Moreover if her sword were in play against her enemies, and she were not sick within, one could take a legitimate pride in such accomplishments, and call this a blessed age in which heroic leaders, energetic captains and highly trained generals spring forth everywhere in abundance, as though from the furrows of Thebes.' Guarino was a northern Italian humanist in close touch with humanist and patrician circles in Venice and with the practicalities of the emerging Venetian standing army. He was also one of a group of humanist educators who stressed the moral value of physical, and particularly martial, exercises. The schools of Guarino and his contemporary, Vittorino da Feltre, at Ferrara and Mantua were essentially court schools and aimed at producing the type of rounded Renaissance personality exemplified by Baldassare Castiglione. But their ideals and particularly the emphasis on military virtues and military training were by no means confined to courtly circles. Salutati and Bruni in Florence argued for the importance of military training for the citizens, and Alberti took up the same plea for 'activity' of a specifically military kind.

However, attitudes to war and to soldiers have to be examined in a wider context than that of the intellectual and social elite, and what is particularly interesting about the fifteenth-century chivalric revival is the widespread popularity of its more obvious manifestations. The institution of knighthood remained both popular and prestigious although it tended to lose its specifically military connotations. This was particularly so in fourteenth-century Florence where knighthoods were used as a form of political honour by governments which consciously rejected links with the old feudal nobility and were peculiarly scornful of the contemporary profession of arms epitomised by the foreign companies. It was in this period that Boccaccio and Sacchetti ridiculed the carpet knight; 'if this type of knighthood is valid one might as well knight an ox or an ass—or any sort of beast' commented Sacchetti on the dubbing by Florence of many of its merchant citizens. Ambassadors were knighted in groups to give them added prestige in the diplomatic world, and in 1378 the Ciompi revolutionaries, containing a strong lower middle class element, knighted 67 of their number. But this was an exceptional phase, even for Florence; knighthood in Renaissance Italy continued to carry considerable prestige and to be usually, if not exclusively, associated with the career of arms. The increasing preoccupation and involvement of civilians in military organisation was accompanied by the knighting of commissaries and *provveditori*. In fifteenth-century Florence knighthoods were far more rare than they had been in the fourteenth and were given to the leading citizens only. These men, although basically civilians, were already becoming involved in a growing interest in jousts and tournaments in which they sought to demonstrate that their knighthood was by no means an empty sham.

The whole question of the fifteenth-century interest in jousts and tournaments is a complicated one, but it is important to see that interest as essentially popular. The tournament was not just an elitist phenomenon reflecting the conversion of a merchant *haute bourgeoisie* into an aristocracy; nor was it just an entertainment put on by increasingly autocratic governments to divert popular attention from political affairs. There are three ways of looking at the tournament or joust in the late Middle Ages; first it was the key ceremony in the chivalric world when knighthood was proved and earned, and the favours of fair ladies won; secondly it was the military exercise essential for acquiring and maintaining the practical skills necessary to the main military arm until the end of the fifteenth century—the heavy cavalry; thirdly it was a public spectacle, a moment when pomp and display could be linked to excitement and even possibly danger. These three elements were always present in the development of the tournament in late medieval Italy; a constant contrast between the increasingly courtly and the persistently practical worlds, with considerable public interest in both.

Many festivals in fifteenth-century Italy were celebrated by two separate military spectacles, usually on successive days. One day there would be a joust—a series of single combats fought by a small group of jousters with wooden-headed lances and blunted swords; these were essentially tests of horsemanship and physical strength. On the next day there would be the tournament which frequently took the form of a full scale mock battle fought either by squadrons of cavalry in an open space, or fought for the possession of a mock castle, with weapons which were by no means necessarily blunted. The distinction between the joust and the tournament was not always as clear-cut as this. The tournament, which could be an extremely bloody occasion, gradually itself became more civilised; the hostility of the Church to needless loss of life and the disapproval of the humanists for ostentatious bravura contributed to this. But ultimately it was the decline of heavy cavalry as the main military arm which brought the end of the tournament as a serious exercise. However, this did not happen in the fifteenth century; Italian tournaments of this period, if only rarely fought with full battle arms, were often distinguished from the joust by the use of lances with small three pronged crowns on the end which were less dangerous than the normal battle lance, and by swords with cutting edges but no points. At the same time tournament armour became so strong and refined that severe wounds were reduced to a minimum, although this did not save Federigo da Montefeltro from losing an eye in a tournament.

But beside the practical tradition of the tournament had grown up the more courtly tradition of the joust and the chivalric spectacle like the battles of the *castelli d'amore*. Not that the joust fought with blunted weapons did not continue to serve a practical purpose, and the best jousters in the fifteenth century were all drawn from the ranks of the professional soldiers. But it was in the joust that the formalised skills of the knight could be displayed by men who were knights only in name, and merchants, lawyers, and courtiers in practice.

Jousts and tournaments as genuine military displays and

not just anachronistic pageants were popular throughout Italy in the fifteenth century and nowhere more so than in the merchant cities of Florence and Venice. However, there seemed to be a very real contrast in the attitudes towards these spectacles in the two cities which tells us something about Renaissance society's attitudes towards the military arts in general. In Florence tournaments were common, being held every year after 1406 to celebrate the capture of Pisa, as well as to welcome distinguished foreign visitors. But they were tournaments in which most of the participants were young Florentine patricians. They were much closer to the courtly than to the practical tradition. The leading jousters often had unnamed 'companions' who were usually professional soldiers, but it was the Florentines who held the limelight and won the prizes. Lorenzo de' Medici commented on the tournament held in 1469: 'To follow the custom and do like others, I gave a tournament in the Piazza Sta. Croce at great cost and with much magnificence. I find that about 10,000 ducats were spent on it. Although I was not a vigorous warrior, nor a hard hitter, the first prize was adjudged to me; a helmet inlaid with silver, and a figure of Mars on the crest.' Of the sixteen leading jousters on this occasion, all but four were Florentines and they included Benedetto Salutati, the nephew of the humanist chancellor Coluccio Salutati, whose helmet was made specially for the occasion by Pollaiuolo. These Florentine pageant-tournaments were pale imitations of war, the pseudo-chivalric cavortings of an essentially unmartial society: a society which admired the military virtues and looked with interest and awe on the accoutrements of war, but feared the practice and distrusted the practitioners of it.

In Venice tournaments were far less common, although just as popular. They were held in the Piazza S. Marco to celebrate great victories or the election of new doges. But in

Venice the participants in the tournaments were mostly professional soldiers and not Venetians. The events were genuine
mock battles, which gave Venetians the chance to appraise
the prowess of their troops and to reward the most skilled.
In 1441 Francesco Sforza brought all his condottieri to such
a tournament held in honour of the wedding of the Doge's
son, Jacopo Foscari, and in 1458 it was Colleoni who directed
the proceedings and whose senior captains carried off the
prizes. The final stage of Colleoni's tournament was a battle
between two squadrons of 70 men-at-arms, each fought with
full battle arms for the possession of a wooden castle erected
outside the Doge's palace. This tradition of large-scale and
serious tournaments in the city ended about 1480 when horses
were barred from the streets, and was replaced by mock
naval battles and regattas. But it was a tradition which reflected the more practical approach of Venetians to military
affairs than that of the Florentines; it was the tradition of a
society in which all men learnt to use the crossbow and many
had active experience of fighting on the galleys.

Tournaments were by no means the only occasions on
which Renaissance society had a chance to show its interest
in war: war which was regarded as inevitable and in certain
circumstances laudable. An interest in classical and medieval
treatises on war, in new military inventions and devices, in
the portrayal of war by artists, all spread much wider than
the military classes of society. The early printing presses of
Italy turned out innumerable editions of classical military
works, and the first book to be printed in Verona, in 1472,
was Roberto Valturio's *De re militari* written twenty years
earlier for Sigismondo Malatesta. The early cannon quickly
received their patron saint, St. Barbara, and were embellished by artists and glorified by writers. All the major architects of the fifteenth century spent much of their time working on fortifications, and battle scenes were amongst the most

popular themes for the decoration of wedding chests. As Professor Hale remarked: 'the more complex war becomes, the more veins of interest it taps', and warfare in the fifteenth century certainly became more complex.

Nor was the distinction between soldiers and civilians, between foreign mercenaries and citizen employers, as clear-cut in the fifteenth century as used to be thought. In Naples and the Papal States the majority of the army leaders were always subjects of the Neapolitan crown or the pope, and this majority became larger in the second half of the fifteenth century. In Milan the noble families had always played their part in military affairs. Venetian patricians were occasionally to be found amongst the captains employed by Venice; Michele Gritti, who commanded a large company in the 1430's and 1440's, was a notable example, and in the 1470's two of the senior commanders of the *lanze spezzate* were members of the Badoer and Malipiero families. Venice also came to rely increasingly on the nobility of her newly acquired Terraferma cities to command her troops, thus utilising the new subjects of her expanded state. Florence has no known exceptions to the rule of not employing native citizens as captains in the fifteenth century, but like Venice offered contracts to the minor nobility of the expanding Tuscan state.

Even more important than the growing tendency to employ new subjects as condottieri was that of turning condottieri into new subjects. The process by which the Italian states domesticated their condottieri with rewards, enfeudations and grants of citizenship, has been fully discussed and must have served to blur the distinctions between subjects and soldiers. A new feudal nobility was created, particularly in Milan and Venice, which quickly began to merge with the old.

The use of nobility from the outer fringes of the new territorial states and the settlement of condottieri on estates in those areas were ways in which the exclusiveness of the group of military leaders was being eroded by the late fifteenth century. However, although the profession was a difficult one for a newcomer to succeed in and was exclusive in this sense, it was not the case that the condottieri were a group apart from the rest of society in the purely social sense. They were certainly not upstarts; success in the military sphere depended very largely on getting a good start to one's career, either by belonging to a noble family with an active military tradition, and hence having estates from which to recruit and an established company to inherit, or by acquiring a company early by marriage to the daughter of an established captain. Promotion from the ranks was of course possible, but very few of the leading condottieri of the fifteenth century in fact rose from the bottom of the profession. The majority of these men came from the upper classes, although of course that social position had been won in some cases by a successful soldier in the family in the thirteenth or fourteenth centuries.

It is not possible in the space available to analyse closely the social status of the leading captains of the fifteenth century, but a very brief glance can show how few were genuinely 'new men'. Gattamelata and Niccolò Piccinino were said to be the sons of a baker and a butcher respectively, but tradition has it that Piccinino's uncle was Podestà of Milan. The Sforza–Attendolo clan, probably the most extensive of all condottiere families, were descended from wealthy and influential Romagnol middle class landowners; the Fortebracci were Perugian nobility, as were the Baglioni and the Michelotti; the Orsini, Colonna, Savelli and Conti families, which produced so many leading soldiers, were also the leading families in the Roman nobility; the Malatesta, Manfredi and Ordelaffi families had long been established as rulers in the

Romagna and the Marches, as had the Montefeltri. Part of the great success of Federigo da Montefeltro was to be attributed to the exceptionally good start he was given not only by birth as the son of a leading soldier and the Lord of Urbino, but also by inheriting, in addition to his father's troops, a half share of the large company of his father's principal lieutenant, Bernardino della Carda. The Sanseverineschi, the Gonzaga of Mantua, the Esti of Ferrara, the Bentivogli of Bologna, the Brandolini of Bagnacavallo, the Martinengo of Bergamo—all were unquestionably noble families by the fifteenth century, and Colleoni and Carmagnola also came from the ranks of the minor nobility. Even in the middle ranks of the profession, genuine success stories are hard to find; the Venetians had a clear policy of promoting squadron leaders in the companies of senior condottieri to command of their own companies, but none of these men ever reached the top of the profession.

It is true that success in the military profession could give a minor noble and his family a prestige and a precedence which they could not otherwise have enjoyed, and in this sense there was a *nouveau* quality about the soldiers. But Italian Renaissance society as a whole was somewhat more fluid than that in northern countries; this was where much of its vitality and originality lay. But it was not a society in which birth did not count nor one in which 'a servant can easily become a king' as Pius II suggested. The discussions of the military writers on the qualities of a good commander are instructive on this point. Vegetius, the great classical authority, made no mention of birth as significant, but by the early sixteenth century Italian writers were adapting the great authority, and Jacopo da Porcia in his *Precepts of War* remarked that noble birth was amongst the necessary qualifications for good commanders. Here, as elsewhere, the writers and theorists were a long way behind practical developments.

The Italian military leaders of the fifteenth century formed a group whose aspirations and behaviour corresponded closely to those of other sections of the upper class. Their non-professional interests lay in the acquisition of lands, the patronage of culture, the accumulation of status and wealth through good marriages and dowries, and the preservation of *reputazione*. Pensions and estates gave them a security in their old age which did not have to be won and protected by force. They were increasingly not just a military caste but a social group who were linked closely to other sections of society.

At a practical level, the contacts between soldiers and civilians were often friendly and positive. Civilian military administrators developed close links with the permanent professional soldiers of Milan and Venice; many of the Milanese administrators were ex-soldiers under the Sforza dukes. At the court of Ludovico Sforza, after 1480, there was an almost complete fusion of talents and interests; the governors of the *lanze spezzate* sat on the ducal council, condottieri served as ambassadors. In Venice fortress commanders were elected indiscriminately from a group of Venetian citizens, long-serving infantry constables, and retired condottieri. A number of the *provveditori* established close links with Venetian condottieri, despite occasional legislation against such contacts. There were in fact laws forbidding Venetians from entertaining soldiers or buying property from them, but these were clearly only spasmodically enforced. The situation in which civilian officials spent long and repeated periods in the camps of a permanent army, and in which condottieri were billeted for years on end in the subject cities, was clearly not one in which a separation between soldiers and civilians could be maintained. Andrea Giuliano was a close associate of the captain Luigi da Sanseverino and was selected to negotiate with him on a number of occasions. Gherardo Dandolo, another of the active *provveditori*, had links with Alvise dal Verme, and in 1454 was the intermediary between Jacopo Piccinino and the Senate. Andrea Morosini was recognised to be a confidant of Bartolomeo Colleoni and handled the secret negotiations for the return of Colleoni to Venetian service in 1454. Bartolomeo Pisani married the daughter of the captain general, Michele Attendolo, and was one of a number of patricians who had close links with the Sforza family. At one stage this particular connection became a dangerous and suspect one, when Francesco Sforza deserted Venice in 1447. An investigation by the Council of Ten revealed that a number of patricians including the Doge's son, Jacopo Foscari, and possibly even the Doge himself, had been rather too friendly with Sforza and had received money from him. This was one of the causes of the disgrace of Jacopo Foscari and also led to the hurried exile of the Doge's son-in-law, Andrea Donato, who was recalled from his post as Doge of Candia and tried by the Ten for receiving 900 ducats from Sforza. Andrea Donato had been *provveditore* with Sforza's army early in the 1440's, and his contact with the condottiere probably dated from that time.

In Florence there is far less evidence of practical, personal contacts of this sort. Cosimo de' Medici was the financial backer of Francesco Sforza and had a close association with him, nevertheless the suspicion of such contacts was on the whole greater in Florence. Amongst the reasons for the dramatic defenestration and execution of Baldaccio d'Anghiari were that he had insulted the Gonfalonier of Justice, Orlandini, and was too friendly with the anti-Medicean Capponi family. But many soldiers figured amongst the correspondents of Lorenzo de' Medici, and his marriage to Clarice Orsini brought one of the largest condottiere families into the Medicean circle. In Rome the Orsini were papal courtiers as well as soldiers, and many of the influential officials of the Apostolic Camera had experience as army paymasters and administrators. In Naples the fusion of military and civil functions amongst the leading personalities of the court was as complete as in Milan. Diomede Carafa, aristocrat, soldier, royal adviser, writer, building patron, and collector of antiquities, was a notable example of this fusion.

The involvement of soldiers in the cultural world of Renaissance Italy is a whole subject on its own to which justice cannot be done within the limited confines of these pages. The very considerable place of martial motifs and interests in fifteenth-century art has already been briefly touched upon. Fortresses and fortifications figured largely amongst the architectural achievements of the age; Mars ranked high amongst the ancient gods depicted by Renaissance artists; soldiers tended to predominate amongst the subjects of major funerary monuments. Battle scenes were painted, armour embellished, and cannon ornamented by some of the major artists of the day. But little of this was a result of encouragement by soldier patrons. The condottieri, like other groups in Renaissance society, turned to cultural patronage as a means of asserting their status and prestige; this was not because they lacked birth or had surplus wealth, but because it was accepted behaviour. Many of them as second or third generation captains had received a humanist education and had a real interest in literature and the arts. But that interest was on the whole a general one; the condottiere patrons were not concerned to cut out special niches for themselves as the creators of a specifically military culture; they conformed to the patterns of taste and behaviour of the upper class of the day. It can be argued that the condottiere princes of the Gonzaga and Este families played a particular part in the popularisation of chivalric styles in the mid-fifteenth century, but even this is an idea which should not be pushed too far. Gianfrancesco Gonzaga, Venetian captain general and a leading soldier of his generation, was the patron of Vittorino da Feltre and Alberti, as well as of Pisanello.

A glance at the major cultural creations of soldiers' patrons of the fifteenth century bears out this contention. Sigismondo Malatesta, the arch-rival of Federigo da Montefeltro as the foremost captain of his generation, attached more importance to the building of the classically inspired Tempio Malatestiano designed by Alberti, than he did to that of his fortress at Rimini. The fortress, although hailed by some contemporaries as a major step in the development of a new military architecture, was at first a rather traditional castle and probably only received its sophisticated outworks at the beginning of the sixteenth century. The Tempio on the other hand was a major Renaissance monument and epitomises the breadth of humanistic culture at Sigismondo's court. Similarly Federigo, although also a builder of fortresses, was more concerned with the construction of his great palace at Urbino and the creation of his library and his collections of art. The depiction of him by Justus of Ghent sitting reading in his library clad in full armour emphasises the fusion of civic and military virtues for which Federigo and many of his colleagues stood. Federigo was a product of Vittorino da Feltre's school at Mantua set up with the encouragement of Gianfrancesco Gonzaga, and this school can be described as another of the major creations of condottiere patronage. Ludovico Gonzaga, who became the senior Milanese commander in the later years of his life, was also a pupil of Vittorino and the patron of Mantegna. Francesco Sforza took a considerable interest in the expansion of the Visconti library which he inherited with the Duchy of Milan, but his major contribution was the building of the Castello Sforzesco, a palace as much as a castle. Bartolomeo Colleoni created at Malpaga, south of Bergamo, a cultured court and a fortified country retreat of considerable elegance. The early frescoes which he commissioned there have strong French affinities and it seems likely that he brought French or Burgundian artists to execute them. His favourite sculptor, Giovanni Amadeo, worked both round Malpaga and on that other important condottiere 'creation', the Colleoni chapel at Bergamo.

It could be said that these men were all condottiere princes whose tastes were inevitably broader than those of lesser captains who were also patrons. But this does not seem to be the case; what we know of the patronage of the minor figures shows the same breadth of interests. Religious patronage came high on the list of any soldier patron as one might expect. There were few of the prominent captains of the day who did not devote money either during their lifetimes or in their wills to building and endowing chapels and commissioning votive paintings. The list of such works would be endless from the major creations of Sigismondo Malatesta, Colleoni and Braccio Baglioni to the 25 small Umbrian churches mentioned in the will of Antonio, Count of Marsciano. Manuscript collecting was another favourite cultural occupation of soldiers, and not just the collecting of military treatises and other works relevant to their profession as one might expect. The libraries of condottieri of which we have knowledge were balanced collections in which military works appear no more frequently than in the libraries of civilians. Even a man like Antonio, Count of Marsciano, an archetypal Venetian professional soldier, whose small collection of 40 manuscripts and printed books showed an unusual concentration of military works, also included a selection of contemporary humanistic works by Francesco Barbaro, Guarino and Matteo Palmieri.

That soldiers were participators in as well as patrons of the intellectual and cultural life of the day needs also to be stressed. There were poets and writers of considerable skill as well as leaders of courts amongst the Italian soldiers of the fifteenth century. Malatesta Malatesta wrote Petrarchan sonnets of recognised merit, and the intellectual accomplishments of his brothers Pandolfo and Carlo have already been discussed. Alessandro Sforza, the brother of Francesco, married one of the most brilliant intellectual women of the day, Costanza Varano, and their son Costanzo, a soldier of note, was also a poet of some repute. Bartolomeo d'Alviano was the friend of the Venetian humanists Navagero, Fracastoro and Pietro Bembo, and wrote a military treatise when in a French prison after Agnadello.

This is inevitably a very impressionistic view of the culture of the condottieri, but just as it is a mistake to regard the Italian military commanders as social upstarts, so it is unwise to see them all as unlettered boors.

But in the last resort it is the total impact of war on society which it is important to assess. Fifteenth-century war was limited war, but how far does this mean that it left civilian society unaffected? Once again it seems that the isolation of war has been exaggerated. The approach of war meant large-scale recruiting drives, particularly to fill the ranks of the infantry. It is true that the cavalry companies were fairly permanent bodies of which the core was made up of men-at-arms often recruited from the condottiere's estates and home area. Thus mobilisation and preparation for war for these companies did not on the whole mean recruiting from the areas which they were being called upon to defend. But with the infantry the picture was rather different. In most fifteenth-century Italian armies a considerable proportion of the infantry constables and of the rank and file infantry were subjects of the employing state. The proportion of course varied and was higher in Florentine and papal armies than in those of north or south Italy. This indicates the other factor which has to be borne in mind when considering the problem of recruiting in Italy, the extent to which certain specific areas were good recruiting grounds. It is often held that mountainous areas produce the best infantry both because the men are hardier and because the agriculture of such areas does not require the full attention of the whole male population. But an analysis of a sample of 350 infantry constables during the fifteenth century shows that while it is true that there was a tendency for greater numbers of them to come from central Italy, from Tuscany and the Papal States, it does not seem to be the case that the poorer, more mountainous parts of these areas produced the best infantry. In fact the whole of central Italy, with the exception of few limited fertile areas, was poor land for agriculture. Most of the area was afflicted by a degree of rural under-employment, and it was not necessary to go deep into the Apennines to find infantry recruits. At the same time, if the declared towns of origin of the infantry constables are anything to go by, many of these men came from in and around the larger towns of the region. Umbria and Tuscany alone produced nearly one-third of the constables in this sample, and in those areas it was Borgo San Sepolcro, Terni, Città di Castello, Spoleto and Narni which predominated as the native cities of the men. None of the cities of the Marches produced as many constables as those in Umbria and south-east Tuscany, and the Romagna was surprisingly unproductive considering its reputation as a recruiting area. Outside this central area, Bologna and Rome stand out from the other cities, and a notable feature also of the sample is the large number of non-Italians amongst the constables: thirteen Slavs and Albanians, thirteen Spaniards, nineteen Corsicans, odd Germans and Frenchmen, and one Englishman.

There are two obvious dangers in attempting statistical analyses of this sort. In the first place the declared place of origin of a man can only be taken to be the nearest sizeable town to his birthplace; Niccolò da Bologna was not necessarily an urban dweller from Bologna but could have been a countryman from the *contado* of Bologna. Thus, although a majority of constables nominate large towns as their places of origin this is by no means an indication that a majority of them came from urban families. However, and this is also the second reservation that we must have, one is here dealing with the constables, the infantry leaders—and it is reasonable to assume that these were the more intelligent and the more facultied members of the profession. One would therefore expect to find a higher proportion of townsmen amongst this group than amongst the rank and file infantry.

However, to return to the original point, a significant proportion of the infantry in any Italian army were local men, and this proportion of course increased enormously when one looks beyond the professional infantry to the militia. Militia levies were used by all the Italian states in the fifteenth century, if only as pioneers. In Venice and Milan by the 1470's they were being put on a semi-permanent, trained basis and described as *provisionati* rather than *cerne*. All the Romagna condottiere princes used militia levies, and papal cities were occasionally called upon to produce them for local service. Not even in Florence did the rural militia organisation disappear completely as the humanists thought, although the levies were usually largely used for pioneer duties.

However, even given this degree of local participation in the army, one is not implying something approaching a national army nor suggesting that many men were fighting for home and country. The militia were conscripts and usually unwilling ones; the desertion rate was high and they could not be relied upon to move far from their homes. The professional infantry, like the men-at-arms of the condottiere companies, served for a variety of reasons, amongst which personal gain ranked high, but not necessarily highest. The wages were, in theory, quite good, the chances of a real windfall in the form of booty or a rich captive, slim, but always possible. Excitement, adventure and the companionship of military life were always attractions. But often it was negative pressures which were the most important: the need to escape from a situation of rural under-employment, or of urban social repression; the need to escape from justice or from creditors; the need to escape from a stifling family environment. Most men served in Renaissance armies not because they enjoyed fighting and looting, but because it was a profession like any other; the chances of advancement were perhaps greater than in some professions but should not be exaggerated; the degree of freedom from normal social ties and commitments was an attraction in a society which was still basically hierarchic. But the soldiers of Renaissance Italy did not live in a world apart from the civilians, even though the concept of a national army still lay far in the future.

If the civilian population of an Italian state was not untouched by the preparations for war, they became crucially involved in the financing of war. The escalating costs of war and defence, particularly in the first half of the fifteenth century, far outstripped the normal resources of the Italian states. This accelerated the growth of loan financing, and huge profits could be made by successful and fortunate financiers. But in the end the revenues themselves had to be increased and the collection of them made more efficient. The imposition of the Florentine *catasto*, one of the first comprehensive tax systems in Europe, arose directly out of the financial crises created by the wars with Milan and Lucca. In 1427–8 Florence was said to have spent three and a half million florins on this war, and this represented over ten times the normal revenue of the state. This was the background to the decision to accept the *catasto*, and also more importantly to the financial and administrative confusion which led to the rise to power of the Medici financiers. Venice also moved towards a *catasto* in the late 1450's under pressure of the accumulated war debts of the Milanese wars and the impending war with the Turks. Her army in the late 1440's was costing nearly a million ducats a year, a sum which even on the most optimistic estimates could only be produced by devoting almost the entire revenue to it. In the 1470's and 1480's even the peacetime standing army of Milan cost half the total revenue of the Milanese state. In the Papal States while Martin V's campaigns of 1421/2 and 1428/9 cost about 160,000–170,000 ducats each, the siege of Rimini by Paul II in 1469 cost about half a million. This last figure was about double the papal revenue for the year.

The financial impact of war was not just one of added fiscal burdens and improved fiscal administration. The condottiere princes relied heavily on their earnings as soldiers to subsidise their administrations and finance their patronage. The wealth and cultural prominence of cities like Ferrara, Mantua, Urbino and Rimini owed much to the profits from war. In a sense one of the effects of fifteenth-century warfare was a distribution of wealth from the main commercial centres to some of the lesser cities. Similarly amongst individuals, great fortunes could be made out of war loans, and at a lower level the money poured back into the economy as soldiers spent it and repaid their debts.

The impact of the practice of war on society does not need to be stressed further. If the greater cities were largely immune from siege and sack, this was a period when an increasing section of their populations were becoming the owners of country properties which were by no means immune. In the countryside, Italian farming was peculiarly vulnerable to military devastation; olives, vines and herds could be destroyed with much greater effect than arable crops, and one passage of an army could ruin the rural economy for years. This could lead to complete migrations

of the population, abandonment of villages and total transformation of the rural scene. The pattern of rural settlement
in an area like that north of Rome was crucially affected by
warfare. The original villages were sited in inaccessible and
often basically uneconomic positions in order to defend
themselves. Nevertheless, in the confused period of the
Schism between 1378 and 1420, many of these villages were
destroyed and whole areas of the Roman Campagna and the
Patrimony fell out of cultivation. As security returned towards the middle of the fifteenth century, so the whole
pattern of rural settlement began to change. Defence became
less important, and the villages were able to expand beyond
their natural defences, and even move out into the open
country. In the area of Pisa, which was often described as
singularly desolate in the fifteenth century, much of the
trouble was caused by the constant passage of armies, which
not only devastated the economy, but also broke down the
banks of the important drainage ditches and this led to
flooding. Once again life in the cities could not remain untouched by these conditions in the countryside. Refugees
poured in to seek the shelter of the walls, creating new and
urgent social pressures and problems. Prices were inevitably
affected; interrupted trade routes, destruction of crops, and
the need to supply large armies were factors which must
at times have exercised more influence in this area than
seasonal fluctuations. No study of prices in fifteenth-century
Italy can be complete without a careful analysis of the moving
tide of war and armies.

Certainly when war was over or a victory won, the whole
population of a city joined in the rejoicing. Alms were distri-
buted to the poor, jousts were held, and soldiers honoured.
Once again the whole life of the civilian community was
affected by the cessation of war. The chronicles of the period
are filled with war and for this they are often criticised as

sources; but it is not so much their preoccupation with war that is at fault but their concentration on the heroic aspects of it. War was an unpleasant but ever-pressing reality; however, it was not the battles, the heroic deeds and the martial individuals which demand attention but the real impact on society as a whole.

———◦⊂⊃◦———

CHAPTER NINE

ITALY AND EUROPEAN WARFARE

In the autumn of 1494 the French King, Charles VIII, launched his famous invasion of Italy, and by February 1495 he was the master of the kingdom of Naples. No one would dispute the importance of this date and these events in Italian history; the political scene was never to be quite the same again. For forty years France and Spain struggled for predominance in the peninsula, and when in the 1530's Spain emerged as the victor large parts of Italy had already learnt to accept the fact of foreign control. What particularly perplexed contemporary Italian writers was how it had happened so quickly; how had Charles been able to brush aside the resistance of three major Italian states and occupy one of them within six months? The first answer for writers like Machiavelli and Guicciardini lay in the weakness of Italy's military defence. This was the basis for much of their attack on the condottiere system—that it had failed Italy in its time of need. Italy, sheltered behind the Alps, had lost touch with contemporary European military developments and the condottieri were still living in the anachronistic world of the medieval cavalry charge. Thus, when confronted with the fury of the French attack and the novelty of French military methods, their morale collapsed and they were unable to resist.

These are charges to which we must return in more detail, as they are a key to the whole understanding of Italian fifteenth-century warfare, but for the moment it is important to assess how true the basic premise is. To what extent had Italian warfare developed in a vacuum, isolated from ultramontane developments? How far is it true that since the departure of the foreign companies in the fourteenth century, and the death of Hawkwood, Italy had had no experience of foreign military methods?

There is, of course, some truth in it. There was no major invasion of Italy as a whole by a foreign army during the fifteenth century—until 1494; very few of the condottieri were non-Italians. However, as we have seen, quite a high proportion of the infantry constables were foreigners, and by the 1480's large numbers of Albanian stradiots and even Turks were being used as light cavalry. Furthermore the history of Naples in the fifteenth century had been one of a constant struggle between Aragonese and Angevins. Several Angevin expeditionary forces had entered Italy during the century and the core of the armies with which Alfonso won the crown of Naples was Spanish. Nor had the activities of these French and Spanish troops been entirely confined to Naples. There was, in fact, a series of encounters throughout the century in which Italians had met foreign troops, from the battle of Brescia in 1401, when the Milanese army had defeated a German force, to the appearance of the Duke of Lorraine with 250 French lances as one of the Venetian commanders in the War of Ferrara.

Brescia in 1401 was the only major intervention by German troops in Italy during the century, and on this occasion the German cavalry was defeated by Facino Cane and Jacopo dal Verme. In 1411 and 1418 the Venetians faced massive Hungarian invasions and successfully countered both of them, and in 1422 Carmagnola with a Milanese army won a notable victory over the Swiss at Arbedo. Four thousand Swiss had crossed the St. Gothard pass in an attack on Bellinzona and Domodossola. They were met by Carmagnola with an army of about 5,000 cavalry and 3,000 infantry. The Swiss formed a square of pike infantry in their traditional custom, but soon found themselves surrounded. Carmagnola dismounted his men-at-arms and launched them at the square in a manner reminiscent of Hawkwood. Refusing to accept the Swiss offers to surrender, he succeeded in completely shattering them. This was a blow which was remembered in Switzerland for many years and perhaps contributed in some degree to the relatively few appearances of Swiss troops in Italy for the rest of the century.

In 1447 and 1449 it was the turn of Colleoni to meet foreign invaders. French troops under the Duke of Orleans invaded Milan in alliance with the Venetians attacking from the east, and were met by Colleoni at Bosco Marengo. On this occasion he abandoned his normal Braccesco technique of wearing the enemy down with squadrons used in succession, and threw his whole army into a sudden impetuous charge. The French were taken by surprise and broken, leaving about 1,500 dead on the field. Two years later, another French expeditionary force was met by Colleoni at Romagnano Sesia, but this time he fought a carefully planned tactical battle in the Italian style against them and again won a complete victory. These two battles were the bases of Colleoni's considerable international reputation and account for the great efforts which Charles the Bold made to obtain his services in later years.

In 1452 an Angevin force joined the Milanese in the war in Lombardy, but completely failed to give a good account of itself. The French troops were reluctant to engage in the slow and uncomfortable siege warfare which characterised this campaign; nor were they prepared to fight on into the winter as Francesco Sforza expected his troops to do. In fact it was only in their cruelty towards civilians that this French army proved itself superior to the Italians. In 1461 the French suffered another major defeat when they attempted to reimpose French rule in Genoa after a revolution in the city. The Genoese aided by a Milanese force repelled the French attack and inflicted very heavy casualties on the French knights from a prepared defensive position.

The record of Italian encounters with foreign armies was not entirely one of victories. In 1478 10,000 Swiss invaded the Ticino and, when forced to retreat by a larger Milanese army, succeeded in luring the Italians into the valley of Giornico, where, surrounded and subjected to a hail of fire from the encircling hills, the Milanese army was badly defeated. This defeat was avenged in 1487 when it was the turn of the Milanese led by Renato and Gian Jacopo Trivulzio to trap a large Swiss force at Ponte di Crevola. On this occasion, the Milanese army was largely made up of light cavalry and the new Milanese conscript infantry, and it proved itself more than a match for the Swiss force of over 5,000 men which was completely routed. The last major frontier battle before 1494 was that at Calliano (1487), north of Verona, when the Venetians, having turned back an Austrian invasion, sought to capture Trento. Roberto da Sanseverino commanded the Venetian army which had the difficult task of moving up the narrow valley of the Adige against heavily defended fortifications. He succeeded in bypassing two castles, but then as he crossed the Adige with a bridge of boats his army was attacked by a mixed force of Swiss and the new German *Landsknechte* trained to fight in the Swiss manner. Their commander was Friedrich Kappler, a veteran of the Burgundian Wars, and he succeeded in catching the Venetian army as it was half across the river. The centre of the Venetian cavalry was routed and driven back into the river where many, including Roberto himself, were drowned. But the Venetian right wing led by Guido Rossi counter-attacked and forced the Swiss and German infantry to retire. In that they lost their commander and were unable to continue their advance, this encounter must be regarded as a defeat for the Venetians. But both here and at Ponte di Crevola Italians had met, and to some extent gained an advantage over, the troops who were regarded as the masters of the European battlefields at the time.

Finally throughout this period, Italians had the unenviable experience of fighting the Turks. It was not only the Venetian army in Greece and on its own frontiers in Friuli that faced this enemy, since in 1480 a Turkish force occupied Otranto and the Neapolitans under Giulio Acquaviva and the Duke of Calabria had to conduct a protracted siege to evict them. After this 1,500 Turkish cavalry were hired by Naples and put in an appearance in northern Italy in the War of Ferrara.

There is another side to this question of military contacts and that is the appearance of Italian commanders and Italian troops in wars outside Italy. The Genoese had the reputation of being the best crossbowmen in Europe and were hired in large numbers as mercenaries, particularly for the French army. But even more significant was the reputation which Italian captains enjoyed in the second half of the fifteenth century. In 1465 a Milanese expeditionary force took part in the War of the Commonweal in France. It consisted of about 3,000 men led by Gaspare da Vimercate and the Sforzesco infantry captain, Donato del Conte, and was also accompanied by Galeazzo Maria Sforza, the eldest son of Francesco. The army had no artillery with it, but nevertheless was able to do some useful work in the Rhone valley for the royal cause, besieging and taking a number of small castles.

After the final collapse of the Angevin cause in Naples in 1462, a number of leading captains who had fought for the Angevins retired into exile in France and Burgundy. Cola di Monforte, Count of Campobasso, was probably the most notorious of these because his desertion of Charles the Bold before the battle of Nancy earned him the outraged censure of Philippe de Commynes in his memoirs, and subsequent re-incarnation in the pages of Sir Walter Scott. 'There is no treachery which the human mind can imagine for which his body and spirit are not well fitted', was Scott's comment, but in fact Cola di Monforte's desertion of the Burgundian cause was an exceptional moment in the career of an otherwise faithful soldier. He served the Angevins in Italy, in France and in Spain, and only moved to Burgundian service after the death of Jean d'Anjou in 1470. The Burgundian army in the 1470's was filled with Italians; Charles the Bold in his deter-mination to create a permanent fighting force to match the French had not only recruited exiles like Monforte and his colleague, Jacopo Galeota, but had also sent recruiting agents into Italy to hire the best men available. Colleoni was approached, but Venice refused to release him; Troilo da Rossano was lured from the Sforza army, and Orso dall'Anguillara from the Papal States. The Italians numbered 1,000 lances in Charles' army at this time, and Commynes regarded them as the core of the army.

After the defeat and death of Charles the Bold at Nancy Galeota took service with the French. For a further ten years he was a leading commander in the army of Louis XI until killed by an artillery shot in the Brittany campaign. With him in French service was another Neapolitan and Angevin condottiere, Boffillo del Giudice. Boffillo, on the death of Jean d'Anjou, had offered his services to Louis XI and for a time was in high favour with the king. He was a royal council-lor and principal Italian adviser to Louis, and fought a success-ful campaign in Roussillon. After the death of Louis, he began to fall from favour, but retained his position of Governor of Roussillon where he maintained a picked company of 92 Italian men-at-arms. Both Galeota and Del Giudice were approached by Venice and offered command of the Venetian army in the late 1480's, but the death of the former and the declining fortunes of the latter made the negotiations abortive.

In addition to the presence of considerable numbers of Italian troops and Italian captains in northern armies, one must remember also the sophisticated diplomatic reporting of which the Italians were acknowledged masters. Milanese and Venetian ambassadors in France, Burgundy and Germany kept their governments fully informed of the strength and dispositions of the ultramontane armies. In the light of all this evidence, it is absurd to argue that the Italians were unaware of the military developments beyond the Alps or insufficiently prepared to meet the challenge of the Swiss infantry or the French artillery.

Nor do the events of 1494 and the subsequent years bear out the view that Italian warfare was notably degenerate and anachronistic. The invasion of Italy by Charles VIII was opposed by three of the five major Italian states and half-heartedly supported by one, Milan. The recent and uneasy alliance of Naples, the Papacy and Florence omitted two of the best armies in Italy. The Milanese army with its permanent core of household cavalry and conscript infantry was on the French side, while the Venetian army, perhaps the most experienced and certainly the best organised, remained neutral during the opening campaign. Of the three allies, Naples had by far the largest army with a readily mobilised potential of about 18,000 men. However, the Barons' War, which had recently torn Naples apart, had damaged the morale and the leadership of the army, and its organisation does not seem to have been highly developed. Nevertheless, the three most experienced condottieri in Italy were in Neapolitan pay: Niccolò Orsini, Count of Pitigliano, Virginio Orsini and Gian Jacopo Trivulzio. It is significant perhaps that two of these men were Orsini, and yet were not leading the papal army. This army had rather declined since the days of

Paul II and Sixtus IV and, although Alexander VI was making great efforts to build it up again, its strength was relatively small. The Florentines had done little to put right the years of despite and neglect of a permanent military establishment and had to start recruiting hurriedly to catch up.

These were the armies which faced the French in 1494, and they represented probably less than half Italy's fighting strength. However, even then the military imbalance was a good deal less than is sometimes imagined. The total French force which crossed the Alps consisted of about 30,000 men, roughly equally divided between cavalry and infantry. The bulk of the cavalry were heavy cavalry organised into lances of six men each; thus the total figures included the usual proportion of non-combatants. The infantry included about 5,000 of the famous Swiss, but these were outnumbered by native French infantry of whom the majority were Gascon crossbowmen. Finally the artillery train consisted of at least 40 pieces of heavy siege artillery, which were both more mobile and had a greater hitting power than contemporary Italian guns. In addition the French had the static and rather lukewarm support of the Milanese army, and were augmented, as the invasion proceeded, by a growing number of Italian 'deserters', notably the Colonna and their troops, who abandoned the pope at an early stage.

The French army, when fully assembled, was the largest army that had been seen in Europe for more than a century, but much of its strength was rapidly dispersed in garrisons, and the army actually in the field rarely outnumbered the Italians opposed to it. Indeed, at the first major battle of the wars in 1495—Fornovo—the French were themselves considerably outnumbered.

Charles VIII launched his invasion relatively late in the campaigning season. After being held up by a bout of small-pox at Asti, he did not actually leave friendly Milanese soil

until late October. By this time the allied military dispositions were complete and by no means doomed to failure.
They were based on the justifiable assumption that the easiest
route southwards lay through the Romagna, whilst any
attempt to march down the west side of Italy would involve
crossing the Apennines and dealing with the powerful Florentine fortresses of Sarzanella, Pietrasanta, and, ultimately,
Pisa. Thus the main Neapolitan–papal army was concentrated
on the eastern route, while the Florentines were expected to
hold the Apennine passes. The chief threat to this comprehensive defensive plan was an amphibious landing further
south, but the Neapolitan fleet was strong and could be
expected to prevent such a possibility.

Charles and his generals, however, elected to attack on the
western side given the lateness of the season and the need
to go for the most direct route southwards, and also perhaps
sensing that Florence was the weak link in the alliance. The
French army, about 17,000 strong at this stage, tackled the
Apennine passes and the Florentine fortresses without its
siege artillery which had to be sent by sea, while a small
detachment with the Milanese kept the Neapolitan main
army engaged near Bologna. At this stage, political factors
began to play their part. After the French had succeeded in
taking the small fortress of Fivizzano by treachery and ruthlessly sacking it, Piero de' Medici took fright and began to
negotiate. He surrendered his major fortresses without a
fight and allowed Charles a free passage through Tuscany.
The fact that he immediately found himself ousted from
power in Florence did not alter the situation that the Neapolitan–papal army in the Romagna was now outflanked and had
no alternative but to retreat.

Rome now lay undefended as the pope hurriedly recalled
his contingents from the eastern front. To add to his difficulties, the Colonna chose this moment to desert, seize Ostia

(another modern fortress which would have been a real test for the French artillery), and thus provide the cover for a small French force to be landed south of Rome. Therefore, although the combined army got back in time to defend Rome itself, the French, now reunited with their siege artillery, were pouring into the Papal States and had already outflanked the city. Alexander VI decided, probably rightly, that Rome was now indefensible and advised the Neapolitan army to continue its withdrawal southwards while he came to terms. On 30 December 1494 Charles VIII entered Rome having scarcely fired a shot.

The Neapolitans still had a chance to defend their own frontiers, but by now morale was low and internal divisions rife. Charles' army had been joined by some of the most experienced Italian captains, notably Prospero and Fabrizio Colonna, who took the lead in a rapid flanking march through the Abruzzi, which again bypassed the main Neapolitan defences. The French at last unmasked their guns to crush the small fortress of Monte S. Giovanni, and the terror which the ensuing sack produced was sufficient to make the populations of much more powerful cities, like Capua, refuse to co-operate in their defence. King Alfonso had already abdicated in favour of his son, and the will to resist had gone. On 20 February the French entered Naples and the long march was over.

Charles VIII had indeed 'conquered Italy with the chalk of his billeting officers' as Alexander VI put it, but this was not the fault of the soldiers. The chances to resist had been undermined by political indecision and civilian weakness. The Swiss, who only made up about a third of the French infantry, had played no part in the campaign; the artillery had scarcely been used. No reasonable chance of a genuine military confrontation had offered itself. It is true that the Italian armies did not hurl themselves into forlorn counter-attacks as they

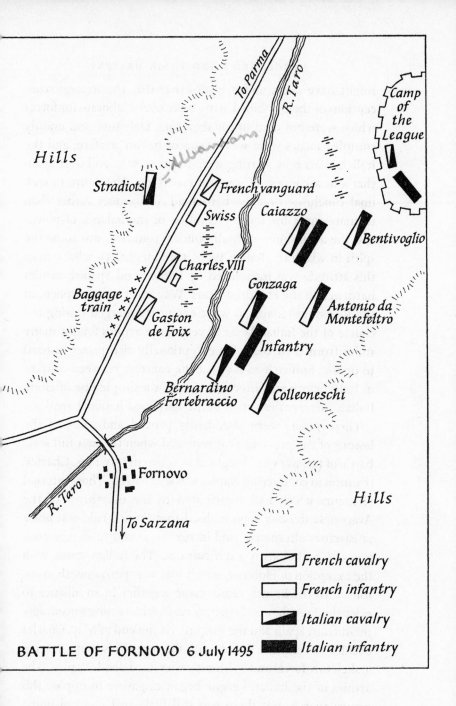

BATTLE OF FORNOVO 6 July 1495

Hills

To Parma

R. Taro

Camp of the League

Stradiots

Albanians

French vanguard

Swiss

Caiazzo

Bentivoglio

Charles VIII

Baggage train

Gonzaga

Antonio da Montefeltro

Gaston de Foix

Infantry

Bernardino Fortebraccio

Colleoneschi

Fornovo

R. Taro

Hills

To Sarzana

French cavalry

French infantry

Italian cavalry

Italian infantry

might have done, and it is also true that the strategic conceptions of the combined army were over-elaborate for forces which were not used to collaborating. Defensive and unduly complex tactics were weaknesses of Italian warfare, and the Italian Wars now starting were to prove over and over again that a new concept of war was emerging. The desire to seek final conclusions on the battlefield, to conquer rather than to manoeuvre for the preservation of the balance of power and the acquisition of small political counters, was to be the spirit in which the Italian Wars were fought. To what extent this attitude was introduced by French and Spanish armies hardened in the Hundred Years' War and the atmosphere of the Reconquista, and to what extent it emerged during the course of the Italian Wars as very large armies fought many miles from their bases for exceptionally rich prizes, is hard to decide. Suffice it to say that the contrast between warfare in Italy before and after 1494 was not a simple one of effete Italian mercenaries versus battle-hardened national armies.

These points were abundantly proved and some of the lessons of the previous year repeated when the first full scale battle of the wars was fought at Fornovo in July 1495. Charles' triumph in conquering Naples was short-lived. Those internal elements which had contributed to the overthrow of the Aragonese dynasty soon realised that French rule was not a satisfactory alternative, and increasing unrest made the position of Charles' army a difficult one. The Italian states, with the exception of Florence, which was now permanently committed to the French cause, came together in an alliance to evict the French, and began to receive increasing encouragement from Spain and the Empire. At the end of May, Charles decided to return to France with the core of his army, leaving a skeleton force under Montpensier to defend Naples. The armies of the Italian League began to gather to oppose this return march, but there was still little real political unity, as some thought it best to let the French pass on their way out of Italy rather than risk a confrontation with them. However, the opportunity, as Charles marched northwards with a relatively small army, was too good a one to be missed and Francesco Gonzaga, the Marquis of Mantua, Venetian captain general and commander of the combined army, elected to bring the French to open battle rather than simply hold the Apennine passes against them. The latter course would have involved little risk and could well have led either to the eventual surrender of the army as it was cut off from its base, or at least to a hazardous transhipment by sea. It would have been a strategy very much in the Italian tradition, but Gonzaga felt both sufficiently confident and sufficiently determined to achieve the personal glory of defeating the French, to go for a crushing victory.

The French retreated along the route they had come in the previous year. This meant crossing the Apennines between Sarzana and Parma by the Cisa Pass, and coming down into the valley of the Taro at Fornovo. Here, below the town where the valley widened out, the huge Italian army was waiting for them in a camp fortified with a ditch and a palisade. Gonzaga described his army as 'the finest and most powerful that has been seen in Italy for many years'. It numbered about 25,000 men of whom about 5,000 were in Milanese service and the remainder in that of Venice. Two thousand two hundred heavy cavalry lances of five men each formed the core of the army, but there were also about 2,000 light cavalry, mostly stradiots, and 8,000 professional infantry. Four thousand Venetian militia had also arrived, although the bulk of the militia forces were still on the march, as was most of the Venetian heavy artillery. The French numbered about 900 lances of heavy cavalry, 3,000 Swiss infantry, 600 archers of the royal bodyguard and 1,000 artillerymen, a total of about 10,000 men.

When it reached Fornovo, the French army crossed the Taro and began to move down the left bank of the river in front of the Italian camp. Its left flank was thus protected by the hills and its right by the river. In the circumstances the French not surprisingly expected the main assault on them to come from straight up the valley, and to counter this the Swiss marched in a tight square close behind the cavalry advance guard. Two further large columns of cavalry completed the order of the march with the King commanding the centre himself and the rear led by Gaston de Foix. The baggage train laden down with loot from the campaign was placed towards the rear and close to the line of the hills; the artillery moved on the right flank along the river bank.

The Italian battle plan was drawn up by Ridolfo Gonzaga, uncle of the Marquis and himself a veteran of the Burgundian wars, with just these dispositions of the enemy in mind. The tactical conception was masterly, although the details for its execution were over-elaborate. Basically the plan was to block the French advance with a holding force and launch the main attack across the Taro on the flanks of the centre and rear columns. This would have the effect of pinning the enemy against the hills, splitting his extended line of march, and destroying the columns in detail. To carry out this operation the Italian army was divided into nine divisions. The Count of Caiazzo, with the main body of the Milanese cavalry and supported by a mixed infantry force and a large cavalry reserve, was to cross the Taro in front of the French and engage the vanguard. Gonzaga himself with his personal troops was to cross in the centre, engage the French centre, and split it off from the vanguard. Bernardino Fortebraccio had command of the third prong of the attack, made up of the leading Venetian cavalry squadrons, and was to attack the rearguard. In close support to Gonzaga and Fortebraccio came the cream of the Venetian infantry, and then in reserve two further columns of cavalry. The first of these comprised the *lanze spezzate* known as the Colleoneschi and commanded by the son-in-law of the legendary Colleoni, who had died nearly twenty years earlier. The second reserve column was led by Antonio da Montefeltro, the illegitimate son of that other leading figure of the preceding generation, Federigo. While all these divisions were attacking directly from across the Taro, the stradiots were to pass right around the rear of the enemy and attack the vanguard downhill, thus causing further confusion and preventing stragglers from escaping into the hills. Finally a strong guard of cavalry and militia was left in the camp.

The intelligent use of reserves has sometimes been described as one of the distinguishing features of modern military tactics, and the concept was certainly one that had been widely explored by the condottieri. But in this case there was too much emphasis on reserves. Whether this was because Gonzaga had more men than he knew what to do with or whether it was a sort of natural caution is hard to say. However, part of the intention was clearly to prevent the reserves being committed too early or all at once, and the leaders of the various reserve divisions had strict orders not to enter the fray until called forward by Ridolfo Gonzaga and no one else.

The battle opened in mid-afternoon with a brief artillery duel across the Taro. But heavy rain had dampened the powder and the guns on both sides were more than usually ineffective. The rain had also swollen the river suddenly, and this was seriously to affect the Italian plan. When the signal to advance was given the three spearhead columns began to cross the river. The Count of Caiazzo attacked the van with indifferent success; his infantry were badly cut up by the Swiss who outnumbered them, and elements of his troops were soon fleeing towards Parma. However, he achieved his task of keeping the French vanguard occupied. The stradiots also reached their first objective and harried the French left flank. But when two of their leaders were killed, they drew off and began to plunder the baggage train, which their encircling movement had placed at their mercy. In the centre Gonzaga found it impossible to cross the river where he had intended and moved further upstream to cross close to Fortebraccio's troops. This led to delay and some confusion; but above all it meant that instead of striking the gap between the French centre and the already committed vanguard, he crossed between the centre and the rearguard, thus exposing his flank to the full weight of the French centre. Here in the space of less than an hour the battle was decided. The element of surprise was lost by the delays, and Gonzaga and Fortebraccio found their squadrons depleted by the difficulties of crossing the river. They bore the full brunt of the counter-attacks of the French and no reserves came forward, as Ridolfo Gonzaga was mortally wounded at the height of the battle. Thus more than half the Italian army never got into action at all. The heavily mauled divisions of Gonzaga and Fortebraccio gave almost as good as they got; the two leaders particularly fighting with exceptional gallantry. At one point they came close to capturing Charles, but so furious a battle could not last for long. Both armies drew back to regroup, and then approaching darkness prevented a resumption of fighting.

The outcome of the battle appeared uncertain, and both sides claimed a victory. The French had achieved their aim of opening a road northwards, as they were able to resume their march stealthily the next night. They had inflicted the heavier casualties on Gonzaga's army which lost over 2,000 men, including a number of captains. The Italians could claim to be the masters of the field as the French drew off, and they captured the French baggage, including Charles' personal illustrated record of his many amorous conquests. They also took more prisoners. These perhaps, in terms of Italian warfare, were indications of victory; but Fornovo was fought for specific objectives, and Gonzaga failed to achieve his objective; so he can be said in real terms to have lost the battle. But he lost it not because the Swiss infantry and French artillery were invincible; neither of these elements played much part. Nor did he lose it because the French fought better or with more determination. He did not even lose it because a part of his army got out of hand, notably the stradiots, and another part, the Milanese, did not press their attack (perhaps on instructions from Milan), although these were the excuses given for the lack of success. Three factors really contributed to the Italian failure. First there was the sudden rising of the Taro which badly disrupted the Italian plan and caused last minute confusion. Secondly both Francesco Gonzaga and his uncle elected to lead the army, and thus no one was really in a position to direct the whole battle. Gonzaga, although he showed great personal bravery and many of the ideal qualities of a subordinate commander, had not appreciated that so large and complex an army needed to be directed from behind. This was by no means a typical Italian mistake; neither Braccio nor Sforza would ever have allowed themselves to make it. Finally the sheer size of the army and complexity of the battle plan frustrated success. This sudden attempt to translate tactics which could work well with a small army used to cooperation to a large composite army which had come together for the first time, was bound to run into difficulties. More traditional tactics would probably have won the day by sheer weight of numbers, which is a curious reflection on the theory that Italian methods were outdated and superseded.

Fornovo was one of the two major battles in the whole period between 1494 and 1530 when a largely Italian army met the invaders in the open field. It is therefore one of the few occasions when one can seek to assess the relative merits of Italian and ultramontane military methods. For the rest of the time the political disunity of Italy and political weakness of most of the states made combination against the invaders and a real trial of strength impossible. Italians fought, some-times distinguished themselves, and occasionally disgraced themselves, on both sides in the wars, but the warfare was increasingly becoming international rather than Italian. It only remains therefore to analyse briefly the Italian contri-butions to the changes which were taking place during these protracted wars.

Charles VIII did not renew his attempts to dominate Italy, and the forces which he left in Naples were gradually over-run with the help of increasing numbers of Spanish troops. The Aragonese dynasty was re-established in Naples, but a Spanish army led by Gonsalvo de Cordoba, the Great Captain, became a permanent part of its defences. The next French invasion of Italy came in 1499 after Louis XII had succeeded Charles and added the Orleanist claim to Milan to the Ange-vin interest in Naples. The four year lull between the two invasions was filled by serious fighting in only one part of the peninsula, and this was the long war fought by Florence for the recovery of Pisa.

Pisa had declared her independence following Florence's surrender to Charles VIII in 1494, and for fifteen years its recovery was the main preoccupation of Florentine policy. This war was an interesting one in a number of respects. It saw two states totally committed to war for a protracted period; not only the Pisans, subjected to almost continuous siege, but also the Florentines found that every aspect of the life of their cities was subject to the effects of war. In this situation Florence became to some extent reconciled to the problem of standing forces, but her suspicion of the condottieri remained. It was the sort of war in which condottiere cavalry could not be seen to best advantage. Paolo Vitelli, who was executed in 1499 for failing to take Pisa, was no more unsuccessful than the French troops hired two years later for the same purpose. The problem was of course not just a military one; the Pisans received support in turn from every state in Italy, together with France and Spain, as each struck at Florence through this running sore in her side. The solutions were therefore diplomatic—to avoid offending potential allies of Pisa and isolate her diplomatically—as well as military. In the latter sphere Florence turned to increasingly permanent companies of infantry, and eventually to Machiavelli's militia, to surround Pisa and starve her into submission. But she still failed to build up the comprehensive military organisation which had long existed in Venice. She was still at the mercy of a military attack, such as those mounted against her by Cesare Borgia in 1501 and 1502, and even more conclusively by the Spanish in 1512. The sack of Prato in the latter year, and the complete humiliation of Florence's new national militia by the Spanish troops, was not so much an indication of Italian military weakness as a justification for the faith which continued, for many years to come, to be placed in professional mercenary troops rather than embryo national armies.

Nor was the success of Cesare Borgia in winning control of the Romagna in a series of campaigns between 1499 and 1503 an example of the effectiveness of militia troops as Machiavelli seemed to think. Cesare's army was essentially a mercenary army. He relied heavily on contingents of French and Spanish troops, and even in July 1502, when he was said to have assembled the best troops in Italy, his army was made up largely of the condottiere companies of men like Vitellozzo Vitelli, Oliverotto da Fermo and the Orsini, and his own Romagnol mercenaries. Cesare, like a number of other Italian commanders, was experimenting with mounted arquebusiers and, with the aid of Vitellozzo, he had assembled a fine artillery train, but the Romagnol militia, paraded briefly in the last weeks of 1502, contributed little to his military success.

Cesare Borgia's army was an effective military weapon for his limited purposes; he had some troops who would have undoubtedly given a good account of themselves against the French or the Spanish, and the French in particular went to considerable trouble to secure his assistance. But he did not have a monopoly of the good Italian troops or the effective Italian captains in the first years of the sixteenth century. The second French invasion of 1499, having absorbed Milan easily, led to a confrontation with Spain in Naples. On both sides in this war Italian commanders played a considerable role. In April 1503 at Cerignola the French and Spanish armies met for the first time in a major battle. In the French army were considerable numbers of Italian troops, but acting only in a supporting role to the French cavalry and the Swiss. On the Spanish side Gonsalvo de Cordoba relied heavily on Prospero and Fabrizio Colonna, who not only led his cavalry forces but also designed the powerful field fortification which contributed greatly to the Spanish victory. Cerignola was one of the most significant battles of the Italian Wars in that it demonstrated in the most complete fashion the answer to the problem of how to deal with the Swiss infantry square. Machiavelli was still obsessed by this problem twenty years later when he wrote his *Arte della Guerra*, but this was only an indication of the unreality of the theoretical framework within which he was writing. The Swiss were never the masters of the battlefields of the Italian Wars as they had been twenty years earlier; Spanish strength linked to the tactical conceptions of the Italian condottieri saw to that, and Cerignola was the turning point.

At Cerignola the Colonna brothers prepared a long ditch and rampart in front of the Spanish position. Behind this were placed the infantry made up of *Landsknechte* in the centre and large numbers of crossbowmen and arquebusiers on the flanks. Further out on either flank were stationed bodies of light cavalry, while the heavy cavalry was held in the rear in reserve under Prospero Colonna. The French attacked this position without fully reconnoitring it. First the heavy cavalry and then the Swiss were held up by the ditch and caught in a murderous crossfire from the arquebusiers. Confusion quickly spread, and, when the Spanish and Italian cavalry charged in on both flanks, the Swiss square was already broken and defenceless. The combination of field fortifications, hand firearms and light cavalry had proved the answer, and Cordoba and the Colonna brothers in finding that answer were profiting from the experiments of earlier condottiere warfare.

Cerignola was also the turning point in this war in Naples. The French, demoralised, began to retreat and were badly defeated again at the battle of the Garigliano later in the year. On this occasion Francesco Gonzaga had command of the French army, and proved no match for the tactical skill of Cordoba, the Colonna, and now also Bartolomeo d'Alviano, who proved himself a master of light cavalry tactics.

Most of the Italians involved in this campaign were Neapolitan and papal troops; the army of Venice was still waiting on the sidelines, committed to a war with the Turks until 1503. Venice had supported the French invasion in 1499 and still remained allied to France, although taking no serious part in the wars, until in February 1508 her northern Alpine frontiers were invaded by an imperial army anxious to participate in the spoils of a division of Italy. The imperialists were weak and the invading army contained no more than 5–6,000 Swiss and German infantry. It was completely out-manoeuvred and utterly defeated by Bartolomeo d'Alviano near Pieve di Cadore. This was a notable victory for an Italian army largely composed of infantry and light cavalry, and it established d'Alviano alongside the Colonna brothers and Gian Jacopo Trivulzio, who now commanded the French forces in Milan, amongst the leading captains of the day.

But this humiliation of the Emperor and Venice's refusal to accept foreign control of Italy brought down on her in the last months of 1508 a combination of all the foreign powers together with the pope, Julius II, in the League of Cambrai. The decision to partition Venice and her large mainland empire was put into operation with less alacrity and determination than might have been expected, so that in the spring of 1509 it was only the French army attacking from the east which posed an immediate danger. This led to the second and final confrontation between a completely Italian army and the invaders at Agnadello.

The opposing armies at Agnadello were fairly evenly matched. The Venetians, commanded by Pitigliano and d'Alviano, had 10,000 cavalry and 22,000 infantry in the field; the infantry consisted of 9,000 militia dressed in their uniforms of red and white, and a core of Romagnol pike infantry trained in the manner of the Swiss. The French began to cross the frontier line of the Adda with almost 40,000 men including 15,000 heavy cavalry and 8,000 Swiss. The opportunity to attack the French while they were crossing the river was lost, as Pitigliano, the supreme commander, preferred to dig himself in and await the French assault in a powerful fortified camp. Pitigliano was an experienced condottiere of the old school; he lacked the confidence and the panache of d'Alviano, but there is no reason to suppose that, had he been allowed to keep to his plan, he would not have made the French pay dearly for an attack on his position. The French were certainly aware of this and hesitated in their advance; d'Alviano was all for ignoring the French army and making a swift counter-move against Milan itself. But this daring idea was rejected and, on orders from Venice, Pitigliano began to move his army cautiously forward, intending to occupy new fortified positions in a more commanding position. The move from one fortified camp to another was the undoing of the Venetians because it enabled the French to attack them in the open. In fact it was the Venetian rearguard, commanded by d'Alviano himself, which took the brunt of the French attack, and initially repelled it with heavy losses. However, the Venetian army was too spread out to take advantage of this situation, and the column next to d'Alviano's, commanded by Antonio Pio da Carpi, did not move to his assistance. Indeed, when it was itself attacked by the ever-increasing concentration of French forces, the newly arrived militia from Brescia which made up a large part of the column, broke and fled. This left d'Alviano and his rear-guard completely isolated with Pitigliano still some two kilometres away and reluctant to commit the remainder of the army to this dangerous situation. D'Alviano was now in a hopeless position; he and his small force of cavalry were surrounded and captured; his infantry fought on desperately. Surrounded by overwhelming numbers of Swiss and Gascons, their leaders soon all killed, they were eventually annihilated.

The defeat at Agnadello had some similarities to Fornovo. In this case the Italian army was caught in a disadvantageous position, but again it was the failure to coordinate properly a large army which materially affected the result. Most of the troops actually involved gave a very good account of themselves. The flight of the Brescia militia was decisive, but other militia elements fought with outstanding heroism, and the condottiere troops stood equally firm. D'Alviano did all that could be done by one man to retrieve the situation;

Pitigliano's judgment and caution could certainly be questioned, but his action had some justification, and the fact that half the army was saved was to be an important factor in the subsequent campaign. The heroic defence of Padua two months later was made possible because so much of the army, and particularly the Romagnol infantry, had been preserved intact.

In the remaining battles of these wars, Italian troops and Italian leaders were heavily involved, but never again as a complete army. At Ravenna in 1512 the Ferrarese artillery of Alfonso d'Este played a major part in the French victory, while a large contingent of papal infantry, led by Ramazzotto da Forlì, fought gallantly on the Spanish side. The commander of the Spanish light cavalry at this battle was the Marquis of Pescara, an Aragonese–Neapolitan nobleman who was to become one of the most famous leaders in the later campaigns.

At Marignano in 1515, when the French recovered Milan, it was Trivulzio, who had been a decisive leader at Agnadello, who still led the French army, and d'Alviano with the Venetian cavalry who delivered the *coup de grace* to the Swiss. At Bicocca in 1522, the victorious Spanish army was commanded by the Marquis of Pescara and Prospero Colonna, and owed their victory to Colonna's field fortifications and massive numbers of Spanish arquebusiers. On the French side, between two enormous squares of Swiss in the front line, were the mounted arquebusiers of yet another Italian leader, Giovanni de' Medici, the famous Giovanni delle Bande Nere. But by the time of Pavia in 1525, the last of the major battles of these wars, the battle at which French hopes of Italian conquest finally faded and at which the French king, Francis I, was captured, the role of the Italians was somewhat reduced. There were probably 3,000–4,000 Italian troops on each side, of whom the most notable were the Black Bands of Giovanni de' Medici, who were described as being amongst the finest troops in the French army. But Giovanni himself was wounded just before the battle and his companies, although they fought gallantly, were overwhelmed and largely destroyed by German *Landsknechte*. With Francis I was Teodoro Trivulzio, cousin of the more famous Gian Jacopo but a far less experienced commander. On the imperialist side was still Pescara, and his nephew Alfonso d'Avalos, Marquis del Vasto, with a few Neapolitan troops. But it was many years since any of these men had fought for an Italian state, and the links with the military scene of limited numbers and limited objectives before 1494 were becoming more and more remote.

Italian soldiers and Italian traditions had contributed much to military developments during these wars, but the only field in which they still predominated was in that of military engineering and architecture. Most of the fortifications built were the work of Italian architects. Francesco di Giorgio Martini, who had designed fortresses and siege works for Federigo da Montefeltro, was still active in Naples in the 1490's. With him was Fra Giocondo, the Veronese architect who later designed the Venetian fortifications at Padua. The successor to Fra Giocondo in Venetian service was Sanmicheli, who was trained in Rome in the tradition of Bramante and the Sangallos and whose fortification work can still be seen all over the Veneto and the Venetian overseas empire. In central Italy the fortresses built by the Sangallo family stretch from Poggio Imperiale (1488) and the Fortezza del Basso (1534) in Tuscany to Civita Castellana (1494) and Nettuno (1502) in the Papal States. Leonardo da Vinci was inspector of fortresses for Cesare Borgia, and Michelangelo strengthened the fortifications of Florence in 1529.

But the only Italian army which remained intact in 1530 with traditions reaching back into the fifteenth century was that of Venice. Milan and Naples were now Spanish. Florence, besieged in that year by an imperialist army, had little or no army with which to defend itself. It relied on a hastily formed militia and the mercenaries of Malatesta Baglioni, employed for the occasion. The pope still had an army, but it was small, its components fluctuated, its traditions were few; it had been able to do little to save Rome from sack by the imperialists in 1527. While it would certainly be wrong to end a history of Italian warfare in the Renaissance in 1494, it would be equally wrong to try to continue it beyond 1530.

CHAPTER TEN

CONCLUSION

One of the principal protagonists of the humanistic debate which forms the framework of Machiavelli's *Art of War* was Fabrizio Colonna. Colonna was a leading Italian captain of his day and one of the principal architects of Spain's ultimate victory in the Italian Wars. His role in the *Art of War* epitomises the essential dichotomy in Italian attitudes towards soldiers. On the one side he was the representative of the condottieri, the faithless, violent and unprincipled mercenaries who monopolised Italy's military skills and debased her military virtues. On the other side he represented a late fifteenth-century ideal, the valiant captain who was also a civilised and educated patron and a respected leader of society.

One of the aims of this book has been to consider the relationships and the links between these apparently opposed views. The fifteenth-century condottiere was not the foreign mercenary in the sense that he had often been in the fourteenth century. He was gradually transformed into a relatively faithful, increasingly aristocratic, and highly professional captain. His relationships with his employers evolved in an atmosphere of growing permanence and tightening control. The supposed rape of the Duchess of Bavaria by Sigismondo Malatesta and the abduction of Dorotea Caracciolo by Cesare Borgia were *causes célèbres* and not everyday occurrences. The captain of the late fifteenth century was more likely to spend his idle hours playing chess, listening to his musicians, and gambling, than dreaming of conquests, counting his profits, or torturing his prisoners. Mars was seen less as the warrior god of war than as the lover of Venus.

It may be argued with some truth that all this made the condottiere a less effective soldier, but the Italian soldier at the end of the fifteenth century was hampered by a good deal more than his own increased civility. Nor was the desire for individual achievement and glory entirely stifled. Luigi da Porto commented in his letters that it was better for a soldier to take part in small skirmishes because 'in a small number everybody's *virtù* can be seen'. Similarly the importance attached by both contemporaries and later Italian historians to the chivalric affray at Barletta in 1503, when thirteen Italian knights overcame thirteen French knights in a tournament outside the walls of the besieged city, indicates a continuing stream in Italian military thinking. This lingering emphasis on individual prowess was anachronistic and even positively harmful in the days of the mass armies of the Italian Wars, but it, like the domestication of the condottiere, contributed to that other side of Fabrizio Colonna, the valiant and civilised captain.

But, of course, the ideal of the civilised soldier of Castiglione and Paolo Giovio was as exaggerated, if not as anachronistic, as the caricature of the worthless condottiere of Machiavelli. Fabrizio Colonna was still a mercenary as were the majority of his fellows. The armies of the sixteenth and seventeenth centuries differed little from those of the fifteenth century except in size and improved techniques. Men like the Constable of Bourbon, Pedro Navarro and Colonna himself were as likely to desert their employers as were Sforza and Braccio a century earlier. The armies they commanded were filled with Swiss and German mercenaries.

Machiavelli perceived an ultimate truth not a contemporary reality when he pointed to national armies as the answer to the problem of military strength. In practical terms his militia experiments were a disaster and his detailed tactical conceptions unworkable. Exaggeration is one of the weapons of the rhetorician and Machiavelli was certainly that. In his practical reflections on war his premises were anachronistic and his solutions unrealistic. This is summed up in the probably apocryphal story of his encounter with another of the leading soldiers of his day, Giovanni de' Medici. Giovanni is said to have offered him the services of the Black Bands to try out his ideas on military formations and tactics in practice. After an exhausting morning on a hot parade ground, Machiavelli had reduced these usually disciplined troops to chaos; finally Giovanni himself intervened and with a few quick commands restored order and brought the demonstration to a close.

But it is not at the practical level that one must seek the lasting significance of Machiavelli's writings on war. As so often he was saying nothing that intelligent and well-informed Italians of his day did not realise already, but he was saying it with an urgency and a relevance which impressed and shocked contemporaries and made his writings lastingly influential. He was aware that the dimensions of war had changed even though he was unable to isolate the exact way in which the nature of war was changing.

It was the scale of the Italian Wars which created their enormous impact on European warfare. The emphasis on size and permanence of armies produced not only more disciplined and extensive use of already known weapons and techniques, but also placed a premium on co-ordination and cooperation between arms. The days had passed when a single arm—whether it was the French heavy cavalry or the Swiss pikes—could dominate the battlefield. The later victories of the wars were won by tactical co-ordination between heavy and light cavalry, mixed infantry and artillery. The French had brought to the wars a large permanent cavalry army and the recently acquired strength of the massed pike infantry; both produced an emphasis on the crushing blow, the set-piece battle. The Italians brought smaller more mixed armies and a tradition of attritional warfare which produced an emphasis on manoeuvre and strategy. The Spaniards created a fusion of these traditions and emerged the ultimate victors.

The Italian Wars were a vast melting pot; the heat and flames were new, the ingredients were not. Italy had contributed significantly to those ingredients even though she herself was to be consumed in the flames.

BIBLIOGRAPHICAL NOTES

The main aim of these notes is to provide reference to further reading in English. Only important works in other languages will be mentioned, together with some subsidiary titles which contain the only available treatment of specific points.

The following abbreviations are used in these notes:

ASM.	Archivio di Stato, Milan.
ASV.	Archivio di Stato, Venice.
ASF.	Archivio di Stato, Florence.
ASR.	Archivio di Stato, Rome.
AV.	Archivio Vaticano.
EHR.	*English Historical Review.*
ASI.	*Archivio storico italiano.*
ASL.	*Archivio storico lombardo.*
AMR.	*Atti e memorie della deputazione di storia patria per la Romagna.*
ASPN.	*Archivio storico per le provincie napoletane.*
ASRSP.	*Archivio della società romana di storia patria.*
Boll. Umb.	*Bollettino della deputazione di storia patria per l'Umbria.*

INTRODUCTION

There is a fundamental need for a comparative approach to the history of warfare in this period. Much important work is being done in individual countries, but for an overall view we are still dependent on the completely outdated C. Oman, *The History of the Art of War in the Middle Ages* (London, 1924). Unfortunately the splendid chapters on warfare in the *New Cambridge Modern History* by J. R. Hale only take up the story at the end of the fifteenth century. But P. Pieri, '*Sur les dimensions de l'histoire militaire*', *Annales*, xviii, 1963, has drawn attention to the needs and possibilities of the field, and some of the most recent works from which I have drawn great profit, inspiration and hope are:

K. Fowler, *The Hundred Years' War* (London, 1971)—a useful collection of essays (see p. 88 for my quotation on p. 2);

H. J. Hewitt, *The Organisation of War under Edward III, 1338–62* (Manchester, 1966);

R. A. Newhall, *Muster and Review; a problem of English military administration, 1420–40* (Cambridge, Mass., 1940);

P. Contamine, *Guerre, État et Société à la fin du Moyen Age; études sur les armées des rois de France, 1337–1494* (Paris, 1972);

C. Brusten, *L'armée bourguignonne de 1465 à 1468* (Brussels, 1953);

P. Stewart, 'The Soldier, the Bureaucrat and Fiscal Records in the Army of Ferdinand and Isabella', *Hispanic American Historical Review*, xlix, 1969;

F. Redlich, *The German Military Enterpriser and his Work Force* (Wiesbaden, 1964);

B. D. Lyon, *From Fief to Indenture; the transition from feudal to non-feudal contract in Western Europe* (Cambridge, Mass., 1957).

CHAPTER ONE

The most useful general books in English on thirteenth-century Italy are:

J. K. Hyde, *Society and Politics in Medieval Italy; the evolution of the civil life, 1000–1350* (London, 1973);

P. Partner, *The Lands of St. Peter* (London, 1972);

D. Waley, *The Papal State in the Thirteenth Century* (London, 1961);

D. Waley, *The Italian City Republics* (London, 1969);

S. Runciman, *The Sicilian Vespers* (Cambridge, 1958);

S. Kantorowicz, *Frederick II* (London, 1931);

G. Masson, *Frederick II of Hohenstaufen* (London, 1957).

Thirteenth-century warfare in Italy has received little attention. Again Oman is the only general view available to English readers, but J. Beeler, *Warfare in Feudal Europe, 730–1200* (Cornell, 1971) does have a certain amount to say about the thirteenth century, and O. L. Spaulding, *Warfare; a study of military methods from earliest times* (New York, 1925) describes some of the major battles. A classic work on the period is H. Delpech, *La tactique au XIIIᵉ siècle* (Paris, 1886), but he has relatively little information about Italy. Specifically on Italian warfare are: D. P. Waley, 'Papal Armies in the Thirteenth Century', *EHR.*, lxxii, 1957, and 'The Army of the Florentine Republic from the 12th. to 14th. Century', in *Florentine Studies*, ed. N. Rubinstein (London, 1968).

For the details of the battle of Campaldino, see R. Davidsohn, *Storia di Firenze* (Florence, 1957—Italian translation), ii, pp. 458–65.

CHAPTER TWO

The main works on warfare in fourteenth-century Italy are:

E. Ricotti, *Storia delle compagnie di ventura in Italia* (Turin, 1893—2nd. ed.) 2 Vols. with appendices of documents;

G. Canestrini, *'Documenti per servire alla storia della milizia italiana dal secolo XIII al XVI', ASI.*, xv, 1851;

D. M. Bueno de Mesquita, 'Some Condottieri of the Trecento', *Proceedings of the British Academy*, xxxii, 1951;

D. P. Waley, 'The Army of the Florentine Republic', *cit.*

The most recent survey in English is G. Trease, *The Condottieri* (London, 1970), an unsatisfactory and rather traditional account, but at its best for the fourteenth century.

Biographies in English are limited to those of Hawkwood of which J. Temple Leader, *Sir John Hawkwood* (London, 1889) is still valuable, while F. Gaup, 'The Condottiere John Hawkwood', *History*, xxiii, 1938-9 is less so.

The estimate of the number of Germans in Italy (p. 29) comes from K. H. Schäfer, *Deutscher Ritter und Edelknechte in Italien* (Paderborn, 1914), p. 6.

The description of Fra Moriale's company is from M. Villani, *Cronica*, ed. Montier (Florence, 1825), ii, pp. 146-8.

On the use of militia forces in the fourteenth century, see W. M. Bowsky, 'City and Contado; military relationships and communal bonds in fourteenth-century Siena', *Renaissance Studies in honour of Hans Baron* (Florence, 1971) and S. Salvemini, *I balestrieri del comune di Firenze* (Bari, 1905).

The details of the Florentine campaign against Pistoia in 1302 are in C. Paoli, 'Rendiconto e approvazione di spesi occorse nell'esercito fiorentino contro Pistoia, maggio 1302', *ASI.*, 3rd. ser., vi, 1867.

The account of the war between Siena and Perugia is largely drawn from W. Heywood, 'La guerra di Perugia con Siena, 1357-8', *Bullettino senese di storia patria*, xiv, 1907.

Machiavelli's *Life of Castruccio Castracane* is available in English translation in A. H. Gilbert, *Machiavelli. The Chief Works and Others* (Duke University Press, 1965). For Francesco degli Ordelaffi, see E. Balzani-Maltoni, 'La signoria di Francesco Ordelaffi', *Studi Romagnoli*, xv, 1964, and for the wider political background of Ordelaffi and his fellow Romagna princes, J. Larner, *Lords of the Romagna* (London, 1965).

CHAPTER THREE

The Italian political scene between 1378 and 1424 is both confused and poorly treated in English. There are two fundamental detailed studies: D. M. Bueno de Mesquita, *Giangaleazzo Visconti* (Cambridge, 1941) and P. Partner, *The Papal State under Martin V* (British School at Rome, 1958). The ideological implications of the struggle between Florence and Milan are discussed by H. Baron, *The Crisis of the Early Italian Renaissance*

(Princeton, 1966—rev. ed.). A useful recent survey of the period is B. Pullan, *History of Early Renaissance Italy* (London, 1973). Vols. V and VI of the Fondazione Treccani, *Storia di Milano* (Milan, 1955) are useful to fill some of the gaps.

On the condottieri in this period of transition the works of Ricotti, Canestrini, Mesquita and Trease cited above remain important, but from this point onwards the fundamental work for the understanding of Italian warfare is P. Pieri, *Il Rinascimento e la crisi militare italiana* (Turin, 1952—2nd. ed.). This is a book which is not untouched with nationalistic bias and it tends to exaggerate the Italian role in wider military developments, but it remains a seminal re-appraisal of the military scene in Italy and is equipped with excellent bibliographies.

Only N. Valeri, *La vita di Facino Cane* (Turin, 1940) carries much weight amongst the various full-length biographies of condottieri of this period, but the gap is beginning to be filled by the *Dizionario biografico degli italiani* where the Attendoli receive reasonable treatment.

On Boldrino da Panicale there are two useful articles: G. Franceschini, 'Boldrino da Panicale (1331?–91)', *Boll. Umb.*, xlvi, 1949, and G. Cecchini, 'Boldrino da Panicale', *Boll. Umb.*, lix, 1962.

For the Malatesta family C. Yriarte, *Un condottiere au XVᵉ siècle; Rimini* (Paris, 1882) is still useful. However the full resources of the rich collection of Malatesta documents and administrative volumes in the state archive in Fano have not yet been fully exploited, particularly for Pandolfo Malatesta. The quotation about Carlo Malatesta on p, 64 comes from *Le commissioni di Rinaldo degli Albizzi*, ed. C. Guasti (Florence, 1867–73), i, p. 460.

For the Venetian army in the early fifteenth century, see M. E. Mallett, 'Venice and its condottieri, 1404–54', in *Renaissance Venice*, ed. J. R. Hale (London, 1973), while Florentine military affairs in this period are treated from a rather different angle by C. C. Bayley, *War and Society in Renaissance Florence* (Toronto, 1961).

A recent account of the life of Pippo Spano is in C. Ugurgieri della Berardenga, *Avventurieri alla conquista di feudi e di corona, 1356–1429* (Florence, 1962), pp. 117–224.

The quotation describing Musio Attendolo Sforza comes from the *Cronaca universale di Gaspare Broglia*, f. 153, in the Biblioteca Gambalunga, Rimini.

CHAPTER FOUR

The general works on the condottieri cited at the beginning of the notes on chapter II serve also as background to this chapter, although they rarely touch on the organisational aspects of the relationships between soldiers and employers. Some of the older biographies of fifteenth-century condottieri are still useful, eg.: L. Collisen-Morley, *The Story of the Sforzas* (London, 1933); L. Bignami, *Francesco Sforza* (Milan, 1938); G. Eroli, *Erasmo Gattamelata da Narni; suoi monumenti e sua famiglia* (Rome, 1877); B. Belotti, *Vita di Bartolomeo Colleoni* (Bergamo, 1933—2nd. ed.); R. De la Sizeranne, *Le vertueux condottiere, Federigo da Montefeltro, Duc d'Urbino* (Paris, 1927); J. Dennistoun, *Memoirs of the Dukes of Urbino, 1440–1630* (London, 1902—rev. ed.); G. Franceschini, *I Montefeltro* (Milan, 1970); C. Yriarte, *Un condottiere au XVe siècle; Rimini* (Paris, 1882); E. Hutton, *Sigismondo Malatesta, Lord of Rimini* (London, 1906).

It is surprisingly difficult to find either detailed discussion or publication of *condotte*. R. Predelli, *I Libri Commemoriali della Repubblica di Venezia, Regesti* (Monumenti storici pubblicati dalla R. Deputazione veneta di storia patria, 1st. Ser., Documenti, 1883–) provides summaries of many Venetian *condotte* and A. Theiner, *Codex diplomaticus dominii temporalis S. Sedis* (Rome, 1882) publishes a number of papal *condotte*. But the similar Milanese publication, L. Osio, *Documenti diplomatici tratti dagli archivi milanesi* (Milan, 1874–1887) has only a very few Milanese contracts. However, both Ricotti and Canestrini, *cit.*, publish some.

Micheletto Attendolo has attracted a good deal of attention recently because of the discovery in Arezzo of a large collection of the records of his company kept by his treasurer, Francesco di Viviano da Arezzo. These remarkable accounts are being studied by Prof. Mario del Treppo, who intends to publish a detailed report on them in the near future. I have not yet been able to examine them in detail and rely for my information largely on the kindness of Prof. Del Treppo and the material communicated by him to the Gattamelata congress held at Narni in 1970, the proceedings of which will also be published shortly. There is a useful biographical sketch in the *Dizionario biografico degli italiani*, iv, pp. 542–3, although this was written before the Arezzo documents were discovered.

My account of Micheletto's negotiations with Florence in 1431 is derived from F. C. Pellegrini, *Appendice di documenti tratti dal R. Archivio di Stato di Firenze relativi alla tesi di F.C.P.* (Pisa, 1891) pp. lviiii–lx, xcvii, cxiii, and ASF. Miscellanea Repubblica, 5 (13 April 1431). Micheletto Attendolo's *condotta* of 13 Nov. 1432, which was a renewal of the one discussed in the previous year, was published by Canestrini, *op. cit.*, pp. 133–45. The quotations about Micheletto on pp. 77 and 103 come from Pellegrini, pp. lviiii and cxiii. For an account of another interesting controversy between a condottiere and his employer later in the century, see C. M. Ady, *The Bentivoglio of Bologna* (London, 1937) pp. 76–7.

There are no general studies of the activities of *provveditori* and commissaries. The *Commissioni di Rinaldo degli Albizzi*, ed. C. Guasti (Florence, 1867–73) give an idea of the occasional involvement in this capacity of one particular Florentine politician, while S. Troilo, *Andrea Giuliano; politico e letterato veneziano del Quattrocento*, in Biblioteca dell'Archivum Romanicum, ser. I, 16–18 (Florence, 1931–2) discusses a Venetian who frequently served as *provveditore*. For the general view of the *provveditori* quoted on pp. 88–9, see Ricotti, *op. cit.*, ii, p. 18. For the relations between Sigismondo Malatesta and Andrea Dandolo, see G. Soranzo, 'Sigismondo Pandolfo Malatesta in Morea e le vicende del suo dominio', *AMR.*, 4th. ser., viii, 1918.

On reward systems, see M. E. Mallett, 'Venice and its condottieri', *cit.* Milanese condottiere fiefs are discussed by D. M. Bueno de Mesquita, 'Ludovico Sforza and his vassals', *Italian Renaissance Studies*, ed. E. F. Jacob (London, 1960).

Some of the treacheries and executions of condottieri are covered by a mass of detailed, and often polemical, literature, particularly the deaths of Carmagnola and Jacopo Piccinino. The confession of Giovanbattista da Narni, chancellor of Tiberto Brandolini, is to be found in ASM. Autografi 204, fasc. 55, while the affair of Baldaccio d'Anghiari is discussed in L. Passerini, 'Baldaccio d'Anghiari', *ASI.*, 3rd. ser., iii, 1866.

The material on Carmagnola's rows with the Venetian senate comes from ASV., Senatus secreta, reg. 11 and 12, *passim*.

Florence's financial difficulties in the 1450's can be explored through ASF. Dieci, Deliberazioni, condotte e stanziamenti, 19 and ASF., Signoria e Collegi, Condotte e stanziamenti, 9. Alessandro Sforza's letter from which I quote on p. 101 is in Biblioteca Ambrosiana (Milan), Z. 226 sup. fasc. 7.

Bernardino da Todi's letters were published by G. Degli Azzi Vitelleschi, 'Un condottiere tuderte al servizio dei fiorentini; Bernardino da Todi', *Boll. Umb.*, xix, 1915.

The quotation attributed to Filippo Maria Visconti and cited on p. 105 comes from Ricotti, *op. cit.*, ii, p. 50.

CHAPTER FIVE

There is no general work to which one can refer for a discussion of the organisation of Italian warfare, and indeed the very existence of military administrators has been largely ignored by historians. On the organisation of companies the recently discovered records of Micheletto Attendolo's company are likely to be of fundamental importance. No similar collection of material is available for any other condottiere company, and the works on individual condottieri have rarely been able to say very much about their companies. The muster roll of Piero Gianpaolo

Orsini's company is to be found in ASR. Soldatesche e galere, 80, 4, ff. 44–82, and that of Tiberto Brandolini's company in ASM. Autografi 204, fasc. 55.

On the French reforms, see Contamine, *Guerre, État e Société, cit.*, pp. 277–290, and for the impact of these on popular opinion, see P. D. Solon, 'Popular Response to Standing Military Forces in Fifteenth-Century France', *Studies in the Renaissance*, xix, 1972. Philippe de Commynes' comments on these reforms came in his *Memoires*, ed. F. Calmette (Paris, 1924), ii, pp. 289–90.

The story of the emergence of permanent forces outside the company organisation in Italian armies has to be pieced together from scattered references. The Milanese *provisionati* of the fourteenth century were described in C. Capasso, 'I *provisionati* di Bernabò Visconti', *ASL.*, 4th. ser., xv, 1911. The Milanese army lists of the second half of the fifteenth century, of which a number are scattered through ASM., Miscellanea storica, make clear the important role of these troops by this time. The famous 1472 list was published by E. C. Visconti, 'Ordine dell'esercito ducale sforzesco, 1472–4', *ASL.*, iii, 1876. Prior to this references to the *famiglia* are to be found in *Storia di Milano*, vol. VI and in M. Sanuto, *Vite de' duchi di Venezia*, Rerum Italicarum Scriptores, xxii (Milan, 1733), p. 1088. Sanuto is also the source for a number of lists of Italian army strengths in this period. P. Pieri's chapter in *Storia di Milano*, VIII, is a valuable account of Milanese military organisation in the second half of the fifteenth century; the reference to the ambassador's report (p. 118) is to be found in P. M. Kendall & V. Ilardi, *Dispatches of the Milanese Ambassadors in France and Burgundy, 1450–83* (Athens, Ohio, 1970), i, pp. 230–1.

On the emergence of permanent elements in the Neapolitan army, see Ricotti, *op. cit.*, ii, p. 95 and P. Gentile, 'Lo stato napoletano sotto Alfonso I d'Aragona', *ASPN.*, lxii–iii, 1937–8. The reference to Alfonso d'Avalos comes from F. Trinchera, *Codice* Aragonese (Naples, 1866), i, p. 38.

The main sources for a study of the papal army in this period are the scattered records in ASR. Soldatesche e galere, 80–6. Some material from these had been put together by A. Da Mosto, 'Ordinamenti militari delle soldatesche dello stato Romano dal 1430 al 1470', *Quellen und Forschungen aus italienischen Archiven und Bibliotheken*, v, 1902. The accounts of the Camera Apostolica (AV. Introitus et Exitus) also give some impression of the men who were being employed in the papal army, and a number of volumes of *condotte* survive in AV. Diversa Cameralia. Administrative records for the Venetian army in the fifteenth century have not so far come to light, but a good deal of material can be found in the Senate proceedings (ASV. Senatus Secreta, Senatus Misti, and, after 1440, Senatus Terra). I am at present preparing a full-length study of the Venetian army, in collaboration with J. R. Hale, which will be published shortly.

In Florence, also, there are no complete series of military administrative records, but a fair number of *condotta* records, pay accounts and muster rolls remain in the archives of the Signoria and the Ten of War.

Little has been written about military administrators in the fifteenth century. For a brief account of the role of the Milanese *collaterali*, see C. Santoro, *Gli Offici dell' amministrazione centrale del comune di Milano e del dominio Visconteo-Sforzesco* (Milan, 1968), pp. 218 and 259–60, and on Orfeo da Ricavo there is a brief note in L. Cerioni, *La diplomazia Sforzesca* (Rome, 1970), i, pp. 164–5. For the detailed references to Belpetro Manelmi's career, see my article on the Venetian condottieri published in *Renaissance Venice, cit.*; Chierighino Chiericati has received notice in G. Zorzi, 'Un vicentino alla corte di Paolo II; Chierighino Chiericati e il suo trattatello della milizia', *Nuovo archivio veneto*, ns. xxx, 1915. Diomede Carafa was the subject of a recent article by J. D. Moores, 'New light on Diomede Carafa and his "perfect loyalty" to Ferrante of Aragon', *Italian Studies*, xxvi, 1971, and his treatise, together with that of Orso Orsini, was studied by P. Pieri, 'Il "Governo et exercitio de la militia" di Orso degli Orsini e i "Memoriali" di Diomede Carafa', *ASPN.*, xix, 1933.

Luca di Maso degli Albizzi's diary describing his period with the army is in ASF. Signoria, Otto e Dieci, 5, III; it is discussed in more detail in chapter VII. For Manelmi's comments on the Florentine infantry in 1431, see Pellegrini, *op. cit.*, p. xxviii, and the letter of Gian Jacopo Trivulzio, referred to on pp. 130–1, is to be found in Ricotti, *op. cit.*, ii, p. 132. Philippe de Commynes' remarks are in his *Memoires, cit.*, ii, pp. 272–3.

P. Partner in his *Papal State under Martin V, cit.*, pp. 155–8 has some discussion of military pay scales as does A. Molho, *Florentine Public Finance in the Early Renaissance* (Cambridge, Mass., 1971), pp. 9–21. The latter, however, causes some confusion by mistaking the advance of several months' pay for a monthly rate and thus exaggerates the costs of war and the greediness of soldiers. The details of the pay of Galeotto da Sanseverino's company (p. 138) come from ASM. Autografi 206, fasc. 26, while the story of Ferrando da Spagna in Venetian pay is to be found in ASV. Senatus Terra 2, ff. 41v–42.

The barracks built by Caterina Sforza for her troops are described in Archivio di Stato, Forlì, Consigli generali e segreti, 1, ff. 5–8; Alfonso V's winter quarters are mentioned in G. Forte, 'Di Castiglione della Pescaia, presidio aragonese dal 1447 al 1460', *Maremma*, iii–iv, 1934–5, pp. 24–5.

The arrangements for Venetian demobilisation in 1405 are described in ASV. Senatus Secreta 2, ff. 189v–190v.

CHAPTER SIX

The denigration of Italian warfare has been so general amongst the older writers on the art of war that it would be useless to catalogue all the relevant authors here. A process of rehabilitation started with W. Block, *Die Condottieri; Studien über die sogenannten 'unblütigen Schlachten'* (Historischer Studien, 110, Berlin, 1913) who exposed some of the fallacies of the view of Italian warfare as a bloodless game. F. L. Taylor, *The Art of War in Italy, 1494-1529* (Cambridge, 1921) contributed to a re-evaluation of the condottieri and subsequently P. Pieri, *Il Rinascimento e la crisi militare italiana, cit.*, took up the Italian cause.

On Italian arms and armour the best books are: C. Blair, *European Armour* (London, 1958); A. M. Aroldi, *Armi e armatura italiana* (Milan, 1961); L. G. Boccia and E. T. Coelho, *L'arte dell' armatura in Italia* (Milan, 1967); A. Gaibi, *Le armi da fuoco portatili italiane* (Milan, 1968). There is one old article on the stradiots, E. Barbarich, 'Gli stradioti nell'arte militare veneziana', *Rivista di cavalleria*, xiii, 1904, which I have not been able to consult.

Italian infantry have been little studied. P. Pieri, 'Alfonso V e le armi italiane', in his *Scritti vari* (Turin, 1966) discusses the new sword and buckler infantry, and a number of older writers have tentatively tackled the problem of hand firearms. An impression of the wide use of hand firearms in the second half of the century can be gained from munitions lists to be found scattered through ASM. Miscellanea storica, and also particularly in an interesting munitions book kept by Bartolomeo da Cremona (ASM. Autografi 225, munizioni d'arme, fasc. 14).

The standard works on Italian artillery in this period are: C. Promis, *Dell'arte dell'ingegnere e dell'artigliere in Italia dalla sua origine* (Turin, 1841); A. Angelucci, *Documenti inediti per la storia delle armi da fuoco italiane* (Turin, 1869); C. Montu, *Storia dell'artiglieria italiana* (Rome, 1934); A. Pasquali-Lasagni, 'Note di storia dell'artiglieria dello stato della Chiesa nei secoli XIV e XV', *ASRSP.*, lx, 1937. However, for many perceptive comments on the role of artillery and reactions to it, see J. R. Hale, 'Gunpowder and the Renaissance; an essay in the history of ideas', in *From the Renaissance to the Counter Reformation: Essays in Honour of Garrett Mattingley*, ed. C. H. Carter (London, 1966), from p. 115 of which I quote on p. 163.

The classic work on Italian fortification is E. Rocchi, *Le fonti storiche dell'architettura militare* (Rome, 1908), but recently late medieval and Renaissance fortifications have been attracting considerable interest and a number of valuable monographs have appeared, notably: A. S. Weller, *Francesco di Giorgio, 1439-1501* (Chicago, 1943); G. De Fiore, *Baccio Pontelli, architetto fiorentino* (Rome, 1963); G. Severini, *Architetture militari di*

Giuliano da Sangallo (Pisa, 1970). Of particular value for the whole problem of early gunpowder fortification is J. R. Hale, 'The Early Development of the Bastion; an Italian chronology, c.1450–c.1534', in *Europe in the Late Middle Ages*, ed. Hale, Highfield & Smalley (London, 1965), to which I owe much of my information.

For the career of Domenico da Firenze, see G. Fasolo, 'Domenico di Benintendi da Firenze; ingegnere del secolo XV', *Archivio veneto*, lvii, 1927. Sanmicheli's report on the defence of Friuli was published by V. Joppi, 'Discorso circa il fortificar della città di Udine', *ASI.*, ns. xiv, 1861.

The dispatch of ambassador Panigarola from Paris in 1465 is published in B. De Mandrot, *Dépêches des ambassadeurs milanais en France sous Louis XI et Francois Sforza* (Société de l'Histoire de France, 1920), iii, p. 330. I am indebted to Dr. Martin Lowry for drawing my attention to this dispatch.

Little has been written on river warfare in this period, but see L. Rossi, 'La flotta sforzesca nel 1448–9', *Bollettino della società pavese di storia patria*, 1912 and 'Gli Eustachi di Pavia e la flotta viscontea e sforzesca nel secolo XV', *ibid.*, xiv, 1914. My information about Venetian river fleets is largely drawn from references in the senate proceedings.

The 1438–9 campaigns in Lombardy are described by G. Soranzo, 'L'ultima campagna del Gattamelata al servizio della repubblica veneta (1438–41)', *Archivio veneto*, lx–lxi, 1957 (at p. 96 he discusses Piccinino's Soave ditch).

F. L. Taylor has a useful discussion of military treatises, and those of Carafa and Orsini are fully examined by Pieri in his article cited above. For the battle of Caravaggio, see Ricotti, *op. cit.*, ii, pp. 79–82.

CHAPTER SEVEN

Luca di Maso degli Albizzi's account of the short campaign which culminated in the battle of S. Romano is to be found at ASF. Signoria, Otto e Dieci, 5, III. A short biography of Luca appears in M. E. Mallett, *The Florentine Galleys in the Fifteenth Century* (Oxford, 1967), pp. 195–201. Micheletto Attendolo's letters and others written from his camp in 1432 are in ASF., Mediceo avanti il Principato.

For Gattamelata's and Sforza's activities in 1438–9, see Soranzo, 'L'ultima campagna del Gattamelata', *cit.*

The camp regulations referred to on p. 188 were published by Eroli, *Gattamelata*, *cit.*, pp. 331–3. A similar set of regulations is to be found in Biblioteca Ambrosiana, Z 226 sup., fasc. 1. English army regulations are discussed by R. A. Newhall, *The English Conquest of Normandy*, 1416–24 (New Haven, Conn., 1924), pp. 224–30, and Niccolò de' Favri's report is mentioned in C. G. Cruikshank, *Army Royal. Henry VIII's invasion of France, 1513* (Oxford, 1969) p. 103.

The quotation from Guicciardini on p. 192 is to be found in F. Guicciardini, *Storia d'Italia*, ed. C. Panigada (Bari, 1929), ii, p. 138.

Francesco Sforza's method of sack was described in a letter of Donato del Conte to be found in A. Bertolotti, 'Spedizioni militari in Piemonte di Galeazzo Maria Sforza', ASL., X, 1883, pp. 161–2. The siege of Volterra is fully discussed by E. Fiumi, *L'impresa di Lorenzo de' Medici contro Volterra (1472)* (Florence, 1948), that of Piombino in 1448 by Forte, 'Castiglione della Pescaia', *cit.*, pp. 29–32.

Machiavelli's views on the weaknesses of Italian warfare have attracted a good deal of attention. They appear throughout his writings, particularly the *Florentine History*, in chapter XII of the *Prince*, and in the opening pages of the *Art of War*. A full-length but unduly favourable discussion of them is M. Hobohm, *Machiavellis Renaissance der Kriegskunst* (Berlin, 1913); more balanced in its approach is F. Gilbert, 'Machiavelli; the Renaissance of the art of war', in *Makers of Modern Strategy*, ed. E. M. Earle (Princeton, 1952). For a re-evaluation of Machiavelli's remarks about Cesare Borgia's militia, see J. Larner, 'Cesare Borgia, Machiavelli, and the Romagnol Militia', *Studi Romagnoli*, xvii, 1966, while the whole idea of bloodless battles has been subjected to critical scrutiny by Block, *Die Condottieri, cit.*, from which the casualty figures cited here are largely drawn.

A full biographical survey of the Italian captains of the fifteenth century is gradually emerging from my notes, but it is not possible, for reasons of space, to justify here the figure of 170 major commanders with the necessary lists and statistics. A starting point for such a survey is C. Argegni, *Condottieri, capitani e tribuni* (Milan, 1936), 3 vols, but this is a very inadequate source based almost entirely on secondary material, and it is being gradually superseded by the *Dizionario biografico degli italiani*.

On medical services in Italian armies, see F. Pellegrini, *La medecina militare nel regno di Napoli* (Verona, 1932), and the important diary of Alessandro Benedetti, chief doctor with Francesco Gonzaga's army at Fornovo in 1495, recently edited and translated by D. M. Schullian, *Diaria de Bello Carolino* (New York, 1967). The details of Giovanantonio di Gattamelata's wounds and recovery are in Cristoforo da Soldo, *Cronaca*, Rerum italicarum Scriptores, new ed. xxi, III, pp. 115–6.

The treatment of prisoners after Brentelle is discussed by R. Cessi, 'Prigionieri illustri durante la guerra fra Scaligeri e Carraresi', *Atti della R. Accademia delle scienze di Torino*, xl, 1904–5, and the case of Astorre Manfredi by P. Zama, *I Manfredi, Signori di Faenza* (Milan, 1955), pp. 182–185.

The problems of the Renaissance poisoner can be appreciated if one remembers that a popular and influential treatise on poisons was still Petrus de Abano's *De Venenis*, written in the late thirteenth century, in which the list of 'poisons' is quirkish in the extreme. For the poison plots of the Venetian Council of Ten, see ASV. Misti del Consiglio de' Dieci, 11, ff. 28v–32; 13, ff. 107–9, 163v, and 181; 14, ff. 18, 60 and 65v. The story of Pietro Brunoro and Troilo Orsini can be found in Ricotti, *op. cit.*, ii, pp. 57–8.

The quotation on p. 205 is part of a letter of Antonio, Count of Marsciano to Lorenzo in ASF. Mediceo avanti il Principato, XXXIX, 95 (4 Mar. 1484). For the best general treatment of the problem of military conventions, see M. H. Keen, *The Laws of War in the late Middle Ages* (London, 1965), however he has relatively little to say about Italy.

CHAPTER EIGHT

The theme of humanist dislike of mercenaries is developed by C. C. Bayley, *War and Society in Renaissance Florence*, cit., pp. 178–95; see also p. 107 for the remarks of Alamanno Salviati. A valuable treatment of popular attitudes to war in the latter part of the century is J. R. Hale, 'War and Public Opinion in Renaissance Italy', in *Italian Renaissance Studies*, ed. E. F. Jacob (London, 1960).

The thirteen clans cited on p. 209 are Sforza–Attendolo, Fortebracci–Piccinino, Orsini–Anguillara, Colonna, Da Sanseverino, Gattesco–Brandolini, Mauruzzi, Malatesta, Gonzaga, Manfredi, Este, Montefeltri, and Dal Verme.

The quotation on p. 210 from Guarino is to be found in Guarino da Verona, *Epistolario*, ed. R. Sabbadini (Venice, 1916–9), letter 796; I am indebted to Mr. John Law for drawing my attention to this.

Knighthood in Florence is the subject of G. Salvemini, *La dignità cavalleresca nel comune di Firenze* (Florence, 1896). On tournaments in fifteenth-century Italy, see R. Truffi, *Giostre e cantori di giostre* (Rocca S. Casciano, 1911); M. Tosi, *Il torneo di Belvedere in Vaticano e i tornei in Italia nel Cinquecento* (Rome, 1945); J. R. Gage, *Life in Italy at the time of the Medici* (London, 1968), pp. 138–149; A. Angelucci, *Ricordi e documenti di uomini e di trovati italiani per servire alla storia militare* (Turin, 1866), pp. 77–79—a description of the 1458 tournament in Venice.

The Council of Ten investigation into the associations between Venetian patricians and Francesco Sforza is to be found in ASV., Misti del Consiglio de' Dieci, 13, ff. 62–73v.

The cultural patronage of Italian soldiers has aroused interest from a number of directions. Two recent works which have useful bibliographies are: G. Lanza Tomasi, *Ritratto del Condottiero* (Turin, 1967); G.

Paccagnini, *Pisanello alla corte dei Gonzaga* (Milan, 1972). Another obvious starting point for an enquiry into soldiers' patrons is the literature on Federigo da Montefeltro and Sigismondo Malatesta. For discussion of the library of Antonio, Count of Marsciano, see M. E. Mallett, 'Some Notes on a Fifteenth-Century Condottiere and his Library; Antonio, Count of Marsciano', in *Studies in the Italian Renaissance; a collection in honour of P. O. Kristeller*, ed. C. H. Clough (Liverpool University Press, forthcoming).

Once again, as with condottieri, it is impossible to set out here the statistical base for the discussion of infantry constables on pp. 225–6. This is a study which is at an even more preliminary stage than that of the cavalry leaders and my remarks at this point must be seen as very tentative.

For a discussion of war finance, see Molho, *Florentine Public Finance, cit.*, pp. 9–21. M. Becker in a number of his writings has also drawn attention to this crucial aspect of the relationships between war and society; see particularly his 'Some common features of Italian urban experience (c.1250–1500)', *Medievalia et Humanistica*, ns. I, 1970.

The remarks about the impact of war on the countryside can be amplified from: *Villages desertées et l'histoire économique* (Paris, 1965) with a chapter on Italy by C. Klapisch and J. Day; P. J. Jones, 'Agrarian conditions in late medieval Italy', in *Cambridge Economic History of Europe*, vol. I (Cambridge, 1969); M. E. Mallett and D. Whitehouse, 'Castel Porciano; an abandoned medieval village of the Roman Campagna', *Papers of the British School at Rome*, xxxv, 1967.

CHAPTER NINE

The best account of the Italian Wars in English is still F. L. Taylor, *The Art of War in Italy, cit.* That a Cambridge Ph.D thesis written fifty years ago and long out of print could be thus described, is remarkable considering the European significance of these wars. The fundamental work of P. Pieri, *Il Rinascimento e la crisi militare, cit.*, and a number of more or less useful accounts of individual battles and captains do something to fill the gap, but little has been written on wider aspects of warfare in this period apart from J. R. Hale's chapter in the *New Cambridge Modern History*, vol. I.

The details of the various battles in which Italians met foreign armies in the fifteenth century are largely drawn from Pieri, whose bibliography is still the best guide to the available literature.

The Milanese expedition to France in 1465 is described in P. Ghinzone, 'Spedizione sforzesco in Francia, 1465–6', *ASL.*, 2nd. ser., vii, 1890, while the Italians in Burgundian armies are emphasised by De La Chauvelays, *Mémoire sur la composition des armées de Charles le Temeraire* (Paris, 1879), *passim.*

For information on Jacopo Galeota and Boffilo del Giudice, see the two articles of P. M. Perret, 'Jacques Galeot et la république de Venise', *Bibliothéque de l'Ecole des Chartes*', lii, 1891 and 'Boffile de Juge, Comte de Castres, et la république de Venise', *Annales du Midi*, iii, 1891. Sir Walter Scott's reference to Cola di Monforte is in *Anna of Geierstein*, and the best discussion of this figure is B. Croce, *Un condottiere italiano del Quattrocento; Cola di Monforte, Conte di Campobasso* (Bari, 1936).

The numerous accounts of Charles VIII's army in 1494 are summed up in F. Lot, *Recherches sur les effectifs des armées francaises des guerres d'Italie aux guerres de religion, 1494–1562* (Paris, 1962), pp. 15–21. The most complete account of the expedition in English is J. S. C. Bridge, *A History of France from the Death of Louis XI* (Oxford, 1921–36), while the French artillery has recently been the object of a special study by P. Contamine, 'L'artillerie royale francaise à la veille des guerres d'Italie', *Annales de Bretagne*, lxxi, 1964. The battle of Fornovo has a vast bibliography which can largely be found in D. M. Schullian's edition of Benedetti's *Diaria de bello Carolino, cit.*

For a discussion of Cesare Borgia's army, see Larner, 'Cesare Borgia, Machiavelli, and the Romagnol militia', *cit.* A more detailed account of his campaigns and other political and military aspects of the period can be found in M. E. Mallett, *The Borgias* (London, 1969).

The Italian captains of this period have been better served than some of their predecessors by biographers. C. de Rosmini, *Nell'istoria intorno alla militare impresa e alla vita di Gian Jacopo Trivulzio* (Milan, 1815) and L. Leonii, *Vita di Bartolomeo d'Alviano* (Todi, 1858) are both still useful, as is P. Gauthiez *Jean des Bandes Noires* (Paris, 1901).

For the battle of Agnadello, it is again to Pieri that I turn for description and bibliography.

CHAPTER TEN

The best edition of Machiavelli's *Arte della Guerra* is that edited by S. Bertelli in the Biblioteca di classici italiani (Milan, 1961); Bertelli cites the story of Machiavelli and Giovanni de' Medici on p. 317. An adequate translation is provided by A. H. Gilbert, *Machiavelli. The Chief Works and Others, cit.*, and a rather acid comment on the value of the treatise is to be found in S. Anglo, *Machiavelli; a dissection* (London, 1969), pp. 116–142.

Luigi da Porto's comment is in his *Lettere storiche*, ed. Bressan (Florence, 1857), p. 214.

For comments on the continuing role of mercenaries in sixteenth century warfare, see V. G. Kiernan, 'Foreign mercenaries and absolute monarchy', *Past and Present*, xi, 1957, and M. Roberts, *The Military Revolution, 1560–1660* (Belfast, 1956).

INDEX